D0077049

THE PRESS OF
THE YOUNG REPUBLIC,
1783–1833

Also available in
The History of American Journalism

The Early American Press, 1690–1783
Wm. David Sloan and Julie Hedgepeth Williams

THE PRESS OF
THE YOUNG REPUBLIC,
1783–1833

Carol Sue Humphrey

WITHDRAWN
FROM
UNIVERSITY OF PENNSYLVANIA
LIBRARIES

**THE HISTORY OF AMERICAN JOURNALISM,
NUMBER 2**

James D. Startt and Wm. David Sloan,
Series Editors

GREENWOOD PRESS
Westport, Connecticut • London

PN
4855
H57
1994
no.2

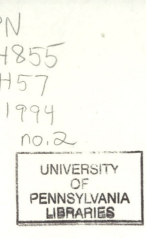

UNIVERSITY
OF
PENNSYLVANIA
LIBRARIES

Library of Congress Cataloging-in-Publication Data

Humphrey, Carol Sue.
  The press of the young Republic, 1783–1833 / Carol Sue Humphrey.
    p.   cm. — (The history of American journalism, ISSN 1074–4193 ;
  no. 2)
  Includes bibliographical references and index.
  ISBN 0–313–28406–7 (alk. paper)
  1. Journalism—United States—History—18th century.
  2. Journalism—United States—History—19th century.   I. Title.
  II. Series.
  PN4861.H86   1996
  [PN4855]
  071'.3'09033—dc20   96–7140

British Library Cataloguing in Publication Data is available.

Copyright © 1996 by Carol Sue Humphrey

All rights reserved. No portion of this book may be
reproduced, by any process or technique, without the
express written consent of the publisher.

Library of Congress Catalog Card Number: 96–7140
ISBN: 0–313–28406–7
ISSN: 1074–4193

First published in 1996

Greenwood Press, 88 Post Road West, Westport, CT 06881
An imprint of Greenwood Publishing Group, Inc.

Printed in the United States of America

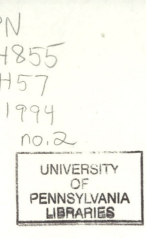

The paper used in this book complies with the
Permanent Paper Standard issued by the National
Information Standards Organization (Z39.48–1984).

10 9 8 7 6 5 4 3 2

Copyright Acknowledgments

The author and the publisher gratefully acknowledge permission to reprint the following materials:

Excerpts from the William Henry Brodnax Papers, Richard Keith Call Letter, Francis Asbury Dickins Papers, Fontaine Family Papers, James Mercer Garnett Papers, Robert Selden Garnett Papers, Gooch Family Papers, Greene Family Papers, Hugh Blair Grigsby Papers, William Hammett Papers, Harrison Family Papers, Haxall Family Papers, Henry Lee Papers, Mercer Family Papers, John Stuart Skinner Papers, and Spragins Family Papers appear courtesy of the Virginia Historical Society, Richmond, Virginia.

Material from Carol Sue Humphrey, *"This Popular Engine": New England Newspapers During the American Revolution, 1775–1789* (Newark: University of Delaware Press, 1992) appears courtesy of the University of Delaware Press.

Materials from Carol Sue Humphrey, " 'Little Ado About Something': Philadelphia Newspapers and the Constitutional Convention," *American Journalism* 5 (1988): 63–80, and Carol Sue Humphrey, "Greater Distance = Declining Interest: Massachusetts Printers and Protection for a Free Press, 1783–1791," *American Journalism* (forthcoming), appear courtesy of *American Journalism*, Athens, Georgia.

Material from Carol Sue Humphrey, " 'That Bulwark of Our Liberties': Massachusetts Printers and the Issue of a Free Press, 1783–1788," *Journalism History* 14 (Spring 1987): 34–38, appears courtesy of *Journalism History*, Las Vegas, Nevada.

Excerpts from the Joel Barlow Papers, the Book Trades Collection, and the Isaiah Thomas Papers appear courtesy of the American Antiquarian Society, Worcester, Massachusetts.

Materials from *Aurora* Office Account Books, the Robert and Francis Bailey Records, the Meredith Papers (*Port Folio* Group), and the Woodhouse Collection appear courtesy of The Historical Society of Pennsylvania, Philadelphia, Pennsylvania.

P. O. 227960

For Edna Hyder,
Whose love for history was so contagious

Contents

Series Foreword

Since the renowned historian Allan Nevins issued his call for an improved journalism history in 1959, the field has experienced remarkable growth in terms of both quantity and quality. It can now be said with confidence that journalism history is a vital and vitalizing field full of scholarly activity and promise.

The new scholarship has widened the field's horizons and extended its depth. Today, especially with new bibliographic technologies at their disposal, journalism historians are able to explore literature pertinent to their studies to a greater extent than was previously possible. This expansion of literary sources has occurred in conjunction with other advances in the use of source materials. Today's historians incorporate primary and original records into their work more than was common when Nevins issued his call, and they also utilize sources produced by the electronic media. As the source foundation for journalism history has grown, so its content has undergone a substantive expansion. Previously neglected or minimized subjects in the field now receive fairer and more concerted treatment. Contemporary journalism history, moreover, reflects more consciousness of culture than that written a generation ago.

Growth, however, has created problems. Abundance of sources, proliferation and diversity of writing, and the stimulation of new discoveries and interpretations combine to make scholarship in the field a formidable task. A broad study covering journalism history from its beginnings to the present, one combining the rich primary materials now available and the older and newer literature in the field, is needed. *The History of American Journalism* series is designed to address this need. Each volume will be written by an author or authors who are recognized scholars in the field. Each is intended to provide a coherent perspective on a major period, to facilitate further research in the field, and to engage general readers interested in the subject. A strong narrative and interpretive element will be found in each volume, and each contains a bibliographical essay pointing readers to the most pertinent research sources and secondary literature.

This is the second volume in the series, the first having dealt with printing and newspaper publishing in the American colonies and during the Revolutionary War. The present volume begins with newspapers following the American victory in the Revolution and takes the story into the presidency of Andrew Jackson, as the party press began to be replaced by the mass-oriented penny newspapers of the 1830s. As subsequent volumes will do, it focuses on the nature of journalism during the years surveyed, chronicles noteworthy figures, examines the relationship of journalism to society, and provides explanations for the main directions that journalism was taking.

The remaining four volumes will complete *The History of American Journalism* in chronological order and are scheduled to appear over the next four years.

Preface

In the fifty years following the end of the Revolution, the American press grew and expanded. It capitalized on the lessons learned during the war and enlarged on them. Mechanically, newspapers improved immensely, becoming both more readable, with the introduction of new equipment and new type styles, and more available, as they expanded in circulation and frequency of publication. The year 1783 witnessed the first attempts at a daily newspaper, the *Pennsylvania Evening Post*; by 1833, eighty-eight dailies had appeared in the United States. Furthermore, the press diversified in type and content as magazines became an established part of the publishing business.

The press also reflected the growth of the country as it moved westward after the Revolution. In 1783, no newspapers were published west of the Appalachian Mountains. By 1833, publishers operated their presses from New York to beyond the Mississippi River and almost everywhere in between.

Finally, newspapers reflected the growth and the development of the nation internally through the ever-increasing diversification of labor. Newspaper offices went from small, one-person/one-family operations to large concerns with publishers, editors, correspondents, and printers, each with their own specific job to do. By the time Benjamin Day inaugurated the "penny press" in 1833, the American press had blossomed into a widespread, well-established institution that played an important role in keeping people informed about events in the world outside their own little community.

The half century following the fight for independence witnessed a period of growing pains for the press as printers became editors and sought their niche in American society. Newspapers played an important political role as the press became a part of the partisanship that characterized most of this period. As political parties grew in the United States, newspapers became an essential part of the communication network for the dissemination of the ideology of each party. As a result, newspapers preached the various party lines, each seeking to convert the public to its way of thinking. The idea of neutrality or objectivity on the part of newspapers did not develop. Later historians, describing the period as the "dark ages of American journalism," criticized these partisan editors because they did not seek to present an objective view of events. However, these newspaper producers saw such an idea as ludicrous because newspapers had to take positions in order to carry out their proper function. This perception of the role of the press as rabidly partisan in the field of politics faded only with expansion in the size and type of publications after the War of 1812. As the press grew, new publications sought new audiences, and politics slowly became only one topic of concern among many. Variety meant growth and development, but it also spelled the end of the partisan press in the United States.

This book considers the variety of this period in American journalistic development. Partisanship dominated the era and provided the measuring stick for contemporary judgments of the press, so politics provides the centerpiece for the book. However, the newspapers and magazines covered more than just party politics, and these issues are considered as well. During this fifty-year period, the definition of the role of the press in society changed. In 1783, newspapers sought primarily to convince people to adopt a particular point of view. By 1833, more and more publishers, whether of a newspaper or a magazine, held the view that the primary function of the press lay in providing news and information to readers. To many people today, the press does not look that different in 1833 from how it had looked fifty years before. Someone like Philip Freneau or John Fenno, however, would have seen the changes occurring and would not have been comfortable with them because the heyday of their strongly political papers was fading into obscurity.

Acknowledgments

Many people have helped in the production of this book. Many colleagues at Oklahoma Baptist University and fellow members of the American Journalism Historians Association supported the work through their encouragement. Shirley Jones proofread the manuscript. Both the Library Company in Philadelphia and the Virginia Historical Society in Richmond supported the research financially through Mellon Fellowships. Finally, as always, my family encouraged me every step of the way.

1

A New Era Begins:
The Confederation, 1783–1789

On November 25, 1783, the withdrawal of the British army from New York marked the end of almost 200 years of colonial rule that had begun at Jamestown, Virginia, in 1607. As the last troops sailed away, the newspapers of the United States rejoiced at the end of British domination and looked forward to a bright and glorious future. The editor of the *Pennsylvania Gazette* in Philadelphia reflected the feelings of most Americans when he exulted: "We congratulate our fellow-citizens on this important day!—It loudly demands LAUS DEO from the United States. . . . May it not be the language of their lips only, but may it be engraven on their hearts, and expressed in their future lives!"[1]

Printers also took time to praise those who had helped win the war. Included in this group were the newspapers themselves because the printers believed strongly, and rightly so, that their small productions had helped rally Americans to the cause of independence and thus to the achievement of final victory.

The road to victory, however, had been paved with many difficulties and losses for everyone, and the press had joined in the suffering. Those who managed to overcome the difficulties, through luck or hard work or both, faced the uncertain future with hope and optimism. For them, the war had served as a testing ground to toughen not only the press, but also all Americans to face the future together. Newspaper printers came out of the Revolution believing that their weekly sheets had played an essential role in the conflict, and they planned to continue that role in the future. The possibilities were almost endless, since newspapers would provide information and encouragement for the new nation as it developed and grew.

In many ways, these hopes for the future proved to be true. The decade of the 1780s marked the beginning of a new era in American journalism because fresh faces appeared among the printers and publishers throughout the country. Having come of age and learned their trade during the Revolution, these younger newspaper producers exuded optimism and believed strongly in the important role of the press in the political arena of the new Republic. With the arrival of peace in 1783, these new printers began to make their presence felt in the young nation. Trained by older artisans during the years of fighting with Great Britain, they assumed that the press had played a central role in the move for independence and would continue to be essential for the maintenance of republicanism in the new nation that emerged from the Revolution. These politically oriented printers would dominate the trade by the 1790s as their predecessors retired or died. While all did not succeed in their newspaper enterprises, they brought new blood into the trade.

Most successful among this newer group was Benjamin Russell, a Bostonian who had learned his craft from Isaiah Thomas[2] in Worcester. Russell, like several other younger printers, had experienced the Revolution firsthand, serving two short tours of military service in 1777 and 1780. In 1782, he received an early release from his apprenticeship, apparently because he served one of his stints in the army as a substitute for Isaiah Thomas. Returning to Boston in late 1783, Russell soon established the *Massachusetts Centinel* in partnership with William Warden. Russell's *Centinel* became one of the most important Boston papers in the years to come, particularly in the 1790s under its new title, the *Columbian Centinel*. Russell proved a staunch Federalist and used his paper to support the policies of the Washington administration. He retired in 1828, ending a long and distinguished career devoted almost exclusively to newspaper publishing.[3]

In conjunction with the appearance of new printers such as Benjamin Russell, the 1780s witnessed considerable growth in the newspaper industry in the United States. When the Revolution ended in 1783, printers produced thirty-five news sheets throughout the young nation, one of them the first attempt at publishing a daily newspaper. By the time of the first national census in 1790, ninety-two publications had appeared throughout the country, including eight dailies. The years of peace had been good for the press, allowing it to increase to almost three times its size only seven years earlier.[4]

Throughout these years of growth, newspaper printers discussed the successes and failures of the new government. Most believed that the structure created by the Articles of Confederation could not succeed, and, thus, they actively supported the move toward a new government, which grew throughout the decade. American newspapers of the 1780s reflected the growing anxieties of the printers for the security and efficacy of the national government, and the continual discussion of such issues encouraged readers to be concerned as well. Such worries, whether based on actual fact or not, helped set the stage for the adoption of a new form of government in 1787–1788.

Visually, the newspapers of the 1780s looked much as they had during the Revolution. Most news sheets were four pages in length, with two or three columns of type per page. Beyond the masthead of the newspaper, which contained the title and the date, the front page differed little from the other pages. News, essays, and advertisements were scattered throughout the paper, although printers increasingly tried to group together materials from one city. Printers continued to label news generally according to the city of origin for the story rather than the place where the event actually occurred. Foreign news about the activities of European governments continued to appear frequently, but domestic news from the states became increasingly common as readers became more interested in events elsewhere around the country. Local news remained of little importance, although it slowly began to occupy a larger percentage of the available space. The biggest change in the newspapers of the 1780s came as printers became more willing to comment on the news and essays they published. Although not clearly labeled as editorials, such opinion statements laid the groundwork for the frequent use of editorials during the party press conflicts of the 1790s.

Following the end of the major fighting in 1781, the American press lost the common interests that had been present during the war years. The newspapers increasingly addressed more issues of local concern, such as western lands in Virginia or pay for the Continental Army in Connecticut. Unlike the newspapers in Britain and France, the press of the United States did not have a center. As a result, the dissemination of news was generally unorganized, and only an issue of major concern or impact would bring the focus of all the newspapers together. As the 1780s progressed, such an issue appeared. Increasingly, the news sheets addressed a worry that was producing a sense of anxiety for many throughout the country: the inability of the government created under the Articles of Confederation to handle the problems facing the new nation.

At the time of the final approval of the Articles of Confederation in 1781, printers rejoiced over the establishment of a permanent government for the United States. Soon, however, some complained of the inadequacy of the current system and urged that changes had to be made. Such comments increased throughout the 1780s until, by the time the Constitutional Convention met, most American printers had concluded that any change at all from the weak Articles of Confederation would be beneficial.[5]

Fears concerning the effectiveness of the Articles had appeared as early as 1782 and had slowly increased in number and intensity throughout the decade.[6] In April 1782, one essayist in Boston's *Independent Chronicle* declared that "the political machine has been improved of late; but it is not yet perfected. It does not answer fully the cogs of national government. The defects are felt in many pernicious consequences."[7] A correspondent in the same newspaper expressed surprise that great care had been taken earlier in forming state governments, but that little time was spent in formulating the national system. He concluded that a flawed government resulted, indicated by the fact that "our national honour, character, and abilities have declined, and are declining under it." He urged a change because "there is a defect somewhere" and "it is our duty, interest and happiness to remove it."[8]

The weakness of Congress and the need to enlarge its powers produced most of the worries about the national government expressed in the newspapers.[9] For example, an essay in the *Freeman's Oracle* of Exeter, New Hampshire, stated that "they may DECLARE every thing but can DO nothing."[10] Benjamin Russell, while lamenting the state of the nation, asserted that "the Confederated States in

Congress assembled have not the power to apply to effect any remedy, however salutary, to cure our national disorders."[11] In Springfield, Massachusetts, the editor of the *Hampshire Herald* averred, "[H]ow absurd, to endow them with power to levy war, to contract loans, and then deprive them of their resources necessary for the discharge of such debts, which the faith of the nation is pledged for."[12] A writer in the *Independent Chronicle* feared that the United States, "by neglecting to vest Congress with necessary powers, are precipitating themselves into an imperial government."[13] In the *Connecticut Courant*, "A.B." concluded that "every one must be convinced of the utility, nay absolute necessity of the powers of Congress being either enlarged, or entirely annihilated—either to support our national dignity, or confess we have none."[14]

Concern over the national government centered primarily on the issue of money and the need to pay the debt produced by the Revolutionary War. The Continental Congress, as empowered by the Articles of Confederation, did not have any direct taxation powers. The Congress could only requisition money from the individual states and hope that they honored the requests. The states' payment of congressional requisitions had been haphazard at best throughout the war and did not improve during the 1780s. As a result, several attempts were made to invest Congress with a method of direct taxation in order to provide money for the payment of the national debt.

The first attempt to give the national government a taxing power took the form of a continental impost proposed on February 3, 1781. The proposed duty received substantial support from both political leaders and newspapers throughout the country. The *Connecticut Courant* commented that no state could dare refuse its approval because to do so would "retard the fulfillment of our public engagements—and most probably end in the creation of some compulsory power on the continent," which would force the states to act together or, even worse, "terminate in a total dissolution of our federal government."[15]

Most of the states apparently agreed with the *Courant* because twelve of them approved the impost. Rhode Island, however, declared the measure a violation of the Confederation and refused to ratify it. Without the approval of all thirteen states, the amendment could not take effect, so Rhode Island's refusal killed the measure. Supporters of the impost did not understand the state's reasoning and severely castigated it for not bending to the rule of the majority. Some felt that the real reason for Rhode Island's refusal lay in the fact that the state raised a large amount of money through its own impost and did not want to lose any of it to Congress.[16] A resident of Rhode Island lamented his state's action in the *Providence Gazette*: "The voice of our legislature has reprobated the measure; but as a citizen of the United States, I deeply regret the consequences."[17] One of a series of essays printed in the *Connecticut Courant* and then throughout the country in 1784 summed up the feelings of numerous people concerning Rhode Island's refusal: "Had Congress purchased the whole state at the expense of the other twelve or had the whole state been annihilated, the other states would have suffered less than they now do in consequence of that refusal."[18]

Failure to approve the proposed impost only served to increase the concerns about the Articles government. "Lycurgus," writing in the *Connecticut Courant*, criticized the Continental Congress as "the only obstacle to the compleat establishment of a perfect democratical constitution" because of its inability to do anything.[19] Some writers urged changes in the Articles because of concerns over the country's international reputation.[20] Lack of a recognizable and functional central government, said an essayist in the *Connecticut Gazette*, would produce European laughter and ridicule: "The Confederal Constitution, while it presents a Comedy to the rest of the world, will prove in the end a Tragedy to ourselves—and our distress will be attended with so much ridicule, that we shall lose the consolation of pity."[21] One writer in the *Independent Chronicle* concluded that only a strong national government could defend America's interests abroad and "protect the United-States from the insults and abuses of barbarians, whether civilized or uncivilized."[22]

Whatever the reason for their anxiety, most newspaper writers who urged changes in the Confederation clearly felt that all the country's problems resulted from a weak government. The Articles of Confederation had failed. The individual states had acted in their own selfish interests, threatening to ruin everything gained during the war with Britain. The establishment of a stable national government was essential for the United States' survival.[23] In fact, this action would constitute the final chapter of the American Revolution. "Nestor," writing in the *Providence Gazette*, insisted that people mistakenly confused the Revolution and the war: "The American war is over, but this is far from being the case with the American revolution; On the contrary, nothing but the first act of the great drama is closed. It remains yet to establish and perfect our new forms of government, and to prepare the principles, morals and manners, of our citizens."[24]

The growing concern over the future of the nation provided a perfect backdrop for Shays's Rebellion. Fueled by economic problems, the revolt began as a minor conflict in Massachusetts, but quickly developed into a national concern. Scarcity of money, intensified by a severe taxation and debt retirement program instituted by the state, created extreme hardships for debtors in rural Massachusetts. Trouble had been brewing throughout rural New England ever since the end of the war. Attempts to force favorable legislation out of state governments occurred in Connecticut and Vermont. In New Hampshire, a mob of disgruntled farmers held the general assembly prisoner for several hours. The greatest unrest, however, occurred in the frontier counties of western Massachusetts. Trying to stave off property seizures for unpaid taxes, residents met in county conventions in the summer and fall of 1786 to petition the Massachusetts state legislature for help. Failing to get a sympathetic hearing in Boston, the men rebelled. Led by Daniel Shays, an ex–Continental Army captain, nearly two thousand of them joined together in a makeshift army that closed the courts and prevented government officials from foreclosing on anyone's property. Finally, in February 1787, the militia under General Benjamin Lincoln clashed with Shays's men near Petersham, bringing an end to the rebellion.[25]

Newspaper printers recoiled in horror at the lawlessness of these events because they considered such actions as adding to, rather than solving, the country's postwar problems. They attributed blame for the insurrection to a variety of causes. After the militia put down the disturbance, one Boston printer asserted that the "late irregularities have proceeded from want of true information respecting the doings of the General Court."[26] A piece in the *Independent Chronicle* reprinted from a Philadelphia paper declared that Massachusetts's troubles were punishment for her continued participation in the slave trade.[27]

Many, however, placed blame for the insurrection on the shoulders of a group of essayists who had spoken out against the legal system. "Honestus," an essayist in the *Independent Chronicle*, received particular criticism. During March and April of 1786, he had written a series of pieces condemning lawyers and the legal system as too expensive and time-consuming and calling for reform of the entire system. Many in western Massachusetts agreed with "Honestus," and the Shaysites demanded similar changes. The similarity in proposals between "Honestus" and the insurrectionists resulted in the accusations against the essayist. "Honestus" defended himself in print, insisting that the grievances he wrote of had existed for a long time and that the failure to solve the problems, rather than his writing about them, produced the rebellion.[28]

Numerous newspaper pieces attacked the Shaysites for taking the law into their own hands.[29] One essayist in Boston's *Massachusetts Gazette* denounced the county conventions as "unconstitutional from the very nature of such assemblies, because they weaken the government, which is feeble at best."[30] Furthermore, concluded editor Isaiah Thomas in the *Worcester Magazine*, "these conventions are void of all authority, and when they assume to give law or direction to the people, or to any branch of government, they usurp the lawful powers of the legislature and are guilty of injuring the majesty of the people." He strongly urged everyone in Massachusetts to work hard "to restore the publick tranquility, that peace and harmony may again prevail, and our numerous inhabitants be united and happy." Furthermore, he hoped that the legislature "will immediately attend to all just complaints of the people, and exert themselves for the general good."[31]

Finally, many people, according to an essay in the *Norwich Packet*, feared that the revolt in Massachusetts would create trouble for the entire United States, possibly even resulting in European intervention: "They will say our division is our weakness; our aversion to taxation is our determination to cheat them; the instability of the confederation, and our diversity of sentiment is our greatest curse; the whole renders them without a friend to assist in case of attack, let us therefore but step forth and that very moment they are conquered."[32] Fearing the worst and urging that something be done to solve the grievances that produced the rebellion, one writer concluded that "our country has stood upon the verge of ruin."[33] In the *Freeman's Oracle*, "Camillus" cried that "this is a crisis in our affairs, which requires all the wisdom and energy of government." He believed that everyone must know that "our disturbances have arisen, more from the want of power, than the abuse of it; from the relaxation, and almost annihilation of our federal government; from the feeble, unsystematic, temporising, inconsistent character of our own State."[34] The editor of the *Norwich Packet* voiced the hopes of many when he prayed that "proper measures may speedily be adopted (for under God they may) to strengthen the declining, jarring, convulsive empire, as well the whole confederate body as the constituent parts."[35]

Shays's Rebellion sent shock waves throughout the country, producing anxiety over the nation's future. As a result, the movement for changes in the national government intensified. For some time, many of the country's leaders had wished that something could be done to strengthen the Confederation. James Madison of Virginia had spearheaded much of the effort to produce a national meeting to review the Articles of Confederation in order to make needed changes. At a meeting in Annapolis, Maryland, in September 1786, Madison convinced the seven states represented to issue a call for a meeting of all states in Philadelphia for the following year. Although mentioned in most newspapers, the Annapolis Convention elicited little direct comment from printers. The occurrence of Shays's Rebellion between the Annapolis and Philadelphia meetings captured people's attention and convinced many of them, including George Washington, that something had to be done in order to prevent the downfall of the national government. The Constitutional Convention of 1787 resulted from such growing concern.

The Convention assembled late in May 1787. The members quickly adopted guidelines and procedures for their discussions, including a resolution that declared that their debates and discussions would be closed to the public. Most of the delegates either agreed with the secrecy rule or did not care what was done concerning the issue. The few who strongly disagreed with the measures quickly found they lacked support for their opposition. Promoters argued that privacy would enable the delegates to speak their minds without fear of being held to their words at a later date—a totally free atmosphere for discussion would produce benefits in the final results of the Convention.[36]

The nation's newspaper printers complained little concerning the secrecy order, even though reports of state legislative debates had appeared throughout the 1780s. Apparently, most pressmen agreed that confidentiality was necessary for the Convention to succeed, and, therefore, they did not disapprove of the secrecy rule.[37]

While this assumption concerning the printers may be true, it does not mean that the newspapers totally ignored the Philadelphia meeting. The Constitutional Convention was the major American news event of the summer of 1787—no newspaper could totally ignore it. The news sheets discussed a variety of topics in their coverage of the Convention, including the names and qualifications of the delegates, when sessions occurred, hopes for the meeting's results, and the decision to meet in secret.[38]

All of the gazettes expressed interest in who attended the Convention. Most of them published a list of the entire membership once the meeting had officially convened.[39] Along with the lists of delegates, Philadelphia printers listed their qualifications. The *Independent Gazetteer* portrayed them as "temperate and very respectable men"[40] and praised them as "men who are qualified from education, experience and profession for the great business assigned to them."[41] The publishers of the *Pennsylvania Packet* tried to relieve any fears their readers might harbor by describing the members as "men in whom you may confide" because "their extensive knowledge, known abilities, and approved patriotism warrant it."[42] Several papers gloried in the fact that "the same hands that laid the foundations of the Temple of Liberty are again employed in this arduous task."[43] In general, all the public prints applauded the Convention delegates, describing them, as did the editor of the *New Hampshire Gazette,* as "sages and patriots." Furthermore, he asserted that the joint efforts of "so distinguished a body of men, among whom will be a Franklin and a Washington, cannot but produce the most salutary measures. These names affixed to their recommendations . . . will stamp a confidence in them" that the opposition "will not dare to attack, or endeavour to nullify."[44]

Although the members of the press heaped praise on all the delegates, they reserved their special commendations for the Convention's president, George Washington.[45] Several publications stated that Washington's presence alone provided reason for hope and confidence in the meeting's results.[46] The original report of his plans to attend the meeting made one contributor to the *Pennsylvania Evening Herald* happy because "this great patriot will never think his duty performed, while any thing remains to be done."[47] A writer in the *Pennsylvania Packet* assumed that "a WASHINGTON surely will never stoop to tarnish the lustre of his former actions, by having an agency in anything capable of reflecting dishonor on himself or his countrymen."[48] The *Pennsylvania Gazette* summed up the feelings of almost everyone in its congratulatory message to Washington for his success as leader of the Convention:

How great . . . must be the satisfaction of our late worthy Commander in Chief, to be called upon a second time, by the suffrages of three millions of people, to save his sinking country?—In 1775, we behold him at the head of the armies of America, arresting the progress of British tyranny.—In the year 1787, we behold him at the head of a chosen band of patriots and heroes, arresting the progress of American anarchy, and taking the lead in laying a deep foundation for preserving that liberty by a good government, which he had acquired for his country by his sword. Illustrious and highly favored instrument of the blessings of Heaven to America—live—live for ever![49]

Alongside their praise for the delegates who attended the Philadelphia assembly, the newspapers made a point of severely chastising any who failed to attend. They particularly criticized Rhode Island for its failure to send anyone at all.[50] Several writers assumed that this action meant that Rhode Island no longer belonged in the Union and that, should she request readmittance, it would be refused.[51] A correspondent of the *Pennsylvania Journal* saw Rhode Island's lack of representation as an occasion for joy because "her delinquency will not be permitted to defeat the salutary object of this body."[52]

Items concerning who attended and when the Convention met constituted the only specific information that the newspapers published. The rule of secrecy proved almost totally inviolable. Beyond the more mundane matters of who and when, the press could only speculate or ignore the whole thing. Printers did not desire to do the latter, so they attempted the former. Most of the guesses in the newspapers between May and September 1787 consisted primarily of hopes and worries about the importance of the Convention and its possible results.

In general, hopes soared high in the press concerning the outcome of the Philadelphia meeting.[53] A writer in the *Providence Gazette* observed "that on the Proceedings of the Federal Convention . . . must these United States depend for political Happiness, and national Honour."[54] The *Pennsylvania Gazette* proclaimed that "under such a Government as will probably be formed by the present Convention, America may yet enjoy peace, safety, liberty, and glory."[55] Several news sheets noted that "the eyes of the whole continent" turned toward Philadelphia.[56] One writer in a Philadelphia paper commented that "every enterprize, public as well as private, in the United States . . . seems suspended," awaiting the outcome of the meeting.[57] The editors of the *Connecticut Courant* insisted that one result of the Convention must be a strong executive power in the national government: "How widely different would have been the character of the union, if in Congress had resided a power to control the selfish interests of a single state, and to compel the sacrifice of partial views, in order to promote the common weal."[58] Many publishers commented that the meeting was "perhaps the last opportunity which may be presented to us of establishing a permanent system of Continental Government; and, if this opportunity be lost, it is much to be feared that we shall fall into irretrievable confusion."[59]

Many people based their hopes for the results of the Philadelphia meeting in reports, like those in the *Connecticut Courant*, that "the greatest unanimity subsists in the councils of the Federal Convention." They prayed that "the United States will discover as much wisdom in receiving from them a suitable form of government to preserve the liberties of the people, as they did fortitude in defending them against the arbitrary and wicked attempts of Great Britain" because "nothing but union and a vigorous continental government, can save us from destruction."[60] Upon reporting the adjournment of the Convention to allow a committee to write up the results, the *Independent Chronicle* declared that "the public curiosity will soon be gratified; and it is hoped, from the universal confidence reposed in this delegation, that the minds of the people throughout the United States are prepared to receive with respect, and to try with a fortitude and perseverance, the plan which will be offered to them by men distinguished for their wisdom and patriotism."[61] Clearly, as stated by the *Connecticut Courant*, "whatever measure may be recommended by the federal convention, whether an addition to the old constitution, or the adoption of a new one," would constitute "a Revolution in Government, Accomplished by Reasoning and Deliberation; an event that has never occurred since the formation of society, and which will be strongly characteristic of the philosophic and tolerant spirit of the age."[62]

The Constitutional Convention adjourned on September 17, its work done. The result of its deliberations was a brief document, which began appearing in the public prints on September 19. Following the four-month news drought, the printers snapped up this document quickly. Every newspaper published the complete Constitution. The members of the press soon inundated their readers with discussions of the proposed new government. Whereas pamphlets had functioned along with the weekly sheets as sources of political information in earlier years, the debates over the Constitution witnessed the establishment of the supremacy of the newspaper as a public forum, a domination that would last into the twentieth century. *The Federalist Papers*, so famous to modern readers, constituted only the best known of hundreds of essays that appeared in the public prints during the ratification struggle.[63]

Overall, the press praised the delegates for their hard work. The newspapers applauded them, according to the *Middlesex Gazette*, because "they have calmly and deliberately formed and adopted a plan of government, which (when we consider the heterogeneous materials afforded for its construction by thirteen distinct states, almost all of them different in their interests, manners and customs) may justly be called a master-piece of human wisdom." Furthermore, "while the revolutions of government in other countries, have given rise to the most horrid scenes of carnage and bloodshed," only the United States could "boast of a Constitution formed by her chosen sages."[64]

Many writers realized the uniqueness of the situation. In urging adoption of the Constitution, "Federalist," an essayist in the *Massachusetts Centinel*, insisted that "America can scarcely hope ever to see so respectable a body of her citizens convened on a similar occasion—so great an unanimity we cannot expect again."[65] In the *Connecticut Courant*, "A Landholder" warned that this might be America's last opportunity "to adopt a government which gives all protection to personal liberty and, at the same time, promises fair to afford you all the advantages of a sovereign empire."[66] The *Independent Gazetteer* declared that such a meeting as the Convention seemed "quite novel in the history of government,"[67] while the *Newport Herald* stated that "the establishment of a Free and Efficient Government by the unbiased suffrages of an extended and numerous people, is without precedent in the old world, and will be an immortal honor to the new."[68] According to a New England correspondent in the *Independent Chronicle*, the events of the summer of 1787 formed "a most unusual spectacle" because the people of the United States had "calmly and deliberately, in time of peace, unawed by arms, and uninfluenced by party faction, appoint[ed] their wisest and best men to form a constitution of government, adequate to the great purposes of the general confederacy, and most productive of the prosperity, felicity, safety and welfare of the whole."[69]

Many printers saw the proposed Constitution as the means for finally completing the Revolution. They almost assumed that all good patriots would support the measure. They endeavored to convince their readers to approve the proposal because a large majority of the American people supported the recommended new government. The *New Hampshire Gazette* reported that "the public prints from every quarter of the United States are filled with accounts of the unanimity" concerning the proposed government "and the great happiness the people feel in the glorious prospect of being speedily relieved from their present feeble and declining state, and being put on a respectable footing among the nations."[70]

Constitution supporters, who became known as Federalists, urged support for the proposal in order to end the suspense over the United States' future. Writing in the *Massachusetts Centinel*, "A Freeman" affirmed that "our country now seems to hang in anxious suspense, not knowing whether she is to have a good and efficient government or none at all, or a despotic one imposed upon her by some daring adventurer."[71] Describing the document as "the best plan of government that ever graced the ancient or modern world,"[72] another writer in the same paper warned that "the consequence of the people's rejecting the federal Constitution, will be Anarchy in the extreme."[73] Furthermore, a third essayist stated that "in anticipating the acceptance of the American Constitution every countenance brightens with the full flow of hope and animating expectation of publick honour, peace and lasting prosperity to our 'Dear Country.'"[74] The *Independent Chronicle* reported that "many people look upon the adoption of the new constitution, as the millenium of virtue and wealth."[75] An anonymous essayist in a later issue of the same publication summed up the feelings presented by most printers in their papers:

Let us then be of one heart, and of one mind. Let us seize the golden opportunity to secure a stable government, and to become a respectable nation. Let us be open, decided and resolute in a good cause. Let us render our situation worthy the ashes of our slaughtered brethren, and our own sufferings. Let us remember our emblem, the twisted serpent, and its emphatical motto, unite or die! This was once written in blood; but it is as emphatical now as then. A house divided against itself, cannot stand. Our national existence depends as much as ever upon our union; and its consolidation most assuredly involves our posterity, felicity and safety.[76]

Many writers praised the Constitution because it offered the "prospect of our national reputation being rescued from opprobrium and disgrace" by preventing breaches of public contracts, according to the *Independent Chronicle*.[77] According to "Common Sense" in the *Cumberland Gazette*, one of the best parts of the proposal was "power, adequate power, to manage the great affairs of the nation, conferred upon the Congress."[78] An author in the *Boston Gazette* insisted that the economic evils that had plagued the country since the end of the Revolution would disappear if the states adopted the Constitution.[79] Praising the proposed government for its "wisdom and sound judgment," the editor of a Connecticut paper rejoiced over the United States' economic possibilities if the Constitution were adopted: "It will set all the springs of action in motion" by empowering the government to protect American trade, and "this will revive ship-building; and we may soon expect to see our rivers lined, as heretofore, with new ships; this gives employment to carpenters, joiners, blacksmiths, and even to every species of tradesmen."[80]

The most famous arguments favoring the Constitution appeared in the *New York Independent Journal* from October 1787 to April 1788. Written to help encourage

the ratification of the Constitution by New York, "Publius" authored the eighty-
five essays collectively known as *The Federalist Papers*. "Publius" was actually
three people—Alexander Hamilton, James Madison, and John Jay. They hoped to
explain the Federalist position and to justify the need for a stronger national government. According to "Publius," a republican form of government had to be established in order to protect the rights of the people from the whims of an
unpredictable majority. A stronger national government would provide protection
for all groups and outlooks, not just those with the largest numbers. Furthermore,
the proposed Constitution would strengthen the overall position of the United
States and enable the country to take its rightful place among the nations of the
world. Although not considered very effective in the ratification struggle for which
the essays were written, *The Federalist Papers* still constitutes one of the best single expositions of the Constitution.[81]

Historians and politicians have long debated the motives behind the move to
change the government of the United States in the 1780s. Answering this question
completely may not be possible, but the newspapers of the era provide some insights. Printers, in urging Americans to push for changes in their government, stated
an interwoven series of reasons for doing so. They clearly believed that the debts of
the United States were great and that something had to be done to pay them.[82] Also,
trade and commercial complications and restrictions could only be handled by a central government with adequate powers.[83] From these perspectives, economic issues
and motives clearly played a part in the move to adopt the Constitution.[84]

However, the newspapers also indicate that more was involved than just money.
Many expressed concerns over the future existence of the new nation, fearing that
the country would be divided into several sections (a proposal seriously discussed
by some) or that a European nation would take advantage of the situation and attempt to conquer the United States.[85] Printers expressed great frustration because
the rest of the world paid little respect to the young nation and its citizens, a fact
that many people blamed on the inability of the national government "to support
our dignity" because of its lack of real power.[86] These fears indicate that the push
for changes in the national government, at least from the perspective of the newspaper printers, also involved an attempt to bolster national pride by creating a political structure that could promote a better public image. An essay to the House of
Burgesses reprinted throughout the country summed up the apprehensions of most
publishers: "The Confederal Constitution, while it presents a Comedy to the rest
of the world, will prove in the end a Tragedy to ourselves."[87] All of these motives—economics, national survival, and a desire just to stand up and not be
pushed around anymore—helped convince many Americans, including most
newspaper printers, to support the Constitution as proposed by the Convention.

Everyone, however, did not wholeheartedly support the proposed new plan of
government. The plan's opponents, who became known as Anti-Federalists, feared
that the Constitution would produce too strong a national government at the expense of the states and the people. One essayist in the *Newport Mercury* charged
that the new plan removed the seat of power too far from the people.[88] Others in-

sisted that it would take away the right to trial by jury, that it did not provide enough protection for a free press, and that it abolished free elections.[89] A writer in the *Freeman's Journal* insisted that "the great names of Washington and Franklin have been taken in vain, and shockingly prostituted to effect the most infamous principles"[90]—just because they both signed the Constitution did not mean that they both gave the document their complete support. Finally, "Algernon Sidney," writing in the *Providence Gazette*, worried that, "if we suffer it to be established, the world will, on account of the gross tyranny which it holds forth, be inclined to suspect, rather than our understandings, our integrity and courage."[91]

Basically, the Federalists and the Anti-Federalists differed over where the center of political power should be located. Even before the Constitutional Convention, many who later became Federalists perceived the United States to be "headless" because the national government had little power.[92] For them, the government of the United States had to have "powers competent to the exigencies of the public."[93] To have a national government too weak to accomplish anything was to have no government at all. They could not understand the hesitations to increase the powers of the national Congress. "Power," wrote an essayist in the *Connecticut Courant*, "is as safe in the hands of Congress, as in the hands of the General Assembly; for the members of both are equally the representatives of the people."[94] The supporters of the proposed new government clearly believed that the nation needed a strong central government structure, and they blamed individual states for the weakness of the United States. "The conduct of the single states," wrote a writer in the *New Hampshire Recorder*, "have been like that of the Prodigal Son in the gospel. They have taken of the portion of their Independence, that should have been lodged forever in Congress, and spent it in riotous living in a far country."[95] Proponents of the Constitution viewed the national government as the key part of the political structure of the United States.

The Anti-Federalists, however, preferred to put their trust in the state governments, which they perceived as the central part of the American system. During the 1780s, as some Nationalists sought to strengthen the national government, several state leaders called for the dissolution of Congress as unneccessary on a regular basis. A special meeting could be called if any national issue or emergency arose.[96] Many who later opposed the Constitution feared that the attempts to strengthen the national government reflected a grasp for power similar to that exhibited by Great Britain during the 1760s.[97] Others declared that attempts to give the national government more money would only make it difficult for citizens to pay their state and local taxes.[98] For these men, the proposed Constitution "with one sweeping clause" destroyed all the state constitutions by establishing "its arbitrary doctrines, supreme and paramount to all the bills and declarations of rights, in which we vainly put our trust, and on which we rested the security of our own often declared unalienable liberties."[99] Those opposed to the proposed new government swore to fight this dangerous proposal, primarily by publishing their questions and reservations in the press.

In overall numbers, however, few essays against the Constitution appeared in American newspapers. The Anti-Federalists expressed great concern over their inability to get their ideas included in the public prints, revealing their belief in the definite impact of the press on the general public. Constitution supporters clearly agreed that newspapers could effect the ratification of the new government because they used economic pressure, such as cancelled subscriptions and discontinued advertisements, against Anti-Federalist printers. Only about a dozen opposition sheets existed in the entire country, and they suffered financially during the year of debate over the Constitution. Edward E. Powars, editor of Boston's *American Herald*, attempted to keep up the fight against the Constitution, but cancelled subscriptions and declining advertising forced him to cease his efforts against the Constitution and move his operation to Worcester in June 1788.[100]

Because of the lack of Anti-Federalist essays in the newspapers, opponents of the Constitution accused printers of being partial in the way they conducted their businesses. All hotly denied the charge, insisting that they published everything they were given and that their papers were "open to all parties."[101] John Carter of Providence, Rhode Island, asserted that, "whatever may have been my private sentiments respecting public measures, I have never suffered them to interfere with what I conceive to be the indispensable duty of an impartial Printer; nor have I at any time suffered myself to become the 'dupe' or 'tool' of a party."[102] Furthermore, Carter concluded that he had "faithfully and impartially handed to the Public every Performance, pro and con, that has been committed to him."[103] It is difficult to determine how truthful Carter was being in his assessment of the situation concerning the publication of materials opposed to the Constitution. Plainly, he believed that his press was fair and open to all, and most Federalist editors agreed, asserting that they printed whatever materials were submitted to them for publication. The Anti-Federalists, however, just as clearly thought that partisan newspaper printers in their communities consciously excluded essays that explained their dislike of the proposed new government.

Whatever the accuracy of Carter's defense, printers who supported the Constitution published few pieces in opposition to the proposed new government. In many cases, ardent Federalist printers probably found what they considered legitimate reasons for not publishing Anti-Federalist pieces. In Connecticut, for example, no public debate occurred because so few opposition essays appeared. Between the publication of the Constitution in September 1787 and its ratification by Connecticut fifteen weeks later, only six articles criticizing the proposed new government appeared in Connecticut newspapers.[104] "Candidus," an essayist in the *Independent Chronicle*, decried this situation. He wrote that "the adoption of the proposed Constitution, being a concern of such magnitude, we are in duty bound to hear with patience, the observations of our fellow citizens, provided their remarks are delivered with calmness and propriety" because discussion and debate "would be the means to unite every man, in embracing a system of Government, which might forever secure the liberties of this Country."[105]

The Anti-Federalists also had to face the problems of delays in the circulation of newspapers. Postmaster General Ebenezer Hazard, in an effort to save money, had restricted the free carriage of newspapers by postal riders. He could not have chosen a worse time for such changes. Printers depended almost completely on mail exchanges for their news. Anti-Federalist writers suspected a conspiracy and castigated Hazard and his employees for attempting to muzzle them. Complaints from opposition printers alone would lend support to the conspiracy theme, but Federalist publishers also complained of delays in the mails.[106] In February 1788, the *Independent Chronicle* stated that "[p]rinters in the northern States have received scarce a single paper, printed beyond the Hudson" since the beginning of the year.[107] A bottleneck had developed somewhere, but no one ever clearly ascertained its source. Because of his inability to solve the problem, Hazard lost his job after George Washington became president.

Although they accorded precious little space to Anti-Federalist pieces, printers did not seem to mind using part of their papers to castigate those who opposed the new government. They freely attacked those who criticized the Constitution, even impugning the characters of such Revolutionary heroes as Richard Henry Lee and Patrick Henry.[108] Equating Anti-Federalists with Tories and insurgents—"enemies of good government"[109] and "Shaysites"[110]—the newspapers described these people as dishonest and ignorant men who desired to welsh on their legal obligations. One correspondent in the *Massachusetts Gazette* assured everyone that the supporters of the Constitution had nothing to worry about: "[I]f the anti-federal cause . . . is as base and contemptible as the scribblers who advocate it, the federalists have very little to fear, for certainly a more despicable junto than the herd of anti-federal writers were never leagued together."[111]

Throughout the ratification struggle, the public prints took a keen interest in the state conventions called to consider the Constitution.[112] In words published in the *Massachusetts Centinel*, they wished for wisdom and understanding to be showered on the delegates: "May the Great Idea fill the mind of every member of this honourable body, that Heaven on this auspicious occasion favours America, with an opportunity never before enjoyed by the sons of men, of establishing a form of government peaceably and deliberately, which will secure to these states all those blessings which give worth to existence, or dignity to man, Peace, Liberty, and Safety!"[113] The *Newport Herald* warned that, "should any state reject this salutary system, unbiased posterity will consign their names to an infamous immortality."[114]

Joyfully, printers reported the ratification of the Constitution by each state. Benjamin Russell, editor of Boston's *Massachusetts Centinel*, introduced an illustration of ratification's progress that became popular throughout the country. Following Connecticut's approval in early January 1788, Russell printed a cartoon of five pillars, one for each state that had ratified. He added another pillar each time a new state voted in favor of the Constitution.[115] Newspapers all over the country reprinted this journalistic innovation—illustrations were rare in the public prints, and a continuing one such as this was unheard of. This cartoon became an easily recognizable symbol of unity for the new nation. A particularly happy day came when news of New Hampshire's approval, the ninth state to do so, arrived because, as the *Newport Mercury* declared, "by this fortunate Event we expect an efficient just and lasting Government will very soon take Place upon such a Foundation as no other Nation can boast of."[116] The editor of the *Cumberland Gazette* prayed, "[M]ay every other State erect a pillar to strengthen this noble building; and may it secure the freeborn sons of Columbia from every attempt to interrupt their peace—and last as long as the sun and moon endure."[117] Isaiah Thomas insisted that "this great event will stand unrivalled in history—a revolution of the kind we have no record of. The present era is one of the most important of our country, and bids fair greatly to promote our political happiness."[118]

In covering the ratification conventions in each state, the Federalist papers ridiculed those states that refused to approve the Constitution, namely, North Carolina and Rhode Island. The printer of the *New Hampshire Spy* reported that "the rejection of the new government by the state of North Carolina is not considered an affair of the first magnitude. Few tears have been shed in consequence of it, and but few people have troubled themselves about it."[119] North Carolina finally ratified the new government late in 1789.

Rhode Island received barbs for throwing "the shadow of a schism on the Bond that unites the great Federal Republic."[120] Rhode Island's reputation had suffered during the 1780s because of its refusal to ratify the proposed continental impost and for its paper money laws.[121] As declared in the *New York Daily Advertiser*, to many people, Rhode Island was "a State verging into anarchy and ruin from democratic licentiousness, while her Representatives are actuated by the most dangerous sentiments of usurpation and despotism."[122] The editors of the *Connecticut Courant* felt that Rhode Island's opposition constituted an "infallible sign of the justice and utility" of the Constitution.[123] Many felt no great loss that Rhode Island no longer belonged in the Union. The problem was a big one because Rhode Island could not really chart an independent course of its own; the possibility of invasion and dismemberment by neighbors was a very real threat.[124] Even prior to the Convention, an out-of-state correspondent in the *Pennsylvania Gazette* warned Rhode Island that "the confederation must take notice of you, and it seems the opinion of many here, that when the convention meets in Philadelphia, that measures will be taken to reduce you to order and good government, or strike your State out of the union, and annex you to others."[125] Rhode Island eventually bowed to the inevitable, ratifying the Constitution in 1790.[126]

In many ways, the push to force Rhode Island to approve the new government reflected a budding sense of nationalism, or at least nationhood, already appearing in the United States. Nationalism as a political force developed in the nineteenth century, but an awareness of unique identity appeared in a variety of countries long before the 1800s. The United States took part in this phenomenon. Although not having a long history of unique identity to call upon, Americans sought to create a history out of the pieces available to them.[127]

The newspapers of the young republic helped tremendously in this endeavor. Numerous descriptions of the glories and blessings of the United States appeared in print.[128] Such descriptions often provided a backdrop for comparisons between the United States and Europe. The newspapers generally downplayed the lack of a long history for the United States by emphasizing how the new nation would surpass the countries of the Old World. As described in the *Hampshire Gazette*: "The cloud which gathers in the European hemisphere serves, as a foil to set off the lustre of the prospect that opens upon America. . . . [T]he dotage of our parent continent is stained with wild ambition and fantastic pride, while the vigorous youth of the confederated states, expands under the influence of reason and philosophy."[129]

Another early effort at history making, one that appeared almost before the nation itself did, was the creation of heroes. George Washington in particular became a national hero almost overnight. Describing him as the "American Fabius"[130] and the "American Cincinnatus,"[131] the newspapers portrayed Washington as the ultimate citizen soldier who did not use his military achievements to gain political power.[132] By the mid-1780s, public celebrations of his birthday occurred throughout the country, an event dutifully reported by the newspapers.[133] By the time the states adopted the Constitution, many saw Washington as one of the greatest human beings ever to live, one clearly destined to be the first president of the new nation. The *Newport Mercury* proclaimed: "Can Europe boast of such a Man?—or can the History of the World shew an instance of such a voluntary compact between the Deliverer and the Delivered of any country, as will probably soon take place in the United States?"[134] The development of such reverence for Washington reflects a romantic impulse that became dominant in the telling of American history in the nineteenth century. Washington, in conjunction with Benedict Arnold, became the first of a series of great heroes and evil villains that people such as historians George Bancroft and Francis Parkman later wrote about in their histories of the United States.

The debates over the Constitution provided another excuse for printers to encourage a sense of nationhood by emphasizing the uniqueness of the entire process. Although those involved in the Glorious Revolution in Great Britain in 1689 would have disagreed, most Americans, including the newspaper printers, described the Constitutional Convention and its aftermath as something totally new and unheard of in world history. Adjectives used included an event that "seems quite novel in the history of governments,"[135] "an event that has never occurred since the formation of society,"[136] and "this great event [that] will stand unrivalled in history."[137] Newspaper printers continually praised the Constitution and the possibilities it promised for the future.[138] Benjamin Russell referred to the situation as "one of those few opportunities which occur in the revolution of human affairs, for the unfolding and displaying the amazing powers of the human mind."[139]

Following ratification and the inauguration of the new government, several editors considered the events of the last several years. The pages of the *Salem Mercury* summed up the reflections of countless persons on the dangers avoided and their prayers for the future:

On contemplating our country, just arrived upon the solid and uniform tract of regular, equitable and effectual government, after having so narrowly escaped the dreadful calamity of anarchy and disunion; while, on one hand, civil disunion yawned for our peace and safety, and on the other, foreign subjugation watched, to devour all that was valuable in life, the present pleasing reverse of affairs must yield delight to every beholder. . . . May the national blessings resulting from this political revolution, continue, and continually expand, from generation to generation, till the last shock of Time buries the Empires of the world in one undistinguished ruin.[140]

With the inauguration of the new government in 1789, Boston's *Herald of Freedom* painted a glorious picture of what the future held for America:

Trade and commerce now raise their drooping heads, the Mechanick brandishes the tool of industry in triumph, and the husbandman repairs to the field with vigour; justice, from her sacred seat, views with pleasure the once benighted prospect, now dawning into brightness resplendent as nature's purest light; while publick faith and honour gladden at the thought of our reviving credit. May America never cease to pay the tribute of gratitude she owes to the bountiful Parent of the Universe; may her citizens prove themselves worthy to enjoy the blessings heaped upon them: and may our country increase in splendour and glory 'till the "course of nature changes, and the sun shall have finished its last diurnal rotation round the skies."[141]

Most American newspaper printers would have agreed. With the new form of government, the United States now stood ready to take its rightful place in the world, and the newspapers of the young government stood prepared to help guide and record the march into a glorious future.

NOTES

1. *Pennsylvania Gazette* (Philadelphia), 3 December 1783.

2. Isaiah Thomas had learned the printing business in Boston from Zachariah Fowle. He established the *Massachusetts Spy* in Boston in 1770 and moved it to Worcester following the Battles of Lexington and Concord in 1775. An important Revolutionary printer, Thomas also earned a place in journalism history by authoring the *History of Printing in America* in 1810 and founding the American Antiquarian Society (AAS) in 1812. The nucleus of the early newspaper collection of the AAS came from Thomas's personal collection of newspapers published prior to 1810. The only book-length study of Thomas is Clifford K. Shipton, *Isaiah Thomas: Printer, Patriot, and Philanthropist, 1749–1831* (Rochester, N.Y.: Printing House of Leo Hart, 1948).

3. Although Benjamin Russell was an important printer and newspaper publisher throughout his career, no detailed biographical studies of his life have been produced.

4. Numbers for 1783 are based on Clarence S. Brigham, *History and Bibliography of American Newspapers, 1690–1820*, 2 vols. (Worcester, Mass.: American Antiquarian Society, 1947); numbers for 1790, from Alfred McClung Lee, *The Daily Newspaper in America* (New York: Macmillan, 1937), 711.

5. See, for example, *Providence* (R.I.) *Gazette*, 24 February, 10 and 24 March, 7 July 1781.

6. John Bard McNulty, *Older Than the Nation: The Story of the Hartford Courant* (Stonington, Conn.: Pequot Press, 1964), 27; *Exchange Advertiser* (Boston), 2 June 1785; *Independent Chronicle* (Boston), 15 February 1787; *New Hampshire Spy* (Portsmouth), 3

April 1787; John P. Kaminski and Gaspare J. Saladino, eds., *Commentaries on the Constitution, Public and Private*, vol. 1, vol. 13 of *The Documentary History of the Ratification of the Constitution* (Madison: State Historical Society of Wisconsin, 1981), 76.

7. *Independent Chronicle*, 18 April 1782.

8. Ibid., 24 July 1783.

9. See, for example, *American Mercury* (Hartford), 6 September 1784, 11 September 1786; *Connecticut Courant* (Hartford), 7 September 1784, 5 February, 19 March, 6 August 1787; *Providence Gazette*, 11 September 1784; *Exchange Advertiser*, 2 June 1785; *Independent Chronicle*, 9, 23, and 30 March, 7 and 20 April, 11, 18, and 25 May, 1, 15, and 22 June 1786; *New Hampshire Mercury* (Portsmouth), 16 August 1786; *Worcester* (Mass.) *Magazine*, third week in May, third week in June 1786; *Boston Gazette*, 19 June 1786; *Independent Ledger* (Boston), 7 August 1786; *Freeman's Oracle* (Exeter, N.H.), 29 August 1786; *Connecticut Gazette* (New London), 8 September 1786; *New Hampshire Spy*, 6 February 1787; *Norwich* (Conn.) *Packet*, 5 July 1787; Merrill Jensen, ed., *Ratification of the Constitution by the States: Delaware, New Jersey, Georgia, and Connecticut*, vol. 3 of *The Documentary History of the Ratification of the Constitution* (Madison: State Historical Society of Wisconsin, 1978), 484.

10. *Freeman's Oracle*, 5 September 1786.

11. *Massachusetts Centinel* (Boston), 13 June 1787.

12. *Hampshire Herald* (Springfield, Mass.), 16 November 1784.

13. *Independent Chronicle*, 8 June 1786.

14. *Connecticut Courant*, 24 July 1786.

15. Ibid., 25 May 1784.

16. E. James Ferguson, "State Assumption of the Federal Debt During the Confederation," *Mississippi Valley Historical Review* 39 (December 1951): 413–14.

17. *Providence Gazette*, 22 February 1783.

18. *Connecticut Courant*, 2 March 1784.

19. Ibid., 26 March 1786.

20. *New Hampshire Mercury*, 7 June 1785; *American Herald* (Boston), 9 March 1786; *Massachusetts Spy* (Worcester), 9 March 1786; *Connecticut Courant*, 26 March, 6 November 1786; *Providence Gazette*, 2 December 1786, 16 June 1787; *Continental Journal* (Boston), 3 January 1787; *Massachusetts Centinel*, 12 April 1788.

21. *Connecticut Gazette*, 21 April 1786.

22. *Independent Chronicle*, 2 June 1785.

23. *Connecticut Gazette*, 28 April 1786; *Exchange Advertiser*, 22 June 1786; *New Hampshire Recorder* (Keene), 28 August 1787; Jensen, *Ratification of the Constitution*, 97, 148; Speech of Joel Barlow, 4 July 1787, excerpts recorded by Reverend Lemuel G. Olmstead, Joel Barlow Papers, American Antiquarian Society, Worcester, Mass.

24. *Providence Gazette*, 30 December 1786.

25. *Massachusetts Gazette* (Boston), summer of 1782, 22 June 1784; *Hampshire Herald*, 2 November 1784, 19 September 1786; *Worcester Magazine*, fourth week in September 1786, third week in December 1786; *Freeman's Oracle*, 26 September 1786; *Norwich Packet*, 5 October 1786; *Boston Gazette*, 23 October, 25 December 1786; *Vermont Journal* (Windsor), 6 November 1786; *Independent Chronicle*, 24 May 1787. Shays's Rebellion and its impact on the move to adopt the Constitution has long been a subject of interest to historians. Most studies of the 1780s, even when not considering the revolt directly, address the results of Shays's Rebellion in some detail. See, for example, Richard Buel, Jr., *Dear Liberty: Connecticut's Mobilization for the Revolutionary War* (Middle-

town, Conn.: Wesleyan University Press, 1980), 288–90; Christopher Collier, *Roger Sherman's Connecticut: Yankee Politics and the American Revolution* (Middletown, Conn.: Wesleyan University Press, 1971), 224–25; Florence Parker Simister, *The Fire's Center: Rhode Island in the Revolutionary Era, 1763–1790* (Providence: Rhode Island Bicentennial Foundation, 1979), 231; Chilton Williamson, *Vermont in Quandary, 1763–1825* (Montpelier: Vermont Historical Society, 1949), 112, 168–71; Jere Daniell, *Experiment in Republicanism: New Hampshire Politics and the American Revolution, 1741–1794* (Cambridge: Harvard University Press, 1970), 196–99; Robert E. Brown, *Middle-Class Democracy and the Revolution in Massachusetts, 1691–1780* (Ithaca, N.Y.: Cornell University Press for the American Historical Association, 1955), 114–23, 184; Irwin H. Polishook, *Rhode Island and the Union, 1774–1795* (Evanston, Ill.: Northwestern University Press, 1969), 178. For an in-depth study of the revolt itself, see David P. Szatmary, *Shays's Rebellion: The Making of an Agrarian Insurrection* (Amherst: University of Massachusetts Press, 1980).

26. *Independent Chronicle*, 4 October 1787. Also printed in *Massachusetts Gazette*, 5 October 1787.

27. *Independent Chronicle*, 29 March 1787.

28. *Independent Chronicle*, 9 March, 15 and 29 June 1786, 18 January 1787, 31 July 1788.

29. *American Mercury*, 4 September 1786; *New Hampshire Mercury*, 6 September 1786; *Providence Gazette*, 9 September 1786; *Worcester Magazine*, third week in September 1786, fifth week in November 1786; *United States Chronicle* (Providence, R.I.), 14 June 1787.

30. *Massachusetts Gazette*, 25 August 1786.

31. *Worcester Magazine*, fourth week in September 1786. See also the first week of January 1787.

32. *Norwich Packet*, 2 November 1786.

33. *Worcester Magazine*, first week in April 1787.

34. *Freeman's Oracle*, 31 March 1787.

35. *Norwich Packet*, 2 November 1786.

36. The best minutes of the Convention are those made by James Madison. He did not indicate that there was active opposition at the time the Convention adopted the restriction. However, in later months, several delegates expressed dislike for the secrecy rule. Luther Martin of Maryland stated publicly his misgivings concerning the restriction after he had withdrawn from the Convention. Also after withdrawing from the Convention, John Lansing and Robert Yates of New York broke the secrecy rule when they told Governor George Clinton that the delegates were exceeding their instructions. William Paterson of New Jersey, a delegate who remained in the Convention, also expressed discontent with the secrecy rule because he wished to confer with the people he represented before the final vote. During the ratification struggle, the Anti-Federalists severely criticized the Convention's decision to operate in secret. Charles Warren, *The Making of the Constitution* (New York: Little, Brown, 1937 (1928)), 137–38, 354, 761; Carl Van Doren, *The Great Rehearsal: The Story of the Making and Ratifying of the Constitution of the United States* (New York: Viking Penguin, 1948), 124–25, 231. In the day of the Freedom of Information Act and open meetings laws, the Convention secrecy rule often strikes a discordant note. However, studies of the decision clearly indicate that the issues produced little real debate or disagreement among the delegates in Philadelphia. For a more detailed discussion of the organizational days of the Convention and the decision for secrecy, see Clinton Rossiter, *1787: The Grand Con-*

vention (New York: W. W. Norton, 1987 (1966)), 167–68; Warren, *The Making of the Constitution*, 134–38; Max Farrand, *The Framing of the Constitution of the United States* (New Haven, Conn.: Yale University Press, 1913), 58; Donald Barr Chidsey, *The Birth of the Constitution* (New York: Crown, 1964), 40; Richard B. Morris, *Witnesses at the Creation: Hamilton, Madison, Jay, and the Constitution* (New York: Henry Holt, 1985), 198–99; Robert Middlekauff, *The Glorious Cause: The American Revolution, 1763–1789* (New York: Oxford University Press, 1982), 628; Jack N. Rakove, *The Beginnings of National Politics: An Interpretive History of the Continental Congress* (Baltimore, Md.: Johns Hopkins University Press, 1979), 399; Van Doren, *The Great Rehearsal*, 28–29; Reid Goldsborough, "Debate in the Press," *Media History Digest* 7 (1987): 18–21; Victor Rosewater, "The Constitutional Convention in the Colonial Press," *Journalism Quarterly* 14 (December 1937): 364–66.

37. Carol Sue Humphrey, "'Little Ado About Something': Philadelphia Newspapers and the Constitutional Convention," *American Journalism* 5 (1988): 63–64, 71–72.

38. For a good discussion of the varieties of materials printed about the Convention, see John K. Alexander, *The Selling of the Constitutional Convention: A History of News Coverage* (Madison, Wis.: Madison House, 1990).

39. See, for example, *Independent Gazetteer* (Philadelphia), 1 and 16 May, 1 June 1787; *Pennsylvania Evening Herald* (Philadelphia), 2, 19, and 30 May 1787; *Pennsylvania Mercury* (Philadelphia), 4 and 18 May 1787; *Pennsylvania Packet* (Philadelphia), 14, 15, 17, 19, 30, and 31 May, 15 and 25 June, 21 July 1787; *Pennsylvania Journal* (Philadelphia), 23 and 30 May, 2 and 16 June, 22 August 1787; *Pennsylvania Gazette*, 25 July, 22 August 1787.

40. *Independent Gazetteer*, 13 June 1787. Also printed in *Freeman's Journal* (Philadelphia), 20 June 1787.

41. *Independent Gazetteer*, 27 June 1787. Also printed in *Pennsylvania Packet*, 28 June 1787; *Pennsylvania Mercury*, 29 June 1787; *Pennsylvania Journal*, 30 June 1787.

42. *Pennsylvania Packet*, 27 June 1787.

43. *Independent Gazetteer*, 16 June 1787. Also printed in *Pennsylvania Journal*, 16 June 1787; *Pennsylvania Gazette*, 20 June 1787.

44. *New Hampshire Gazette* (Portsmouth), 19 May 1787.

45. See, for example, *Independent Gazetteer*, 12 and 14 May 1787; *Pennsylvania Packet*, 14 May, 4 August 1787; *Freeman's Journal*, 16 May 1787; *Pennsylvania Journal*, 16 and 26 May, 11 August 1787.

46. *Independent Gazetteer*, 30 May 1787; *Pennsylvania Gazette*, 30 May 1787; *Pennsylvania Journal*, 30 May 1787.

47. *Pennsylvania Evening Herald*, 12 May 1787.

48. *Pennsylvania Packet*, 23 August 1787.

49. *Pennsylvania Gazette*, 22 August 1787. Also printed in *Pennsylvania Journal*, 25 August 1787.

50. See, for example, *Pennsylvania Packet*, 19 May, 12 and 30 July 1787; *Independent Gazetteer*, 22 May, 6 June 1787; *Pennsylvania Gazette*, 23 May, 1 August 1787; *Pennsylvania Journal*, 23 May 1787.

51. *Pennsylvania Gazette*, 2 May 1787; *Pennsylvania Evening Herald*, 9 June 1787.

52. *Pennsylvania Journal*, 30 May 1787. Also printed in *Pennsylvania Packet*, 5 June 1787.

53. See, for example, *Independent Gazetteer*, 19 and 30 May, 7, 23, and 27 June, 18 and 27 July, 17 August, 1 September 1787; *Pennsylvania Gazette*, 23 and 30 May, 8, 15, 22, and

29 August 1787; *Connecticut Courant,* 28 May 1787; *Massachusetts Centinel,* 30 June 1787.

54. *Providence Gazette,* 11 August 1787.

55. *Pennsylvania Gazette,* 30 May 1787. Also printed in *Independent Gazetteer,* 30 May 1787; *Pennsylvania Journal,* 30 May 1787.

56. *Independent Gazetteer,* 7 August 1787; *Pennsylvania Gazette,* 8 August 1787.

57. *Pennsylvania Gazette,* 29 August 1787.

58. *Connecticut Courant,* 25 June 1787.

59. *Freeman's Journal,* 16 May 1787. Also printed in *Pennsylvania Gazette,* 13 June 1787; *Pennsylvania Packet,* 21 June 1787.

60. *Connecticut Courant,* 25 June 1788.

61. *Independent Chronicle,* 9 August 1787.

62. *Connecticut Courant,* 28 May 1787.

63. See, for example, *New Hampshire Recorder,* 21 August 1787; *American Herald,* Fall 1787; *Salem* (Mass.) *Mercury,* Fall 1787; *Worcester Magazine,* December 1787, January 1788; *Hampshire Gazette* (Northampton, Mass.), 5 December 1787; *Newport* (R.I.) *Mercury,* January–March 1788. There have not been many detailed studies of the coverage of the Convention in the newspapers. Most journalism history textbooks mention the Constitutional Convention, but do not discuss it in any depth. Their discussions focus more on the ratification debates, which occurred in late 1787 and throughout 1788. For example, see Rosewater, "The Constitutional Convention in the Colonial Press," 364–66; Jim Allee Hart, *The Developing Views on the News: Editorial Syndrome, 1500–1800* (Carbondale: Southern Illinois University Press, 1970), 169–73; Willard Grosvenor Bleyer, *Main Currents in the History of American Journalism* (Boston: Houghton Mifflin, 1927), 102–104; Frank Luther Mott, *American Journalism: A History of Newspapers in the United States Through 250 Years, 1690–1940* (New York: Macmillan, 1941), 131–32; Sidney Kobre, *Development of American Journalism* (Dubuque, Iowa: William C. Brown, 1969), 106; Michael Emery and Edwin Emery, *The Press and America: An Interpretive History of the Mass Media,* 6th ed. (Englewood Cliffs, N.J.: Prentice-Hall, 1988 (1954)), 72–73; George Henry Payne, *History of Journalism in the United States* (New York: D. Appleton and Co., 1920), 146; Robert A. Rutland, *Newsmongers: Journalism in the Life of the Nation, 1690–1972* (New York: Dial Press, 1973), 57–58.

64. *Middlesex Gazette* (Middletown, Conn.), 21 July 1788.

65. *Massachusetts Centinel,* 17 November 1787.

66. *Connecticut Courant,* 16 July 1787.

67. *Independent Gazetteer,* 6 July 1787.

68. *Newport* (R.I.) *Herald,* 3 July 1788.

69. *Independent Chronicle,* 19 July 1787.

70. *New Hampshire Gazette,* 16 November 1787.

71. *Massachusetts Centinel,* 29 September 1788.

72. Ibid., 1 November 1788.

73. Ibid., 10 November 1787.

74. Ibid., 29 September 1787.

75. *Independent Chronicle,* 10 January 1788.

76. Ibid., 5 June 1788.

77. Ibid., 4 October 1787.

78. *Cumberland Gazette* (Portland, Me.), 24 January 1788.

79. *Boston Gazette,* 15 October 1787.

80. *Connecticut Gazette*, 26 October 1787.

81. Clinton Rossiter, ed., *The Federalist Papers* (New York: New American Library, 1961), vii–xvi; Kaminski and Saladino, *Commentaries on the Constitution*, 490–94; Francis Newton Thorpe, *The Constitutional History of the United States* (Chicago: Callaghan, 1901), 2: 137–38.

82. See, for example, *Independent Chronicle*, 9 March 1786; *Connecticut Courant*, 13 March, 21 August 1786.

83. *Independent Chronicle*, 2 June 1785; *New Hampshire Mercury*, 7 June 1785; *American Herald*, 20 June 1785; *Worcester Magazine*, third week of June 1786; *Connecticut Gazette*, 8 September 1786; *American Mercury*, 11 September 1786; *Freeman's Oracle*, 7 November 1786.

84. In writing *An Economic Interpretation of the Constitution of the United States* (1913), historian Charles Beard did not use newspapers. It is a detriment to his economic argument that he did not do so because he would have found much support for his ideas. For American printers in the 1780s, economic issues provided the centerpiece of a host of arguments in favor of a new and stronger national government.

85. *Massachusetts Spy*, 9 March 1786; *Boston Gazette*, 19 June 1786; *Freeman's Oracle*, 29 August 1786; *Independent Chronicle*, 15 February 1787; *New York Daily Advertiser* (New York), 24 March 1787; *Connecticut Journal* (New Haven), 18 April 1787; *Essex Journal* (Newburyport, Mass.), 25 April 1787.

86. *Connecticut Courant*, 24 July, 6 November 1786; *Independent Ledger*, 7 August 1786; *Providence Gazette*, 2 December 1786; *Connecticut Journal*, 3 January, 16 June, 11 August 1787; *Pennsylvania Gazette*, 30 May 1787; *Massachusetts Centinel*, 20 October 1787, 12 April 1788; *New Hampshire Gazette*, 16 November 1787; *Boston Gazette*, 10 December 1787, 14 January 1788.

87. Reprinted in *Connecticut Gazette*, 21 April 1786.

88. *Newport Mercury*, 17 March 1788.

89. *Providence Gazette*, 8 December 1787, 29 March 1788.

90. *Freeman's Journal*, 7 November 1787. Also printed in *Providence Gazette*, 24 November 1787.

91. *Providence Gazette*, 29 March 1788.

92. *New Hampshire Spy*, 6 February 1787.

93. *Connecticut Courant*, 5 February 1787.

94. Ibid., 19 March 1787.

95. *New Hampshire Recorder*, 28 August 1787.

96. *Boston Evening Post*, 28 June 1783.

97. See, for example, *Boston Evening Post*, 30 August 1783.

98. *Hampshire Herald*, 7 February 1786.

99. *Providence Gazette*, 8 December 1787, reprinted from *New York Journal* (New York).

100. Rutland, *Newsmongers*, 59, 62–63. As a group, the Anti-Federalists have not received much study. Two good works on their ideas and efforts are Jackson Turner Main, *The Antifederalists: Critics of the Constitution, 1781–1788* (Chapel Hill: University of North Carolina Press for the Institute of Early American History and Culture, Williamsburg, Va., 1961), 250–51; Robert A. Rutland, *The Ordeal of the Constitution: The Antifederalists and the Ratification Struggle of 1787–1788* (Norman: University of Oklahoma Press, 1965), 37–38, 72–74, 135, 138, 267.

101. John Bixler Hench, "The Newspaper in a Republic: Boston's *Centinel* and *Chronicle*, 1784–1801" (Ph.D. diss., Clark University, 1979), 157; *Freeman's Oracle*, 18 January

1787; *American Herald*, 15 October, 17 December 1787, 21 August 1788; *Boston Gazette*, 3 December 1787; *Newport Herald*, 2 October 1788; *New Hampshire Recorder*, 6 January 1789.

102. *Providence Gazette*, 29 December 1787.

103. Ibid., 12 January 1788.

104. J. Eugene Smith, *One Hundred Years of Hartford's Courant: From Colonial Times Through the Civil War* (New Haven, Conn.: Yale University Press, 1949), 63–66; Judith Maxen Katz, "Connecticut Newspapers and the Constitution, 1786–1788," *Connecticut Historical Society Bulletin* 30 (1965): 41; *Connecticut Courant*, 10 and 24 December 1787; *American Mercury*, 24 December 1787.

105. *Independent Chronicle*, 3 January 1788.

106. Rutland, *Newsmongers*, 64–65; Main, *The Antifederalists*, 249–50; Rutland, *Ordeal of the Constitution*, 128–34.

107. *Independent Chronicle*, 21 February 1788.

108. See, for example, Collier, *Roger Sherman's Connecticut*, 223; *New Haven Gazette, and Connecticut Magazine*, 8 February 1787; *Freeman's Oracle*, 29 February 1787, 8 November 1788; *Salem Mercury*, 7 August 1787; *Connecticut Courant*, 22 October 1787, 30 June 1788; *Hampshire Chronicle* (Springfield, Mass.), 25 December 1787, 9 July 1788; *New Hampshire Spy*, 8 and 11 January 1788; *Connecticut Journal*, 9 July 1788.

109. *Norwich Packet*, 13 March 1788.

110. *Boston Gazette*, 22 October 1787.

111. *Massachusetts Gazette*, 29 January 1788.

112. Kaminski and Saladino, *Commentaries on the Constitution*, xxxvii; *Connecticut Courant*, 26 November, 31 December 1787; *Independent Chronicle*, 10 January to 13 March 1788; *Boston Gazette*, 11 February, 12 May, 9 and 23 June, 7 July 1788; *Essex Journal*, 13 February 1788; *Newport Herald*, 14 February 1788; *Salem Mercury*, 10 June 1788; *New Hampshire Spy*, 24 June, 22 July 1788; *New Hampshire Gazette*, 26 June 1788.

113. *Massachusetts Centinel*, 9 January 1788.

114. *Newport Herald*, 27 September 1787.

115. *Massachusetts Centinel*, 9 January 1788.

116. *Newport Mercury*, 30 June 1788.

117. *Cumberland Gazette*, 26 June 1788.

118. *Massachusetts Spy*, 10 July 1788.

119. *New Hampshire Spy*, 26 August 1788.

120. *Connecticut Journal*, 9 December 1789. Also printed in *Connecticut Gazette*, 11 December 1789.

121. Polishook, *Rhode Island and the Union*, 173, 195–96, 208, 211.

122. *New York Daily Advertiser*, 9 April 1787.

123. *Connecticut Courant*, 10 November 1788.

124. *Newport Herald*, 12 April 1787, 26 March 1789; *United States Chronicle*, 1 November 1787; *Salem Mercury*, 15 January 1788; *Massachusetts Centinel*, 26 April, 20 August 1788; *Providence Gazette*, 4 and 23 August 1788; *Norwich Packet*, 8 October 1789; *Newport Mercury*, 23 December 1789.

125. *Pennsylvania Gazette*, 2 May 1787.

126. Polishook, *Rhode Island and the Union*, 230.

127. Henry Steele Commager asserts that Americans created a history for themselves primarily through one of three ways. First, they asserted that "they had no need for ancestors, for they themselves were ancestors." Second, they said that "America had, in fact, the

most impressive of all pasts; ALL Europe was the American past." The first resulted in an almost overwhelming confidence in the future, while the second produced the dichotomy of "New World innocence and Old World corruption." Still, neither of these proved totally satisfying, so the third way appeared—the use of what was available. In this third area, the newspapers played a vital role, as they provided the means to create heroes and heap praise on American successes. Henry Steele Commager, "The Search for a Usable Past," *American Heritage*, February 1965, 4–9, 90–96. Americans also sought to develop their own literature and culture, separate from that of Europe. Newspapers played a significant role in this process by encouraging the overall goal and by publishing works of individual authors. For a good discussion of this change, see Hans Kohn, *American Nationalism* (New York: Macmillan, 1957), Chap. 2.

128. See, for example, *American Mercury*, 21 August 1786; *Newport Mercury*, 28 August 1786; *American Herald*, 30 September 1787; *Middlesex Gazette*, 26 November 1787; *Herald of Freedom* (Boston), 27 November 1788.

129. *Hampshire Gazette*, 10 October 1787.

130. *Continental Journal*, 15 February 1787; *Newport Mercury,* 13 August 1787.

131. *New Hampshire Spy*, 15 May 1787.

132. *Newport Mercury*, 13 August 1787; *Hampshire Chronicle*, 13 August 1788.

133. See, for example, *Continental Journal*, 10 February 1785; *Vermont Gazette* (Westminster), 14 February 1785; *Continental Journal*, 15 February 1787; *Independent Chronicle,* 12 February 1789.

134. *Newport Mercury*, 15 October 1787.

135. *Connecticut Courant*, 16 July 1787.

136. *Independent Chronicle*, 19 July 1787.

137. *Massachusetts Spy*, 10 July 1788.

138. See, for example, *Connecticut Courant*, 3 March 1788; *New Haven Gazette, and Connecticut Magazine*, 19 June 1788; *American Mercury*, 14 July 1788.

139. *Massachusetts Centinel*, 19 January 1788.

140. *Salem Mercury*, 3 March 1789.

141. *Herald of Freedom*, 28 April 1789.

2

The Adoption of the
Bill of Rights, 1789–1791

Although the new Constitution provided for a more stable government than the one established under the Articles of Confederation, many people expressed unhappiness about it. Even before its initial proposal by the Philadelphia Convention, and continuing throughout the ratification process, detractors expressed concern over the failure of the new government structure to provide specifically for the protection of individual rights, including the freedom of the press. "Centinel" summed up the fears of many when he warned his "Friends, Countrymen and Fellow Citizens" to be wary of the government because it limited "certain liberties and privileges secured to you by the constitution of this commonwealth."[1] Although the issue of a bill of rights did not prevent ratification of the Constitution, it slowed down the process and became an issue of concern that the new government had to deal with almost immediately.

The earliest concerns over the need for a national bill of rights appeared during the meeting of the Constitutional Convention in Philadelphia. On August 20, 1787, Charles Pinckney of South Carolina submitted a series of proposals that would have protected a variety of civil liberties, including freedom of the press. The Convention referred the proposal to the Committee of Detail for further study; there it quietly died with no action taken.[2]

The strongest call for protection of civil liberties in the proposed Constitution came from George Mason, author of the Virginia Declaration of Rights.[3] On September 12, the day the Convention began consideration of the final draft of the Constitution, Mason urged the addition of a bill of rights because "it would give great quiet to the people." He further stated that "with the aid of the State declarations, a bill might be prepared in a few hours." Elbridge Gerry of Massachusetts agreed and moved that a committee be appointed to prepare a bill of rights. Mason seconded the motion, but it received little support from other Convention members. Roger Sherman of Connecticut responded that a national bill of rights was not necessary because the state bills of rights would remain unchanged and remain in force after the new Constitution took effect. Mason, apparently fearing the worst, reminded the Convention that the proposed Constitution clearly stated the supremacy of the national government and its law, but his urgings fell on deaf ears. Gerry's motion failed, with not even one state voting in favor of it.[4]

· Although the delegates overlooked Mason's concerns, both Pinckney and Gerry had not given up completely. On September 14, 1787, while the delegates debated and edited the Constitution in detail, Pinckney and Gerry proposed the inclusion of a statement "that the liberty of the Press should be inviolably observed." Sherman immediately responded that such a statement was not needed because "the power of Congress does not extend to the Press." The proposal failed to pass.[5]

Most of the members of the Constitutional Convention clearly felt that the state bills of rights provided enough protection for individual rights, or possibly they were just in a hurry to finish their business so they could go home. It had been a long, hot summer in Philadelphia, and they overlooked or ignored most last-minute proposals at the Convention. However, Mason and Gerry both felt so strongly about their objections to the proposed new government, which included the lack of a national bill of rights, that both of them refused to sign the Constitution when completed. These two men may have had a better sense of the American people at the time because the lack of protection for civil liberties became a major issue during the ratification struggle that followed. When the Constitutional Convention adjourned on September 17, 1787, with a finished document to present to the American public, much of their work lay before them as they worked to gain approval for the proposed new government.

The correspondence of James Madison and Thomas Jefferson following the adoption of the Constitution by the Convention reflected the depth of the debate to come over the lack of a bill of rights in the proposed Constitution for the national government. Madison wrote to Jefferson that he favored a bill of rights, "provided it be so framed as not to imply powers not meant to be included in the enumeration," but that its absence was not "a material defect." However, "it is anxiously desired by others. I have favored it because I supposed it might be of use, and if properly executed could not be of disservice."[6]

Jefferson responded that a bill of rights was absolutely essential if the proposed government was to be fair and honest. In critiquing the Constitution, he felt that the lack of a bill of rights greatly weakened the proposed instrument of governance and that protections for individual rights would have to be included at some point in time: "Let me add that a bill of rights is what the people are entitled to against every government on earth, general or particular, & what no just government should refuse or rest on inferences."[7] Jefferson supported the Constitution in general and hoped that the needed nine states would ratify it quickly. However, he also desired that the remaining four states refuse to ratify in order to force the adoption of a bill of rights to correct the defects he perceived in the proposed government.[8]

Jefferson's concern proved to be a good reflection of public opinion, and the supporters of the Constitution eventually acceded to the demand for a bill of rights in order to achieve ratification. When the Continental Congress discussed the proposed Constitution, Richard Henry Lee of Virginia tried, and failed, to get a bill of rights added prior to the submission of the Constitution to the state legislatures.[9] Lee need not have worried because a number of the state ratifying conventions made the inclusion of protections against arbitrary government action a prerequisite for their approval of the Constitution.

Of the twelve states that ratified the Constitution prior to the approval of the Bill of Rights in 1791, eight urged in some manner that amendments be made to the document in order to protect civil liberties. The proposals varied in content, but all clearly aimed at limiting the actions of the national government in its dealings with individual citizens. Many of the proposals concerned financial and judicial matters, and the freedom of the press did not become a major issue throughout the process of ratification. In fact, only five states (Pennsylvania, Maryland, Virginia, New York, and North Carolina) even considered the issue of a free press. Of these five, only three states ratified with proposed amendments (Virginia, New York, and North Carolina), including a proposal to protect the liberty of the press.[10]

When the First Congress convened in March 1789, the new federal legislators had much on their minds: how to set up the new government structure so that it could operate smoothly, how to raise money in order to pay off the national debt, and how to establish finances on a firm basis. For many of them, the need to amend the new government was low on their list of priorities. For James Madison, the issue of amendments was of paramount importance. He considered it one of the most immediate concerns for Congress to consider for several reasons. First, several states had ratified the Constitution on the assumption that a bill of rights would be added immediately after the new government took office. Second, Madison himself had been elected to the House of Representatives on the basis of a personal promise to secure amendments. For him, the issue of protections for civil liberties could not wait—something had to be done immediately.[11]

On May 4, 1789, Madison informed the House of Representatives that he planned to bring up the subject of a bill of rights in the near future. On June 8, he moved that the House constitute itself a committee of the whole in order to consider proposed amendments. He met with little support for this motion because many congressmen believed that the government had more important matters to consider. Madison, however, refused to yield and continued to remind the legislature that something needed to be done. Finally, on July 21, the House referred the issue of amendments, and Madison's list of proposals, to a select committee for further consideration. The committee reported on July 28, and during the next month, the House debated and discussed the various proposals. Finally, on August

24, 1789, the House of Representatives adopted seventeen amendments and sent them to the Senate for action.[12]

The Senate began considering the proposed amendments on September 2. One week later, it adopted a list that differed somewhat from the group adopted by the House. A conference committee worked out the disagreements, and following some further debate, both houses adopted the conference committee report. On September 25, 1789, Congress sent the proposed twelve amendments to the state legislatures for consideration. The ratification process took over two years, but, finally, on December 15, 1791, Virginia became the last of eleven states needed to ratify the ten amendments that today constitute the Bill of Rights. The First Amendment, actually the third of the twelve proposed by Congress, provided for freedom of the press: "Congress shall make no law respecting an establishment of religion or prohibiting the free exercise thereof; or abridging the freedom of speech, or of the press, or the right of the people peaceably to assemble and to petition the government for a redress of grievances."[13]

The liberty of the press had finally found formal and official protection in the national government, but precedent for such protection reached far back into American history. The individual states based local legal practice on British common law, which provided protection for the press from prior restraint in most cases. In the American colonies, British practices had been expanded and broadened through New World experiences. In New England, the Puritans developed a relatively tolerant outlook concerning freedom of the press because of their strong belief in the need to be able to discuss religious ideas and beliefs.[14] The Puritan belief in the need for a free pursuit of spiritual truth would be strengthened by the ideas of the Enlightenment and its emphasis on a search for rational solutions to problems that appeared in the eighteenth century.[15] America also lacked a rigid class system such as existed in Europe, primarily because the New World had not experienced medieval feudalism.[16] The absence of a dominant landed nobility helped disseminate a variety of rights throughout the entire population. By the time of the American Revolution, the colonials believed that the government was limited in its dealings with the citizens, since all people had certain rights that could not be violated. Among these natural rights was the freedom of the press.

The newly established states sought to protect this and other rights in the documents written to create new governments. By the time the Constitutional Convention met in Philadelphia in 1787, nine of the original thirteen states had provided protection for freedom of expression in their constitutions. The most famous of these state documents, the Virginia Declaration of Rights (1776), stated "that freedom of the press is one of the great bulwarks of liberty, and can never be restrained but by despotick governments." Liberty of the press, not always honored in practice and not made a permanent part of the national government until 1791, had long been an accepted idea in British America.[17]

Given the long history of support for freedom of expression in America, it would be expected for the newspaper printers of the United States to provide a strong push behind any move to provide national protection for the liberty of the press, including the adoption of the Bill of Rights. Initial study, however, shows that this did not prove to be true. Comments published in the 1780s indicated that American publishers had mixed feelings about freedom of the press. By and large, the beliefs of printers concerning freedom of expression reflected those of most Americans, developing out of the British tradition of no prior restraint, but also influenced by the changes encouraged by the American environment, which broadened the possibilities of discussion because of the lack of societal and political controls.

All of the printers clearly believed that "the liberty of the press is the boast of freemen, and essential to the support of a republican government,"[18] but they did not agree about what constituted true freedom of expression. While the newspapers clearly played an important role in keeping people informed of the doings of government, they could be abused if "publications originate from malice and personal pique," as stated by a Rhode Island essayist.[19] The editor of the *Salem Chronicle* stated that "matters of a personal or private nature"[20] were inappropriate for newspaper publications and that printed materials "should be confined within the bounds of decency and politeness."[21] While praising the potential of their weekly publications, most printers also agreed with Thomas Adams and John Nourse, publishers of the *Independent Chronicle*, when they declared that "news-papers may degenerate into instruments for promoting everything base, and for scandalizing everything good."[22] This ambivalence of attitude concerning what constituted a free press would continue in the 1790s as editors sought to justify their own negative comments, while attacking those made by the opposition in the party conflicts between the Federalists and the Republicans.[23]

A case study of Massachusetts finds that printers showed little concern about the potential of the government of the United States to interfere with the workings of the press at the local level. In the decade between the end of the American Revolution and the adoption of the First Amendment, Massachusetts publishers protested loudly against actions of the state government that hurt the press, but expressed little concern over what the national government did.[24]

Throughout the 1780s, Bay State printers had praised newspapers as the major source of news and general information for the public. Benjamin Russell, publisher of the *Massachusetts Centinel*, urged people to save their newspapers in order "to preserve a just, particular, and impartial History of the transactions of the present day."[25] In the *Independent Chronicle*, "Impartialis" declared that a newspaper constituted "the poor man's library," the means by which most people "gain their information of the world at large."[26] A poet in the *Essex Journal* praised newspapers as "the springs of knowledge" for all Americans.[27] "Acirema" declared in the *Worcester Magazine* that "without political knowledge the people cannot secure their liberties, and this necessary information they receive by the medium of News-Papers."[28] At the time of Shays's Rebellion, several printers declared that many of the problems in the backcountry resulted from a lack of communication because few newspapers appeared in the counties where most of the trouble occurred.[29] Clearly, Massachusetts printers believed that the productions of their small presses played an important role in American society.

Because of the importance they attached to their weekly news sheets, publishers also often spoke about the importance of a free press in the operation of a republican government. Many writers praised the role of the newspapers in stirring up the people to revolt against Great Britain.[30] In an essay widely reprinted throughout the United States, "Common Sense" praised freedom of the press as the "Palladium of Liberty, the chief means of diffusing through this wide extended country those generous sentiments which delivered us from British tyranny, and formed the basis of our rising empire."[31] Another widely published piece declared that an open press provided "a security against errors, for where there is a free Press, no false doctrine in religion, policy, or physic, can be broached and remain undetected." Furthermore, a free press was "a great buckler against oppression" and "a standing resource in case of an unforeseen calamity," for publication provided the means of explaining and solving all political problems.[32] According to these pieces published by Massachusetts printers, a free and open press was essential for the operation of a republican government such as the one desired by the American people.

The first major threat to the ability of Massachusetts publishers to operate as they chose came in the form of the state stamp act, passed in the spring of 1785. Designed to help raise money to pay off the war debt, the act resulted in screams of protest from the state's publishers.[33] All of them castigated the legislature for trying to undermine the liberty of the press. In the *Massachusetts Centinel*, "Lucius" declared that "the freedom of the Press is the greatest bulwark of Liberty, and the most sacred right of Freedom." He expressed great shock that his home state had struck "a blow at the root of this inestimable right."[34] John Mycall, publisher of Newburyport's *Essex Journal*, resolved "never to print a News-Paper burdened with a Stamp in a land of Liberty, and where the Press is said to be free!" Rather than submit to the stamp legislation, he would either discontinue his paper or move his printing operation to New Hampshire.[35] Isaiah Thomas, publisher of the *Massachusetts Spy*, was vocal in his opposition to the stamp tax, declaring it to be a "bad policy" that violated the state's bill of rights by interfering with the freedom of the press.[36] The *Boston Gazette* urged the legislature to rethink its action and to "free the public from that bar to political wisdom" by repealing the stamp tax.[37]

The printers continually criticized the state legislature for attempting to limit the liberty of the press, but the issue of money played a role in their protests as well. The stamp tax would raise the cost of their newspapers, and the printers feared that this increase would endanger their business. Several of them stated that the tax would raise the price of their productions by one-third, a change that would make newspapers too expensive for many people to purchase.[38] In addition, because the printers of neighboring states would be able to undersell local publishers, Massachusetts newspapers would be further injured.[39] The result would be the demise of locally published news sheets and the financial ruin of local printers.[40] In the opinion of the editor of the *Essex Journal*, and the rest of the publishers of the Bay State, the disappearance of newspapers because of the state action could only be seen as "a clog to the Liberty of the Press."[41]

The Massachusetts state legislature responded to the protests and repealed the stamp tax. Still needing a source of revenue, however, they replaced the stamp tax with a duty on newspaper advertisements.[42] This measure produced even more complaints because it struck at the financial mainstay of newspapers—advertising. State publishers continued to criticize the assembly for attacking the freedom of the press. Benjamin Edes of Boston and Isaiah Thomas of Worcester led the fight. Both men thought the advertisement tax would destroy the newspapers of Massachusetts and urged its repeal.[43] Edes urged printers to stay out of the state because they could not operate their business freely,[44] while Thomas called on the towns of Massachusetts to instruct their representatives to work for the repeal of the obnoxious legislation.[45] Thomas even went so far as to suspend publication of the *Massachusetts Spy* for over two years. He replaced his newspaper with the *Worcester Magazine*, a type of publication not covered by the act taxing advertisements.[46] Upon resuming the publication of the *Spy* in 1788, Thomas prayed that "Heaven grant that the FREEDOM of the PRESS, on which depends the FREEDOM of the PEOPLE, may, in the United States, be ever guarded with a watchful eye, and defended from shackles, of every form and shape, until the trump of the celestial Messenger shall announce the final dissolution of all things."[47]

Printers criticized the advertisement tax as an infringement on the liberty of the press, but, once more, the issue of money was also clearly involved. The advertisement tax would hurt the financial status of newspapers because increased advertisements enabled a printer to sell his paper more cheaply and so gain a larger circulation.[48] According to Thomas, the tax would "destroy those necessary vehicles of public information, by taking away their only support."[49]

The printers of Massachusetts suffered as a result of the advertisement tax, and many reduced the size of their newspapers in order to continue publication. Six ceased production altogether.[50] Thomas expressed the feelings of all the printers when he declared that, "if therefore the Publication of News-papers is not by Law prohibited, yet if a law is made which takes away the means of printing and circulating News-papers, it amounts to the same thing, and is of course an unconstitutional restraint on the Liberty of the Press."[51] The printers of Massachusetts appealed to the General Court to repeal the act, stating that the money raised from the tax was not enough to justify the financial impact of the legislation on publishers. In 1788, the state legislature finally agreed and repealed the advertisement tax.[52]

With such strong efforts to defend the freedom of the press at the state level, it would not be surprising if the Massachusetts printers had also worked diligently to protect freedom of expression at the national level. That, however, did not prove to be the case. During the late 1780s, the newspapers of the Bay State, as was true in all the states,[53] covered the Constitutional Convention in Philadelphia and the ratification process that followed, but they made few specific suggestions concerning what should be included in the new government.

During the meeting of the Convention, the press urged the delegates to work to solve the problems of the United States through measures that would improve the status of the national government.[54] One editor praised the delegates for their "wisdom and patriotism,"[55] while others urged the people to support the results of the Convention, "whether an addition to the old constitution, or the adoption of a new one."[56]

During the ratification debates, Massachusetts printers strongly supported the adoption of the Constitution because they believed that the new proposed government would improve the stability of the United States.[57] Benjamin Russell, the publisher of the *Massachusetts Centinel*, stated that the Constitution was "the result of much wisdom, candour, and those mutual concessions, without which America can never expect to harmonize in any system of Commerce of Government."[58] A writer in the *Independent Chronicle* called on the American people to "be of one heart, and of one mind" in order to "seize the golden opportunity to secure a stable government, and to become a respectable nation" by ratifying the Constitution.[59] The *Boston Gazette* declared that the nation's problems "will gradually subside, till they finally disappear, if we have but wisdom and firmness speedily to adopt the New Federal Constitution."[60] All the printers seemed pleased when the document had been ratified by enough states to ensure that the new government went into operation.[61]

The newspaper publishers of Massachusetts took particular interest in the actions of their ratifying convention, which met from January 9 to February 6, 1788. Numerous comments concerning the meeting appeared while it was in session, and the printers expressed much pleasure when the state ratified the Constitution.[62] Many delegates to the convention had hesitated to approve the new government because they felt that it did not contain enough protection for individual liberties. They insisted that the Constitution must be amended prior to its taking effect. Delegates negotiated a compromise by which the new form of government was ratified with suggested amendments attached. Many members of the state convention considered the need for amendments crucial, but most of them seemed concerned with state power and financial and judicial issues rather than personal freedoms. The only mention of the liberty of the press during the ratifying convention was an amendment for its protection presented by Samuel Adams on the last day of the convention. The delegates quickly voted down the proposed change and ratified the Constitution (with proposed amendments) by a vote of 187 to 168.[63]

Some newspapers discussed the issue of the liberty of the press and the proposed new national government, but it never became a major issue. Several opponents of the Constitution criticized the press for failing to cover all sides of the issue, but the printers stated that they published whatever materials were presented by the public.[64] "Candidus," an essayist in the *Independent Chronicle*, stated that "freedom of debate in all national questions, has ever been held sacred among a free people; the great subject now submitted to the public, most certainly claims this indulgence, as on its impartial discussion, every thing that is valuable depends."[65] Massachusetts printers apparently agreed with this sentiment, and a lively debate concerning the Constitution took place in several Bay State papers prior to the meeting of the Massachusetts convention.[66] Some newspaper essayists worried over the failure of the document to provide specific protection for a free press, but most writers seemed unconcerned.[67]

Apparently, most people did not worry about the lack of protection for the press in the Constitution because the necessary protections already existed in state bills of rights. The Massachusetts Constitution of 1780 provided that "the liberty of the press is essential to the security of freedom in a State; it ought not, therefore, to be restrained in this commonwealth." The delegates to the ratifying convention considered this provision to be protection enough for the liberty of the press.[68] Bay State printers evidently concurred, since they did not urge the state meeting to include protection for the press in the proposed amendments attached to the state's ratification of the Constitution.[69] Except for the convention proposal of Samuel Adams, the issue of the freedom of the press never came up in Massachusetts during the ratification debates.

Attitudes in the Bay State concerning the need to protect the freedom of the press at the national level had not changed by the time the state legislature considered the proposed Bill of Rights in 1791. Those who had previously supported the Constitution felt that it did not need to be amended, while its opponents still expressed more concern with the issues of state versus national power and judicial rights. Both the House and the Senate of the Massachusetts General Court approved what would later become the First Amendment, but they never passed a joint resolution to finalize their approval. Therefore, the state of Massachusetts failed to ratify the amendment that provided safeguards for the press at the national level.[70] Newspaper printers seemed unconcerned about the failure of the state to ratify the proposed Bill of Rights. The public prints carried very little information about the actions of the state legislature concerning the amendments and expressed no desire that a protection for the liberty of the press become a part of the national government.[71]

Leonard Levy has stated that "the history of the framing and ratification of the Bill of Rights indicates slight passion on the part of anyone to enshrine personal liberties in the fundamental law of the land."[72] This certainly proved true in Massachusetts because no one pushed for the adoption of the Bill of Rights. The printers of the Bay State did not perceive actions of the federal government as any sort of threat to them, as the state taxes of 1785 and 1786 had been. Even the adoption of a postal duty on newspapers failed to generate much excitement. Massachusetts news sheets mentioned the new law, which passed Congress on February 20, 1792, but they did not perceive it as a major threat to their livelihood.[73] Even Isaiah Thomas, the printer who had stopped publication of his newspaper because of the state advertisement tax, saw no problem with the national postal duty. His only comment was that the bill provided for the establishment of a post road from Worcester to Providence, Rhode Island.[74] Clearly, at least in Massachusetts, distance from the government in question made a difference in evaluating the issue of a free press and how much it needed protection. Other states that supported amending the new Constitution included protection for the press among their suggestions, but none of them made a big issue of their concern. A centerpiece of the Constitution for modern-day journalists apparently made it into the law of the land more by accident than plan. Only after its adoption would the press provision of the First Amendment acquire importance in the arena of civil liberties and freedom of expression.

NOTES

1. *Independent Gazetteer* (Philadelphia), 5 October 1787.
2. James Madison's notes constitute the most complete record of the debates of the Constitutional Convention. See James Madison, *Notes of Debates in the Federal Convention of 1787*, ed. Adrienne Koch (Athens: Ohio University Press, 1966), 485–87.
3. Virginia adopted its first state constitution in 1776. The Declaration of Rights formed the introduction. This document, which heavily influenced both the Declaration of Independence and the Bill of Rights, provided protection for freedom of speech, the press, and religion, as well as restrictions against jury trials and unlawful searches.
4. Madison, *Notes of Debates in the Federal Convention of 1787*, 630.
5. Ibid., 640.
6. James Madison, *The Complete Madison: His Basic Writings*, ed. Saul K. Padover (New York: Harper, 1953), 253.
7. Thomas Jefferson, *The Papers of Thomas Jefferson*, ed. Julian P. Boyd et al., 25 vols. to date (Princeton, N.J.: Princeton University Press, 1950–), 12:440.
8. Ibid., 12:569–70.
9. Ibid., 12:282.
10. Margaret A. Blanchard, "Freedom of the Press, 1690–1804," in *The Media in America*, 2nd ed., ed. Wm. David Sloan, James G. Stovall, and James D. Startt (Scottsdale, Ariz.: Publishing Horizons, 1993), 110; Edward Dumbauld, *The Bill of Rights and What It Means Today* (Norman: University of Oklahoma Press, 1957), 10–33.
11. Robert Allan Rutland, *James Madison: The Founding Father* (New York: Macmillan, 1987), 47–49.
12. Dumbauld, *The Bill of Rights*, 33–44.
13. Ibid., 44–50. The First Amendment does not have a special place in the hierarchy of rights because it is "first." The order of the amendments had no special significance, either as proposed or as ratified. James Madison had tried to put them in a sort of hierarchical order, but Congress failed to follow his suggestions and sent them to the states for ratification in a haphazard order that did not consciously go from the most important rights to the least important rights. When considering the First Amendment specifically, one finds that it was just one among many. As originally written by Congress, what became the First Amendment was actually the third proposal. The amendment protecting freedom of belief and expression became the First Amendment only because the states did not ratify the two

proposals on the list prior to it at that time. Oscar Handlin, "The Bill of Rights in Its Context," *American Scholar* 62 (Spring 1993): 181.

14. Wm. David Sloan and Julie Hedgepeth Williams, *The Early American Press, 1690–1783* (Westport, Conn.: Greenwood Press, 1994), 14.

15. Some scholars have concluded that the inclusion of the protection for the press in the same amendment as the protection for religious belief indicates that the Founding Fathers saw freedom of expression as necessary for the preservation of religious liberty. Some American printers would have agreed with this idea, stating that the cement of a republican government was "Religious Toleration and the Liberty of the Press." See *American Herald* (Worcester, Mass.), 22 August 1785; *Salem* (Mass.) *Gazette*, 23 August 1785; *American Mercury* (Hartford, Conn.), 29 August 1785; *Falmouth* (Me.) *Gazette*, 3 September 1785; Archibald Cox, *The Court and the Constitution* (Boston: Houghton Mifflin, 1987), 185–87.

16. Europe had developed a highly structured class society during the Middle Ages. At that time, all the land and political power became concentrated in the hands of a small group of titled aristocrats. Much of their power and influence had been weakened over the centuries because of the appearance of strong monarchies. However, the remnants still remained in the eighteenth century, primarily in the form of special legal privileges. These differences helped produce conflicts throughout Europe during the nineteenth century. Few titled aristocrats came to North America. As a result, the British colonies developed a society consisting primarily of middle-class individuals who considered themselves basically equal with everyone else. Differences existed because of money and talent, but these differences did not become embedded in the legal code as occurred in Europe.

17. Leonard W. Levy, "Bill of Rights," in *Essays on the Making of the Constitution*, 2nd ed., ed. Leonard W. Levy (New York: Oxford University Press, 1987), 290–300; Blanchard, "Freedom of the Press," 91–109. In his study of the press clause in the First Amendment, Leonard Levy concludes that the Founding Fathers were not really clear in what they thought the protection for a free press meant. In many ways, it just recognized and legitimized a pre-existing condition. Freedom from prior restraint was clearly protected, but almost no one believed that the press could print whatever it wished. There is evidence to indicate that they desired to limit what the federal government could do in relation to the press, but that they intended for state courts to continue to punish printers for publishing inappropriate materials and that many of the Founding Fathers assumed that the crime of seditious libel, printing criticism of the government, would continue to be punished by state authorities. Leonard W. Levy, *Emergence of a Free Press* (New York: Oxford University Press, 1985), 220–81.

18. *Massachusetts Gazette* (Boston), 1 January 1788. For other similar comments, see *New Hampshire Gazette* (Portsmouth), 29 May 1788; *Herald of Freedom* (Boston), 15 September 1788.

19. *Providence* (R.I.) *Gazette*, 15 February 1783.

20. *Salem* (Mass.) *Chronicle*, 30 March 1786.

21. *Vermont Gazette* (Westminster), 18 September 1783.

22. *Independent Chronicle* (Boston), 1 January 1784.

23. Such comments reflect the beginnings of concerns about journalistic ethics and the role newspapers should play in society. Hazel Dicken-Garcia's study, *Journalistic Standards in Nineteenth-Century America* (Madison: University of Wisconsin Press, 1989), finds that developed press criticism appeared in the United States in the mid-1830s. However, concerns about the potential negative impact of the press appeared years earlier. Arguments over how far negative comments should go and what constituted truth became more frequent during the partisan debates of the 1790s. In the early nineteenth century,

some editors also became concerned about the potential moral impact of newspapers. For example, the editors of the *Patron of Industry* (New York), in discussing the founding of their newspaper in 1820, declared that

we should shrink from the task of superintending a public journal, did it necessarily involve the publication of the numerous tragical accounts of robberies, murders, and villainies of every description, scandalous stories, neat tricks, and, in short, the details of the most shameless and disgusting vices, and the most atrocious depravities; the constant reading of which is enough of itself to corrupt the taste and deprave the morals of a community. [19 July 1820]

24. Material about Massachusetts study from Carol Sue Humphrey, "Greater Distance = Declining Interest: Massachusetts Printers and Protections for a Free Press, 1783–1791," *American Journalism* (forthcoming).

25. *Massachusetts Centinel* (Boston), 17 March 1787.

26. *Independent Chronicle*, 25 May 1786.

27. *Essex Journal* (Newburyport, Mass.), 8 June 1785.

28. *Worcester* (Mass.) *Magazine*, third week in May 1786.

29. *Boston Gazette*, 16 October 1786, 26 February 1787.

30. *Worcester Magazine*, third week in May 1786; *Boston Gazette*, 17 September 1798.

31. *Massachusetts Centinel*, 19 January 1785.

32. *Massachusetts Spy* (Worcester), 4 December 1788.

33. *Essex Journal*, 11 May 1785; *Independent Chronicle*, 12 May 1785; *Boston Gazette*, 16 and 23 May 1785; Clifford K. Shipton, *Isaiah Thomas: Printer, Patriot, and Philanthropist, 1749–1831* (Rochester, N.Y.: Printing House of Leo Hart, 1948), 42; Clyde Augustus Duniway, *The Development of Freedom of the Press in Massachusetts* (Cambridge: Harvard University Press, 1906), 119–20, 136–37.

34. Essay from *Massachusetts Centinel*, reprinted in *Vermont Gazette*, 11 July 1785. See also Van Beck Hall, *Politics Without Parties: Massachusetts, 1780–1791* (Pittsburgh: University of Pittsburgh Press, 1972), 117; Joseph T. Buckingham, *Specimens of Newspaper Literature*, 2 vols. (Boston: Charles C. Little and James Brown, 1850), 2:33–34.

35. *Essex Journal*, 8 June 1785.

36. *Massachusetts Spy*, 12 May, 2 June 1785.

37. *Boston Gazette*, 30 May 1785.

38. *Essex Journal*, 6 April 1785; *Massachusetts Spy*, 12 May 1785.

39. *Massachusetts Spy*, 21 April, 12 May 1785; *Massachusetts Centinel*, 4 May 1785.

40. *Massachusetts Centinel*, 4 May 1785; *Massachusetts Spy*, 12 May 1785; *Independent Chronicle*, 12 May 1785.

41. *Essex Journal*, 6 April 1785.

42. Hall, *Politics Without Parties*, 118.

43. *Boston Gazette*, 22 August 1785; *Massachusetts Spy*, 26 January, 30 March 1786; *Worcester Magazine*, 5 April 1786, fourth week in July 1786; Buckingham, *Specimens of Newspaper Literature*, 1:197, 242.

44. *Boston Gazette*, 5 March 1787.

45. *Worcester Magazine*, second week in May 1786.

46. Handbill published by Isaiah Thomas, 3 April 1786; *Worcester Magazine*, fourth week in July 1786, fourth week in March 1787, fourth week in March 1788; *Massachusetts Spy*, 3 April 1788.

47. *Massachusetts Spy*, 3 April 1788.

48. *Essex Journal*, 9 November 1785; *Independent Chronicle*, 25 May 1786; Clarence S. Brigham, *Journals and Journeymen: A Contribution to the History of Early American Newspapers* (Philadelphia: University of Pennsylvania Press, 1950), 27; John Bixler Hench, "The Newspaper in a Republic: Boston's *Centinel* and *Chronicle*, 1784–1801," (Ph.D. diss., Clark University, 1979), 93.

49. Handbill published by Isaiah Thomas, 3 April 1786; reprinted in *Essex Journal*, 19 April 1786.

50. *Worcester Magazine*, fourth week in June 1786, fourth week in July 1786, first week in October 1786, fourth week in March 1787; *Essex Journal*, 18 October, 20 December, 10 January 1787.

51. Handbill published by Isaiah Thomas, 3 April 1786; reprinted in *Essex Journal*, 19 April 1786.

52. Boston Printers' Petition, 8 February 1786, copy in Book Trades Collection, American Antiquarian Society, Worcester, Mass., original in Massachusetts State Archives, Senate File 718; Advertising Tax Collections for Suffolk County, Massachusetts, 9 February 1786, copy in Book Trades Collection, American Antiquarian Society, Worcester, Mass., original in Massachusetts State Archives, Senate File 718–3; Committee Report to General Court, 10 February 1786, copy in Book Trades Collection, American Antiquarian Society, Worcester, Mass., original in Massachusetts State Archives, Senate Files 718–2 and 718–4.

53. John K. Alexander, *The Selling of the Constitutional Convention: A History of News Coverage* (Madison, Wis.: Madison House, 1990), 1–9. The most famous discussion of the proposed Constitution, *The Federalist Papers*, was published for the ratification struggle in New York. The issue of protection for a free press was addressed only once at length, in Federalist No. 84, which appeared not in the newspapers, but only as the next to last essay in the book version published on May 28, 1788. Reaction to this particular essay by newspaper printers was nonexistent. John P. Kaminski and Gaspare J. Saladino, eds., *Commentaries on the Constitution, Public and Private*, vol. 1, vol. 13 of *The Documentary History of the Ratification of the Constitution* (Madison: State Historical Society of Wisconsin, 1981), 490–94; Francis Newton Thorpe, *The Constitutional History of the United States* (Chicago: Callaghan, 1901), 2:137–38.

54. *Massachusetts Centinel*, June 1787; reprinted in *Independent Chronicle*, 19 July 1787.

55. *Independent Chronicle*, 9 August 1787.

56. *Massachusetts Centinel*, 13 and 30 June 1787; reprinted in *Independent Chronicle*, 19 July, 9 August 1787.

57. *Massachusetts Centinel*, 29 September, 17 November, 1 December 1787, 1 November 1788; *Boston Gazette*, 15 November, 10 December 1787, 14 January 1788; *Independent Chronicle*, 10 January 1788.

58. *Massachusetts Centinel*, 9 January 1788.

59. *Independent Chronicle*, 5 June 1788.

60. *Boston Gazette*, 15 October 1787.

61. Ibid., 12 May, 9 and 23 June, 7 July 1788; *Massachusetts Spy*, 10 July 1788.

62. *Massachusetts Centinel*, 9 and 16 January, 11 February 1788; *Independent Chronicle*, 10 January to 13 March 1788, 7 February 1788; *Boston Gazette*, 11 February 1788; *Essex Journal*, 13 February 1788; Augustus W. Clason, "The Convention of Massachusetts," *Magazine of American History* 14 (December 1885): 545.

63. Because of the presence of Samuel Adams and his concerns about freedom of the press, the Massachusetts ratifying convention has received much study. See Duniway, *Devel-*

opment of Freedom of the Press, 137–40; Samuel B. Harding, *The Contest over the Ratification of the Federal Constitution in the State of Massachusetts* (New York: Longmans, Green, 1896), 98; Robert A. Rutland, *The Birth of the Bill of Rights, 1776–1791* (Chapel Hill: University of North Carolina Press for the Institute of Early American History and Culture, Williamsburg, Va., 1955), 148; Arthur N. Holcombe, "Massachusetts and the Federal Constitution of 1787," in *Commonwealth History of Massachusetts*, vol. 3, ed. Albert Bushnell Hart (New York: States History Co., 1929), 399–400; Irving Brant, *The Bill of Rights: Its Origin and Meaning* (Indianapolis: Bobbs-Merrill, 1965), 39; Bernard Schwartz, *The Bill of Rights: A Documentary History*, 2 vols. (New York: Chelsea House, 1971), 1:674–75, 681, 707; Clason, "The Convention of Massachusetts," 544. The complete minutes and debates of the Massachusetts Ratifying Convention may be found in Schwartz, *The Bill of Rights*, 2:676–723.

   64. *Boston Gazette*, 3 December 1787.

   65. *Independent Chronicle*, 3 January 1788.

   66. See, for example, *Independent Chronicle*, 6, 13, 20, and 27 December 1787, 3, 10, 17, 24, and 31 January 1788; *Worcester Magazine*, December 1787, January 1788.

   67. *Boston Gazette*, 3 December 1787; *Worcester Magazine*, first week in February 1788.

   68. *Boston Gazette*, 22 October 1787; General Court of Massachusetts, *The Perpetual Laws of the Commonwealth of Massachusetts, 1780–1788* (Worcester, Mass.: Isaiah Thomas, 1788), 1:7; Duniway, *Development of Freedom of the Press*, 130, 136, 138–40; Rutland, *Bill of Rights*, 107, 108, 112; Levy, "Bill of Rights," 267, 299; Jeffrey A. Smith, "Public Opinion and the Press Clause," *Journalism History* 14 (Spring 1987): 8; Schwartz, *The Bill of Rights*, 2:676.

   69. Throughout the ratification debate in Massachusetts, the newspapers often carried materials discussing the need for amendments to the proposed Constitution, but the need to protect the press was not a major issue. See, for example, *Independent Chronicle*, 18 September 1788, 5 February 1789.

   70. Duniway, *Development of Freedom of the Press*, 141; Levy, "Bill of Rights," 287; Denys P. Myers, *Massachusetts and the First Ten Amendments to the Constitution* (Washington, D.C.: U.S. Government Printing Office, 1936), 8–9, 11; Hall, *Politics Without Parties*, 327.

   71. David A. Anderson, "The Origins of the Press Clause," *UCLA Law Review* 30 (February 1983): 486; *Massachusetts Spy*, 17 February 1789. The printers in question never published much about the proposed Bill of Rights, and most of what they did print consisted of copies of the amendments and legislative discussions of them. The average percentage of space allotted to discussion of the Bill of Rights in any one month never exceeded 9.44 percent of total available space. The printers continued to take interest in local free press issues throughout this period. For example, several newspapers gave extensive coverage to the libel trial of Edmund Freeman, printer of Boston's *American Herald*. *Independent Chronicle*, 4 February 1790, 24 February, 3, 10, 17, and 24 March 1791; *Massachusetts Centinel*, 10 February 1790, 26 February 1791.

   72. Levy, "Bill of Rights," 289.

   73. "An Act to Establish the Post Office and Post Roads Within the United States," *The Debates and Proceedings in the Congress of the United States*, 2nd Congress, 1791–1793 (Washington, D.C.: Gales and Seaton, 1849), 1333–41; *Massachusetts Centinel*, 26 February 1791, 5 February 1792; *Independent Chronicle*, 23 February, 8 March 1792; *Boston Gazette*, 12 March 1792.

   74. *Massachusetts Spy*, 8 March 1792.

3

The First Political
Party System, 1791–1800

The establishment of the new government under the Constitution in 1789 opened a new era in American history, and newspapers of the 1790s reflected the changes that occurred. Many people agreed that the United States would be a republic, but they disagreed over how to put republican ideals into practice. As American leaders moved from discussion of political theories to attempts to implement these theories, discord appeared. Arguments and disagreements over how to run the government increased throughout the 1790s, differences that influenced the growth of the press. The French Revolution also influenced the appearance of divisions. Americans had trouble deciding what to do about the changes in France because that revolt took a much bloodier turn than had the American Revolution. Once the Reign of Terror began in 1793, many people simply could not believe that the revolution in France had anything in common with the revolt that had produced the United States.

The contentions over these issues between government officials eventually coalesced into two political parties: the Federalists, led by Alexander Hamilton and John Adams, and the Republicans, led by Thomas Jefferson and James Madison. Each side quickly sought out journalists to support its position because all of these men had learned the potential effect of newspapers during the Revolutionary conflict with Great Britain. Thus developed the first party press in American history. The 1790s were a time of great conflict and great distrust because the United States had not yet developed a concept of "loyal opposition." For most of them, political dissent and faction were dangerous and led to tyranny. People on both sides of any argument quickly accused their opposition of treason and sought to silence them. The newspapers became the major arena for such accusations. It would take a major confrontation over the First Amendment, in the guise of the Sedition Act, before Americans would generally accept the idea that a person could publicly disagree with the national government without advocating treason and revolution.

Political leaders emerged from the Revolutionary War with a growing respect for the possible impact newspapers could produce. As a result, they quickly sought out friendly printers/editors willing to support a particular viewpoint in the columns of their publications. The Federalists and Alexander Hamilton struck first, with the publication of John Fenno's *Gazette of the United States* on April 15, 1789. The first official organ of the Republicans, Philip Freneau's *National Gazette*, did not appear until 1791, primarily because Thomas Jefferson and his supporters hoped for less argument and more cooperation in the newly forming national government. Failing to achieve the goals they desired, the Republicans sought to use newspapers to urge the American people to be watchful of the Federalists and their "monarchical" plans for the future of the United States.

Both parties sought to use the press to influence public opinion because both realized the increasing influence of public opinion in the political arena. Numerous politicians gave active support to various newspapers in an effort to get their ideas out to the public. Republicans who promoted the circulation of various news sheets included Thomas Jefferson, James Madison, Albert Gallatin, John Hancock, and Samuel Adams. Printer John Israel moved to Pittsburgh at the instigation of Hugh Henry Breckenridge to start a Republican paper. By 1800, one report stated that the Republicans had established newspapers throughout the country in order to push Jefferson's election as president. Among the Federalists, Alexander Hamilton led the way in providing financial support for newspapers, but John Jay, Rufus King, and others joined him on several occasions to establish Federalist newspapers in major cities throughout the country.[1]

However, the two groups differed in how they approached the public and in their own estimation of the potential of the people in politics. The Republicans, more supportive of general public involvement in the political system, perceived public opinion as an ally to be influenced and nurtured in order to achieve political success. According to Freneau, "[P]ublic opinion sets the bounds to every government, and is the real sovereign of every free one."[2] The Federalists, however, favored a more limited government, in which those with an investment in society played the most important roles. As a result of this outlook, the Federalists viewed appealing to overall public opinion as an unavoidable necessity.

Both the Republicans and the Federalists saw newspapers as the major mechanism for influencing public opinion. The number of news publications more than doubled during the first decade of the new nation, growing from 92 in 1790 to 234 in 1800. Those published more than once a week multiplied from twenty-two (with eight dailies) in 1790 to fifty-six (with twenty-four dailies) in 1800.[3]

The views of the two leaders of the emerging political parties, Thomas Jefferson and Alexander Hamilton, clearly reflected the growing importance of newspapers in the eyes of national politicians.[4] Jefferson's oft-quoted statement that he would rather have "newspapers without a government" than a "government without newspapers" has produced much discussion concerning his ideas about the press. However, Jefferson's statements concerning the press throughout his political career indicated clearly that he saw newspapers as a key element in the American political process. He perceived the press as the major source of information for the people in the decision-making process. In 1799, he stated that "our citizens may be deceived for awhile, and have been deceived; but as long as the presses can be protected, we may trust to them for light."[5] In one of his last statements concerning newspapers, Jefferson wrote that the press provided "the best instrument for enlightening the mind of man, and improving him as a rational, moral, and social being."[6] Although seldom writing for the newspapers himself, Jefferson continually urged his political friends, particularly James Madison, to enter the fray in support of Republican ideals.[7]

Alexander Hamilton also respected the potential power of the press, but his respect was born out of apprehension. He perceived the role that newspapers had played in toppling governments, and he feared a similar occurrence in the United States. But he also recognized that the press played an essential role in politics and sought to use it to accomplish his own political goals. As a result, Hamilton continually wrote articles for the newspapers and urged others to do the same. Bemoaning the lack of truth concerning the French in American newspapers in 1798, David Ford, a New Jersey militia commander during the Whiskey Rebellion in 1794, agreed with Hamilton, declaring that "I know of no other way to remedy this evil than for the Gentlemen of the Federal Interest to become subscribers . . . and then Write for them, so as that every paper should contain a good piece or two in favor of Gouvernment."[8] Whenever possible, Hamilton provided support to Federalist editors and encouraged all good Federalists to support their newspapers. Although he distrusted the press in many ways, Hamilton proved better able to take advantage directly of its potential than his political rival, Jefferson. Hamilton's premature death in 1804 constituted a major loss to the Federalist Party in its attempt to remain a national contender in the political arena.

Editors agreed with political leaders and always emphasized the power of their publications in influencing public opinion and political action. If for no other reason, the role of the newspapers as the primary source of political information made the press an essential cog in the operation of government. However, editors also believed that the publication of editorial opinion had great influence and played just as important a role in the political arena as did the publication of news and information. Because of this belief, newspaper producers increasingly filled the pages of their publications with more and more political information and opinion in hopes of convincing the public to support the "right" side of the growing political debate on the national government.[9]

For more and more editors, support of a partisan cause became the primary reason for a newspaper's existence because, as stated in the *Newark Gazette*, "the times demand decision."[10] According to William Cobbett, one of the more outspoken newspaper producers of the 1790s, to attempt to be impartial concerning politics was to be "a poor passive fool, and not an editor."[11] For Charles Holt of the *New London Bee*, "to be lukewarm . . . is to acquiesce in slavery."[12] The Republican editor of the Baltimore *American and Daily Advertiser* agreed, declaring that "the American people have long enough been imposed upon by pretended impartiality of printers; it is all delusion."[13] Throughout the 1790s and into the early decades of the 1800s, newspaper editors increasingly agreed with this viewpoint and used both their news reports and their opinion columns to take strong political stands and to encourage their readers to do the same. To do less was to fail as an editor. Clearly, the view of the role of a newspaper had changed from the early 1700s when John Campbell had tried to print everything that came to hand with no comments at all.

Stylistically, Federalist and Republican editors differed very little. As political disagreements increased, both used invective and personal attacks to further their cause. Both accused the other side of accepting bribes and spreading lies as the primary means of political advancement. In his standard work on the era, historian John C. Miller stated that "it was a question which party, in its efforts to gain partisan advantage, gave the lowest blows." Miller overstated the case, since many editors did not choose to use such methods. Still, the leading party journals did not hesitate to attack the enemy in any way possible, and thus used much rumor, innuendo, and personal denunciations in their attempts to win the political loyalty and support of the American people.[14]

Although similar in style, the two political parties and their respective editors did disagree concerning what the role of the press should actually be. Federalist editors continually defended the past and sought to maintain the status quo, while Republican papers increasingly advocated change and more political participation by the people. Both groups sought to support their party and to propagate its ideas, but the respective positions of the two parties in the 1790s influenced how this was done.

Being the voices of the party in office, the Federalist newspapers preached support for the government. John Fenno told his readers that the *Gazette* would attempt, "by every exertion, to endear the GENERAL GOVERNMENT to the people."[15] Furthermore, Federalist editors such as Benjamin Russell sought to point out the dangers to the country inherent in the proposals of the Republicans: "As a Centinel, we will sound the alarm, and faithfully make report of our discoveries of the disposition, force, and movements of our country's foes."[16] Federalists feared the potential influence of the Republicans over the American people and sought to sidetrack their impact by urging the people to allow the national government to operate without change or hindrance.

The Republicans, seeing themselves as the voice of the people, urged expansion of public participation in government in order to "love the Constitution as it ought to be loved" and to fully implement its provisions.[17] In supporting the establishment of the *National Gazette*, Jefferson hoped that Freneau would use his paper to "give free place to pieces written against the aristocratical and monarchical principles"[18] espoused by the Federalists. For the Republicans, newspapers provided information to the members of the public so that they would make the correct politicial decisions at election time. The Republicans did not trust the Federalists any more than the Federalists trusted the Republicans and, as the party out of power, continually urged the people to change their rulers at the next election.

Although many printers and editors took sides during the political party debates of the 1790s, several on each side deserve special attention. Prominent supporters of the Federalists included John Fenno, Noah Webster, William Cobbett, and Benjamin Russell. The most important Republican editors were Philip Freneau and Benjamin Franklin Bache.

John Fenno[19] entered the field of journalism on April 15, 1789, with the first publication of the *Gazette of the United States* in New York. Previously a contributor to Benjamin Russell's *Massachusetts Centinel*, Fenno approached Rufus King in early 1789 about the possibility of establishing a pro-Federalist paper in the nation's capital. Because the *Gazette* was the official organ for the party in power, he received most of the official government printing to help support his business and his newspaper. When the capital moved to Philadelphia in 1791, Fenno moved the *Gazette* there as well.

Fenno's entry into publishing marked the beginning of the development of specialization in journalism. Formerly a school teacher in Boston, Fenno did not enter the publishing field through the traditional way of apprenticeship. He became the first to see himself as an editor, rather than a printer, and he earned his reputation as a writer and an editor. Others would follow in this direction as the multifaceted job of printer splintered into editor, publisher, reporter, and typesetter.

From the beginning, Fenno strongly supported the policies of the Federalist administration of George Washington. Strongly supported both financially and otherwise by Alexander Hamilton, the *Gazette of the United States* spread Federalist ideas, particularly those of Hamilton, throughout the country. As the leading national Federalist newspaper, the *Gazette* circulated to party leaders and printers throughout the United States. As was true of most papers in this era, Fenno published considerable foreign news, but he also carried continuing reports on the debates in the House of Representatives about a variety of issues such as tariffs, taxation, smuggling, and Hamilton's financial proposals. Fenno perceived the purpose of his publication to be support for the government. The contents of his paper should "hold up the people's own government in a favorable light" and "impress just ideas of its administration by exhibiting FACTS," a purpose he tried to fulfill throughout his editorship.[20] When John Fenno died of yellow fever in 1798, the editorship of the *Gazette* passed to his son, John Ward Fenno.

Following the move of the *Gazette of the United States* to Philadelphia, Federalists from New York sought to establish a new journal in order to have a strong voice in their city. Being from New York, Alexander Hamilton in particular felt the need for a new Federalist newspaper in the city. He, along with Rufus King, John Jay, and seven others, contributed $150 each for the establishment of a new publication. Noah Webster[21] moved to New York in order to become the editor of the newspaper, the *American Minerva*, which first appeared on December 9, 1793.

Webster proved himself an ardent supporter of George Washington's administration and Federalist policies in general. Webster stated that he desired that the

Minerva be a "Friend of Government, of Freedom, of Virtue, and of every species of Improvement."[22] He emphasized the importance of the press and praised its wide circulation in the United States: "In no other country on earth, not even in Great-Britain, are Newspapers so generally circulated among the body of the people." Because of their widespread availability, newspapers served as "auxiliaries of governments," "heralds of truth," and "protectors of peace and good order."[23] Webster did better than most in fairly presenting the news, but his publication clearly supported the Federalist Party. He is often credited with popularizing the use of clearly labeled paragraphs of editorial opinion in the local news column.[24] Webster left the *Minerva* in 1798, following the development of a rift between President John Adams and Alexander Hamilton.

By the time Webster ceased editing the *Minerva*, a new editor had appeared to espouse the Federalist cause. William Cobbett, an Englishman, had fled his homeland because he had gotten into trouble for criticizing the government. He lived in the United States for only six years, but during that time, he established a reputation as a caustic writer who spared no words for his political opponents.

Cobbett originally established his reputation as a writer through pamphlets. Encouraged to venture into newspaper publishing, he established *Porcupine's Gazette and United States Advertiser*, a pro-Federalist journal, which first appeared on March 5, 1797, the day of John Adams's inauguration as president. Cobbett made it very clear from the beginning that his paper would be a Federalist publication: "Professions of impartiality I shall make none." He planned for his publication "to be a rallying point for the friends of government," a publication that would never "be an instrument of destruction to the cause I espouse."[25]

Cobbett published 778 issues of *Porcupine's Gazette*, and in all of them, he wasted no words in his attacks on the Republicans and their support of the French in the war in Europe. More than any other editor, he helped establish the reputation of the 1790s as the era of vituperative journalism. He particularly enjoyed attacking the *Aurora* and its editor, Benjamin Franklin Bache. Cobbett described the *Aurora* as a "vehicle of lies and sedition"[26] and characterized Bache as "an impudent scoundrel" and "an evil-looking devil."[27] Such criticism even produced reprimands from other Federalists and eventually got Cobbett in trouble. In 1800, Dr. Benjamin Rush, a Republican, sued the editor for libel. Cobbett lost the case and, rather than pay the $5,000 fine, fled to England.[28] Because he was unpredictable and uncontrollable, there were few people, Federalist or Republican, who were saddened by his departure.[29]

The oldest Federalist paper in the United States appeared in Boston under the editorship of Benjamin Russell. Trained by Isaiah Thomas, Russell founded his newspaper in 1784. A strong supporter of the adoption of the Constitution, he quickly became a strong supporter of the national government and the Federalist policies of Presidents Washington and Adams. Russell even supported the Sedition Act, proclaiming that "it is Patriotism to write in favor of our Government; it is Sedition to write against it."[30] Strongly opposed to Thomas Jefferson, Russell mourned when Jefferson became president: "YESTERDAY EXPIRED, Deeply regretted by MIL-

LIONS of grateful Americans, and by *all* good men, The FEDERAL ADMINIS-TRATION of the GOVERNMENT of the *United States*; Animated by a WASH-INGTON, an ADAMS;—a HAMILTON. . . . Its death was occasioned by the Secret Arts and Open Violence, of Foreign and Domestic Demagogues."[31] The *Centinel* received Federalist Party support, primarily through contracts for publishing state and federal laws, but Russell always remained relatively independent of party influence. He continued to support Federalist ideas well into the 1800s.

Thomas Jefferson and the Republicans entered the journalistic fray in 1791, with the establishment of the *National Gazette* in Philadelphia. First published on October 31, 1791, the *National Gazette* appeared under the editorship of Philip Freneau,[32] a college roommate of James Madison at Princeton. Freneau's journal quickly became the national organ for the Republican Party, reflecting Jefferson's ideas about government and the need to support France in its revolution.

Freneau quickly entered the political debate by attacking Secretary of the Treasury Alexander Hamilton's financial program and his support for using the "general welfare" clause of the Constitution to enlarge the powers of the national government. Freneau showed himself an early advocate of the "watchdog" role of the press,[33] stating that "public opinion sets the bounds to every government and is the real sovereign of every free one."[34] Furthermore, "perpetual jealousy of the government" provided the means to prevent "the machinations of ambition."[35]

Freneau produced one of the best journals of the era, but quality did not keep it alive. Most of Freneau's financial support from the Republicans came through his job as a translator and through printing contracts for the State Department. When Thomas Jefferson resigned his cabinet post in 1793, Freneau lost his patronage, and the *National Gazette* soon ceased publication for lack of financial support.

The disappearance of the *National Gazette* did not leave the Republicans without a journalistic voice. The Philadelphia *Aurora*, edited by Benjamin Franklin Bache[36] since its first publication in 1790, quickly took that spot. Bache, the grandson of Benjamin Franklin, had spent much of his youth with his grandfather in France and, quite naturally, strongly supported the French in their revolution. He quickly attacked anyone and everyone who opposed the French or supported the British.

As it became increasingly clear that President Washington's administration had no intention of strongly supporting the French, Bache began to center his attacks on Washington himself. Responding to the Farewell Address in late 1796, Bache asserted:

If ever a nation was debauched by a man, the American nation has been debauched by Washington. If ever a nation has suffered from the improper influence of a man, the American nation has suffered from the influence of Washington. If ever a nation was deceived by a man, the American nation has been deceived by Washington. Let his conduct then be an example to future ages. Let it serve to be a warning that no man may be an idol.[37]

Following Adams's inauguration, Bache declared that "there ought to be a JUBILEE in the United States" because Washington, "the source of all the misfortune of our country, is this day reduced to a level with his fellow citizens, and is no longer possessed of power to multiply evils upon the United States."[38]

Bache's attacks on Washington constituted only a small part of the verbal abuse he heaped on his political opponents. Because of his vicious verbal attacks on various Federalist politicians, he became one of the first indicted under the Sedition Act in 1798. However, his death from yellow fever before the conclusion of the trial ended the sedition prosecution. Bache's widow and his former assistant editor, William Duane, continued to publish the paper until 1822.

Most of the growing political conflict of the 1790s centered on the role the United States should play in the conflict between Great Britain and France. Although some disagreements over implementing the Constitution surfaced in 1789 and 1790, true discord appeared because of the French Revolution and the European war that resulted. Although President Washington urged neutrality as essential for the survival of the young nation, others stated that the United States should at least support one side or the other ideologically, if not in any other manner. Hamilton and the Federalists affirmed that the United States, with a population primarily of English-speaking descent, had more interests in common with Great Britain than France and urged support for the British. Jefferson and the Republicans, remembering French aid during America's own Revolution and seeing the French Revolution as following the model set by the United States, invoked the names of Lafayette and Rochambeau and urged Americans to support France.

American support for the French cooled somewhat as the revolution took a more violent turn with the Reign of Terror in 1793–1794. It became more difficult for many people to understand how the relatively bloodless American revolt against Great Britain could have much in common with the increasingly violent conflict in France. The actions of the French ambassador, Edmond Genêt, helped worsen this situation and provided the context for the first major conflict in the press between the Federalists and the Republicans. Genêt arrived in the United States in April 1793, and supportive crowds met him wherever he went. Following Genêt's arrival in Philadelphia, Benjamin Franklin Bache stated: "We have no doubt that the affability and popularity of Citizen Genêt will gain him the esteem of the inhabitants of this country and city, and awaken in them sentiments of gratitude for our generous allies, the defenders of the rights of man."[39]

Many American leaders, particularly Republicans, welcomed Genêt and hoped to increase public expressions of support for France on the occasion of his arrival and acceptance as the new French ambassador. Essayists in the Republican newspapers sang Genêt's praises and urged support for the French cause. In the *National Gazette*, "Veritas" claimed that in issuing the Proclamation of Neutrality, President Washington had been misled by "the aristocratic few and their contemptible minions of speculators, tories and British emissaries." He concluded that the "Whigs of 1776 will not suffer French patriots of 1792 to be villified with impunity by the common enemies of both."[40] Such remarks encouraged Genêt in his search for support and aid in the United States. However, he overestimated American support for the French Revolution. Believing that the majority of Americans were supportive of the French cause, Genêt sought to acquire financial and military assistance from private individuals, even though President Washington had clearly declared the United States neutral in the conflict. Furthermore, the ambassador issued commissions for privateers to raid British shipping and sought to develop plans to invade British and Spanish territory in the New World. Such cavalier behavior could not be tolerated. Even Jefferson became increasingly alarmed by Genêt's actions, describing him as "indefensible"[41] and "disrespectful & even indecent towards the P[resident] in his written as well as verbal communications."[42] Finally, President Washington requested that Genêt be recalled.

The Republicans found it difficult to defend Genêt and his actions. His most ardent defender, Benjamin Franklin Bache, concluded that Genêt's actions were appropriate and justified. According to Bache, outfitting privateers did not violate the neutrality of the United States because the right to do so had been granted by the treaty signed with France in 1778. And "as for contravening the President's proclamation," everyone knew that "any proclamation is merely a declaration which owes its little force to the laws, and if it is contrary to treaties, the supreme law of the land, is a perfect nullity."[43] But few joined Bache in such a strong defense of Genêt and his actions. Many Americans perceived the arming of privateers as dangerous to the interests of the United States and as containing the potential for war with Great Britain, something the country could ill afford to wage at that time. The Genêt affair provided the Federalists, led by Alexander Hamilton, an excuse for attacking the Republicans. Hamilton used the press to influence public opinion to protest Genêt's actions and to oppose his Republican supporters, particularly Jefferson. His most effective charge, published under the pseudonym "No Jacobin" in *Dunlap's American Daily Advertiser* in Philadelphia, declared that the French ambassador had "threatened to appeal from the President of the United States to the People" in order to achieve his goals.[44] Protests and public demonstrations against Genêt occurred throughout the United States as Americans responded to what they perceived to be an insult to their government. It appeared that the Federalists had won the first round in the war of words with the Republicans.

Conflict over what the United States should do concerning the European conflict continued to fuel the disagreements between the Republicans and the Federalists. Jay's Treaty of 1795 provided the basis for the next round of arguments. Continuing disagreements over the Ohio Valley between Great Britain and the United States and the issue of neutral rights at sea caused President Washington to send John Jay to London as negotiator in order to try to settle the differences between the two countries peacefully. The resulting agreement, Jay's Treaty, produced a cacophony of criticism from the Republicans and support from the Federalists, most of which appeared in the partisan newspapers of both sides.[45]

Rumors concerning the treaty had existed for months prior to its publication. The president received the treaty in March 1795, but did not submit it to the Senate for approval until June. Washington considered a treaty with Great Britain essential for the survival of the United States, but the one that Jay had been able to negotiate did not please him. The treaty created an international commission to oversee the payment of any debts remaining from the years before the Revolution. Great Britain promised to vacate all posts in the northwest by June 1796. Direct trade between the United States and Great Britain was established on a "most favored nation" status, but trade with British colonies remained limited. The negotiated settlement totally ignored the issue of neutral rights. Following its submission, the Senate reluctantly ratified the document. After its approval, but prior to its official publication, Bache's *Aurora* printed a summary of the treaty and later offered for sale a pamphlet containing the entire contents of the document. It is unclear where the editor learned the contents of the treaty originally, but the publication of a summary in the *Aurora* on June 29 prompted Senator Stevens T. Mason of Virginia to give him a copy of the treaty, which became the basis for the pamphlet advertised on July 1. Bache led other Republican editors in quickly attacking the treaty as a betrayal of American interests. "Americanus" in the *Independent Gazette* stated that the treaty exhibited "the dishonor of America, and the political depravity of her government" because, through it, the United States bowed to the wishes of Great Britain. As a result, the nation surrendered "the most essential political and commercial interests whilst pointing the finger of hostility to France."[46]

Federalist editors, horrified that the contents of the treaty had been leaked to the opposition, sought to shore up public support for the administration. Benjamin Russell denounced the Republicans for seeking to embarrass President Washington, while Noah Webster, Alexander Hamilton, and Rufus King wrote series of essays supporting the treaty. Webster, as "Curtius," wrote twelve essays defending the treaty, while Hamilton and King wrote a more famous series of thirty-eight supportive essays under the pseudonym of "Camillus."[47] Hamilton, in particular, urged support for Jay's Treaty and even support for Great Britain in the war against France because Britain and the United States had so much in common— "the two nations speak the same language, and in every exterior circumstance closely resemble each other."[48] Although the treaty did not have strong or widespread support, the Senate approved it as the best possible result given the current conditions.

Ratification of Jay's Treaty offended the French, and relations deteriorated between France and the United States. By 1797, French naval ships began seizing American vessels carrying British goods. President John Adams (elected in 1796) hoped to avoid war through negotiation. French Foreign Minister Talleyrand sought a bribe of a quarter of a million dollars and a loan of $12 million before he would begin negotiations.[49] In response to this action, two of the three American representatives, John Marshall and Charles Cotesworthy Pinckney, sailed home. This event became known as the XYZ affair because President Adams identified the French representatives as X, Y, and Z in reporting the incident to Congress. This event helped produce the undeclared naval war between France and the United States and provided the premise for the Alien and Sedition Acts, an attack on First Amendment freedoms designed by the Federalists to stifle the opposition, the Republicans. The Sedition Act specifically attacked the press and produced the first serious discussion of the meaning of freedom of the press as protected by the First Amendment. The Alien and Sedition Acts will be discussed more fully in the next chapter. The struggle that followed the adoption of this legislation severely tested the meaning of a republican government in the United States and served to undo the first political party system by weakening the Federalist Party beyond repair. The election of Thomas Jefferson as president in 1800 and the death of Alexander Hamilton in a duel in 1804 heightened the impact of the Alien and Sedition Acts. Although the Federalists continued to exist until the War of 1812, they never again were a major political factor on the national scene.

The newspaper publications of the 1790s are often difficult to judge because so much discussion has been filtered through modern lenses.[50] The press of the first party era was full of vituperation and scurrility, but such language and abuse were common to the era, found not only in newspapers, but also in personal letters, speeches, and other writings.[51] Although both Thomas Jefferson and Alexander Hamilton complained about their treatment in the press, they also both encouraged their supporters to strongly attack the opposition in the newspapers. With no concept of loyal party opposition, only one side was right, while the opposition was lying. Therefore, strong attacks were justified and necessary in order to prevent tyranny or anarchy. Both sides in the growing political debate believed in the influence of the press and sought to use the newspapers to espouse their cause and influence public opinion. For almost everyone concerned, the primary purpose of the press in the 1790s was not to be nonpartisan and present "the news," but to support a political cause and strongly to advocate one side of an issue while attacking the other side. To do less was, as so ably stated by William Cobbett, to be "a poor passive fool, and not an editor."[52] If political partisanship constituted the standard by which to measure the press, the newspapers of the 1790s did a good job.

Furthermore, the newspapers of the 1790s deserve credit for several important journalistic developments. First, the editor appears in the 1790s as a distinct position, one in which the director of the journal is a writer and commentator rather than simply a printer. John Fenno was the first of this new breed of newspaper producer, but he was clearly not the last. If a newspaper was to support a particular cause, the producer had to write not only news, but also opinion to support the cause in question. The concept of the editor as a manager and opinion stater first appeared in the party press of the 1790s and has become the standard for journalism since that time. Along with the development of the position of editor came the regular appearance of a recognizable editorial.[53] Again, the need for political comment led to the appearance of brief, but clearly labeled, editorial comments by the newspaper managers by the mid-1790s. Today, the organized, overt expression of opinion is a major function of a newspaper, a practice that first appeared in the 1780s and had clearly developed by the 1790s.[54] The newspapers of the first decade of the new nation have generally been severely criticized for their scurrility, but this criticism really misses the point. They did a good job of the assignment given them—to support a particular political cause—and in doing so, they established the idea that politics was an important topic worthy of the press's attention and consideration. For that contribution alone, they deserve more credit than they have often been given by many historians.

NOTES

1. Donald H. Stewart, *The Opposition Press of the Federalist Period* (Albany: State University of New York Press, 1969), 9–11.

2. *National Gazette* (Philadelphia), 19 December 1791.

3. Numbers are from Alfred McClung Lee, *The Daily Newspaper in America* (New York: Macmillan, 1937), 711.

4. As major players in the formation of the new nation and the new government, both Jefferson and Hamilton have received much attention from historians. Some of the best biographies of Alexander Hamilton include Nathan Schachner, *Alexander Hamilton* (New York: D. Appleton-Century Co., 1946); John C. Miller, *Alexander Hamilton: Portrait in Paradox* (New York: Harper, 1959); Forrest McDonald, *Alexander Hamilton: A Biography* (New York: Norton, 1979); and Broadus Mitchell's two-volume set, *Alexander Hamilton* (New York: Macmillan, 1957–1962). Jefferson's primary recent biographer is Dumas Malone, who produced a six-volume series, *Jefferson and His Times* (Boston: Little, Brown, 1948–1981). Shorter works include Merrill D. Peterson, *Thomas Jefferson and the New Nation* (New York: Oxford University Press, 1970), and Noble E. Cunningham, Jr., *In Pursuit of Reason: The Life of Thomas Jefferson* (Baton Rouge: Louisiana State University Press, 1987). An insightful study of Jefferson and the partisan press of the 1790s is Michael Lienesch, "Thomas Jefferson and the American Democratic Experience: The Origins of the Partisan Press, Popular Political Parties, and Public Opinion," in *Jeffersonian Legacies*, ed. Peter S. Onuf (Charlottesville: University Press of Virginia, 1993), 316–339.

5. Jefferson to Archibald Stuart, 14 May 1799, *The Writings of Thomas Jefferson*, ed. Paul Leicester Ford, 12 vols. (New York: G. P. Putnam's Sons, 1904–1905), 9:647.

6. Jefferson to Monsieur A. Coray, 31 October 1823, *The Writings of Thomas Jefferson*, ed. Andrew A. Lipscomb, 20 vols. (Washington, D.C.: Thomas Jefferson Memorial Association, 1903–1904), 15:489.

7. See, for example, Jefferson's letter to Madison, 7 July 1793, where he urges Madison to attack the ideas of Alexander Hamilton in the newspapers: "For god's sake, my dear Sir, take up your pen, select the most striking heresies, and cut him to pieces in the face of the public. There is nobody else who can & will enter the lists with him." *The Papers of James Madison*, ed. Thomas A. Mason, Robert A. Rutland, and Jeanne K. Sisson (Charlottesville: University Press of Virginia, 1985), 15:43. Jefferson also encouraged others to write for the press, particularly for the *National Gazette*. Authors who wrote at Jefferson's urging included David Rittenhouse, Joseph Barnes, and George Logan. "Editorial Note," *The Papers of Thomas Jefferson*, ed. Julian P. Boyd, et al. 25 vols. to date (Princeton, N.J.: Princeton University Press, 1950–), 20:733–36. Jefferson himself almost never wrote for the newspapers, believing that he could not achieve the goal he desired if he wrote himself. On several occasions, particularly when defending his support for Philip Freneau and the *National Gazette*, Jefferson hotly denied that he had written anything for the newspapers that did not have his name attached to it. He told Edmund Randolph that he had resolved to follow this course concerning writing for the newspapers early in life and that he had not

veered from this plan. The editors of his papers, currently being published, have found no evidence of Jefferson using a newspaper pseudonym to attack the character of a political opponent. However, they have found evidence of his having written anonymously to the newspapers on several occasions, primarily "to correct misrepresentations, to advance a cause, or . . . to avoid being drawn by 'cavillers . . . personally into contest before the public.'" "Editorial Note," *The Papers of Thomas Jefferson*, ed. Boyd, 20:722. Douglas L. Wilson concluded that Jefferson's personality prevented him from addressing the public directly unless the situation was an emergency, such as when he drafted the Kentucky Resolutions. Douglas L. Wilson, "Jefferson and the Republic of Letters," in *Jeffersonian Legacies*, ed. Peter S. Onuf (Charlottesville: University Press of Virginia, 1993), 72.

8. David Ford to Alexander Hamilton, 11 April 1798, *The Papers of Alexander Hamilton*, ed. Harold C. Syrett et al. (New York: Columbia University Press, 1974), 22:411.

9. For an excellent discussion of the role of the party press, see Wm. David Sloan, "The Early Party Press: The Newspaper Role in American Politics, 1788–1812," *Journalism History* 9 (Spring 1982): 18–24, and Wm. David Sloan, "The Federalist-Republican Press: Newspaper Functions in America's First Party System, 1789–1816," *Studies in Journalism and Mass Communication* 1 (Spring 1982): 13–22.

10. *Newark* (N.J.) *Gazette*, 4 September 1798.

11. *Porcupine's Gazette* (Philadelphia), 5 March 1797.

12. Quoted in *Independent Chronicle* (Boston), 7 August 1798.

13. *American and Daily Advertiser* (Baltimore, Md.), 16 May 1799.

14. John C. Miller, *The Federalist Era, 1789–1801* (New York: Harper & Brothers, 1960), 233; Stewart, *Opposition Press*, 624–25.

15. *Gazette of the United States* (New York and Philadelphia), 15 April 1789, 27 April 1791.

16. *Columbian Centinel* (Boston), 4 March 1801.

17. *Time Piece* (New York), 13 June 1798.

18. Letter to George Washington, 9 September 1792, *The Papers of Thomas Jefferson*, ed. Boyd, 24:356.

19. John Fenno has yet to receive detailed serious study from historians. John B. Hench edited a series of letters from Fenno and his son, John Ward Fenno, in the *Proceedings of the American Antiquarian Society* 89 (1979): 299–368; 90 (1980): 163–234. Two articles that discuss his role in the early party press are Jerry W. Knudson, "Political Journalism in the Age of Jefferson," *Journalism History* 1 (1974): 20–23, and Sloan, "The Early Party Press," 18–24.

20. *Gazette of the United States*, 27 April 1791.

21. Most of the scholarly studies about Noah Webster have dealt with his work in education. The most important of these books are Ervin C. Shoemaker, *Noah Webster: Pioneer of Learning* (New York: Columbia University Press, 1936), and Harry R. Warfel, *Noah Webster: Schoolmaster to America* (New York: Macmillan, 1936). The best study to consider specifically Webster's career as a journalist is Gary Coll, "Noah Webster, Journalist, 1783–1803," in *Colonial Newsletters to Newspapers: Eighteenth-Century Journalism*, ed. Donovan H. Bond and W. Reynolds McLeod (Morgantown: School of Journalism, West Virginia University, 1977), 303–18.

22. *American Minerva* (New York), 9 December 1793.

23. Ibid.

24. Jim Allee Hart, *The Developing Views on the News: Editorial Syndrome, 1500–1800* (Carbondale: Southern Illinois University Press, 1970), 185.

25. *Porcupine's Gazette*, 5 March 1797.

26. Ibid.

27. Ibid.

28. Cobbett had begun his career in England as a radical, calling for more democracy in the government. When he went to the United States, he became more conservative because the republican government he found there did not live up to his expectations. For Cobbett, most of the politicians he found in America were no better than the ones he left behind in England—they were all power-hungry and did not truly support democracy. The violence of the French Revolution only served to reinforce these ideas. Once he returned to England in 1800, Cobbett once more moved in a radical direction in his political thought, primarily because he believed England had degenerated in his absence. Cobbett's idealism concerning democratic government never found fulfillment because no country lived up to his ideal.

29. Besides his materials in the *Gazette*, William Cobbett also wrote numerous pamphlets that discussed his beliefs on government. A good source for these materials is William Cobbett, *Peter Porcupine in America: Pamphlets on Republicanism and Revolution*, ed. David A. Wilson (Ithaca, N.Y.: Cornell University Press, 1994).

30. *Columbian Centinel*, 5 October 1798.

31. Ibid., 4 March 1801.

32. Several excellent biographies of Philip Freneau have appeared. Among these are Mary Austin, *Philip Freneau: The Poet of the Revolution* (New York: A. Wessels, 1901); Samuel E. Forman, *The Political Activities of Philip Freneau* (Baltimore, Md.: Johns Hopkins University Press, 1902); Lewis Leary, *That Rascal Freneau: A Study in Literary Failure* (Brunswick, N.J.: Rutgers University Press, 1941); and James Axelrad, *Philip Freneau* (Austin: University of Texas Press, 1967). A valid study of a particular chapter in Freneau's journalistic career (his coverage of French Ambassador Genêt's efforts to raise military forces in the United States) is Leonard A. Granato, "Freneau, Jefferson and Genet: Independent Journalism in the Partisan Press," in *Newsletters to Newspapers*, ed. Bond and McLeod, 291–301.

33. Axelrad, *Philip Freneau*, 209–34.

34. *National Gazette*, 9 December 1791.

35. Ibid., 9 February 1792.

36. Most of the biographies of Benjamin Franklin Bache have concentrated on the influence of his grandfather on his journalistic career. Included here are Bernard Faÿ, *The Two Franklins: Fathers of American Democracy* (Boston: Little, Brown, 1933); Jeffrey A. Smith, *Franklin and Bache: Envisioning the Enlightened Republic* (New York: Oxford University Press, 1990); and James Tagg, *Benjamin Franklin Bache and the Philadelphia* Aurora (Philadelphia: University of Pennsylvania Press, 1991).

37. *Aurora* (Philadelphia), 23 December 1796.

38. Ibid., 6 March 1797.

39. *General Advertiser* (Philadelphia), 16 May 1793.

40. Quoted in Robert A. Rutland, *Newsmongers: Journalism in the Life of the Nation, 1690–1972* (New York: Dial Press, 1973), 69.

41. Letter to James Monroe, 14 July 1793, *The Writings of Thomas Jefferson*, ed. Lipscomb, 9:164.

42. Letter to James Madison, 7 July 1793, *The Papers of James Madison*, ed. Mason, Rutland, and Sisson, 15:43.

43. *General Advertiser*, 11 July 1793.

44. No Jacobin #1. Reprinted in *Gazette of the United States*, 31 August 1793.

45. Although Jay's Treaty was the first major diplomatic effort of the new government under the Constitution, it has received little direct study from historians. Three works that do concentrate on the treaty are Samuel Flagg Bemis, *Jay's Treaty: A Study in Commerce and Diplomacy*, rev. ed. (New Haven, Conn.: Yale University Press, 1962); Charles R. Ritcheson, *Aftermath of Revolution: British Policy Toward the United States, 1783–1795* (Dallas: Southern Methodist University Press, 1969); and Jerald A. Combs, *The Jay Treaty: Political Battleground of the Founding Fathers* (Berkeley: University of California Press, 1970).

46. *Independent Gazette* (New York), 25 July 1795.

47. Combs, *The Jay Treaty*, 163.

48. Hamilton writing as "Camillus," quoted in Frederick C. Prescott, ed., *Alexander Hamilton and Thomas Jefferson* (New York: American Book Co., 1934), 151.

49. The use of bribes was standard operating procedure in diplomatic circles at the time, and Talleyrand was an expert. A large portion of Talleyrand's personal fortune had come from bribes received as part of foreign negotiations. What was somewhat different in this case was the French insistence that the money be paid before talks even began. Steven T. Ross, *European Diplomatic History, 1789–1815: France Against Europe* (Garden City, N.Y.: Anchor Books, 1969), 174; Franklin L. Ford, *Europe, 1780–1830* (London: Longman, 1970), 58–59; Samuel Flagg Bemis, *A Diplomatic History of the United States* (New York: Henry Holt, 1936), 116.

50. For many years, historians have labeled the early years of the history of the United States as the "Dark Ages of American Journalism." However, recent work in this era has indicated that the partisanship expressed by the press was an accepted and expected part of the role given to newspapers by politicians and editors alike. Particularly important in this area has been the work of David Sloan, who challenged the "Dark Ages" concept in "Examining the 'Dark Ages' Concept: The Federalist-Republican Press as a Model," *Journal of Communication Inquiry* 7 (1982): 105–19, and "Historians and the Party Press: 130 Years of Scholarship," *Studies in Journalism and Mass Communication* 2 (Spring 1983): 27–32.

51. The most useful study of the use of negative language in the newspapers of the 1790s is Wm. David Sloan, "Scurrility and the Party Press, 1789–1816," *American Journalism* 5 (1988): 97–112.

52. *Porcupine's Gazette*, 5 March 1797.

53. "Leading articles," the British name for editorials, had become common on the front pages of newspapers in Great Britain by the middle of the eighteenth century. Colonial newspapers had not followed this development. Instead, opinions, if printed at all, had generally been tacked onto news stories and scattered throughout the newspaper. Editors clearly expressed their opinions beginning in the 1780s, but it was only in the 1790s that the American press developed and made common practice what could obviously be identified as an editorial. Hart, *Developing Views on the News*, 103, 178.

54. Wm. David Sloan, Cheryl Watts, and Joanne Sloan, *Great Editorials: Masterpieces of Opinion Writing* (Northport, Ala.: Vision Press, 1992), 16–18, 24–25.

4

The Challenge of the
Sedition Act, 1798–1800

The party press debates of the 1790s produced the first major confrontation and debate concerning the First Amendment and what its protection of speech and the press actually meant. Although not completely defined at the time, a libertarian concept of freedom of expression developed during the conflict over the Alien and Sedition Acts and has provided the bedrock for the liberty of the press ever since.

Congress passed the Alien and Sedition Acts as a response to the growing political party conflicts that developed out of the disagreements over how the United States should respond to the French Revolution. Jay's Treaty with Great Britain had warded off war with that country, but it also angered France and sparked what President John Adams called "the half war with France." Perceiving the treaty with Britain as a violation of the Revolutionary alliance between the United States and France, the French republic began aggressively raiding American shipping in 1796. President Adams attempted to negotiate the conflict through the appointment of special envoys, but the French refused to discuss the issue without a promise of American loans and a bribe. The resulting scandal developing out of the attempted bribery became known as the XYZ affair. It not only ruptured American-French diplomatic ties for a time, but also provided the grounds for an attack by the Federalists on their Republican opponents.

The break in diplomatic ties between the United States and France came quickly following the publication of the documents related to the XYZ incident. Many believed that war was just a matter of time. French ships took advantage of American military weakness and raided merchant ships all along the Atlantic Coast. The president did not ask for a declaration of war, but Congress prepared for the worst. It appropriated money for the completion of three frigates already under construction and the addition of forty more ships to the navy. It also purchased arms and ammunition and strengthened harbor defenses, as well as tripling the size of the regular army. The government cut off trade with France and declared the treaties of 1778 suspended.[1]

American patriotism reached fever pitch as these war preparations took place. People overwhelmed President Adams with numerous addresses praising the actions of the government and calling for an even firmer stand in the face of French insults. News of American naval victories over French ships in the Caribbean produced public celebrations throughout the states. This growing dislike of France and anything French hurt the Republican Party, and the Federalists triumphed in the congressional election of 1798, the last time they would win a national election.[2]

As news of the XYZ affair spread, the Federalists quickly moved to identify the Republicans as the French party, using the newspapers to brand them as traitors for supporting France and opposing the policies of the United States government. Thomas Jefferson, vice-president and leader of the Republican Party, received most of the criticism. William Cobbett, editor of *Porcupine's Gazette*, attacked Jefferson as "the head of the democratic frenchified faction in this country."[3] Failure to oppose the French and their actions was tantamount to treason. A New York paper stated that any "man who does not warmly reprobate the conduct of the French must have a soul black enough to be 'fit' for 'treasons strategems' and 'spoils.'"[4] A group of Federalist militia summed up the hopes of many of their fellow party members in their Independence Day toast: "May all party spirit be lost in the common cause of national independence."[5] In the face of the growing French threat, the only hope for the nation was the eradication of party divisions. The Federalists in Congress stood ready to use the XYZ affair as grounds for legislation to cripple the Republican Party.

The Federalists designed all of the Alien and Sedition Acts to limit the influence of the Republicans. Of four laws, the first three dealt with foreigners living in the United States. Two laws enabled the president to deport legal aliens, during either war or peacetime, while the naturalization bill lengthened the residency requirement for citizenship from five to fourteen years. The Sedition Act, designed to silence criticism of the government, constituted the biggest threat to the Republicans because it would silence the party's main means of communication with the voting public. Under the terms of the legislation, "if any person shall write, print, utter, or publish . . . any false, scandalous and malicious writing . . . against the government of the United States, or either house of the Congress . . . or the said President . . . or to excite against them the hatred of the good people of the United States . . . or to resist or oppose, or defeat any such law," that person would be subject to two years' imprisonment and a $2,000 fine.

Even before its adoption, the Sedition Act came under attack as a severe violation of the First Amendment.[6] The congressional debates made it clear that the legislation threatened punishment to anyone who criticized the government in any way. The *Aurora* stated in late June that, if Congress adopted the Sedition bill then being debated, "to laugh at the cut of a coat of a member of Congress will soon be treason."[7] Several days later, Bache condemned the proposed legislation for "making it criminal to expose the crimes, the official vices or abuses, or the attempts of men in power to usurp a despotic authority."[8] Such concerns, however, went unheeded, and President Adams signed the Sedition Act into law on July 14, 1798. Although ostensibly designed to control the enemies of the United States, the expiration date of March 3, 1801, which coincided with the end of President Adams's term in office, reflected the political nature of the legislation.

The congressional debates over the Sedition Act revealed a disagreement among Americans concerning the definition of "freedom of the press." Although the Federalists clearly had political motives in their support for the Sedition Act, they also believed that true liberty of the press did not include the right to be overcritical of the government. As stated by Harrison Gray Otis, "[E]very independent Government has a right to preserve and defend itself against injuries and outrages which endanger its existence."[9] The Sedition Act, designed only to protect the government from unwarranted criticism, would not constitute a violation of the First Amendment. The Republicans disagreed, perceiving the legislation and its potential restrictions on open discussion in the newspapers as the embodiment of despotic government. Albert Gallatin, Republican spokesman in the House of Representatives, charged that similar laws had previously been used by rulers "to prevent the diffusion of knowledge, to throw a veil on their folly or their crimes, to satisfy those mean passions which always denote little minds, and to perpetuate their own tyranny."[10] Clearly, the Federalists intended to use the Sedition Act to muzzle their oppositon and "to perpetuate their authority and preserve their present places."[11] The adoption of the act did not end the argument. As officials arrested Republicans for violation of the Sedition Act, the debate over the meaning of freedom of the press continued.

Attempts to quiet the Republican opposition press actually began before the adoption of the Sedition Act. During the congressional debates over the proposed restrictive legislation, Federalists branded two vocal Republican newspapers as the worst examples of a bad breed. The Philadelphia *Aurora*, the nation's largest Republican paper, and the New York *Time Piece*, the fastest-growing opposition publication, both received criticism and were singled out as examples worthy of suppression under the proposed Sedition Act. During 1798, local authorities indicted the editors of these two newspapers, Benjamin Franklin Bache and John Daly Burk, under common law for the offense of seditious libel.

As the editor of the *Aurora*, Bache was the leading target of the Sedition Act. However, his opponents chose not to wait for the new legislation. On June 26, 1798, the day the Senate first discussed the bill, officials arrested Bache and charged him with seditious libel against the president and the executive branch of the government.

For several years, Bache and his newspaper had been criticized for disloyalty by the Federalists. William Cobbett, editor of *Porcupine's Gazette*, stated that "[t]he most infamous of the Jacobins is BACHE Editor of the *Aurora*, Printer to the French Director, Distributor General of the principles of Insurrection, Anarchy and Confusion, the greatest of fools, and the most stubborn sans-cullotte in the

United States."[12] For his opposition to the Federalist administration, congressional leaders barred Bache from the floor of the House of Representatives in 1797.

Prior to the charge of seditious libel, Federalists tried other methods to silence Bache and his criticism of the Adams administration. Withdrawal of advertising from the *Aurora* made the paper less lucrative. Early in 1798, Thomas Jefferson expressed fear that the paper would fold and urged fellow Republicans to continue to support it. In May 1798, mobs attacked Bache's house on two separate occasions. Also in 1798, the editor was assaulted twice, first by Abel Humphreys and then by John Ward Fenno. Both men were sons of political opponents of Bache. Such attacks, however, failed to silence his criticism of the administration. Finally, in June 1798, Bache provided his opponents with enough published materials to justify, at least in their opinion, an indictment for seditious libel.[13]

On June 16, 1798, Bache published a secret letter from French Foreign Minister Talleyrand two days before the government presented it to Congress. The Federalists quickly accused him of being in the pay of France because there seemed no other way that he could have acquired the letter. Government officials seized Bache's mail and sought to gather evidence of treason on the part of the newspaper editor. Bache cleared himself of these charges, but in the process criticized the actions of cabinet members Oliver Wolcott and Timothy Pickering. These critical comments provided the basis for the common law indictment for seditious libel. Authorities arrested Bache and charged him on June 26.[14]

Following his arrest, Bache stated in the *Aurora* that the government would not win its case. Furthermore, he promised that "prosecution no more than persecution, shall cause him to abandon what he considers the cause of truth and republicanism; which he will support, to the best of his abilities, while life remains."[15] Bache remained true to his word, continuing to publish the *Aurora* and use its pages to question the actions of the national government. Court officials set the trial for October, but it never took place. Deciding not to cease publication of the newspaper during the summer's yellow fever epidemic, Bache remained in Philadelphia. He caught the fever on September 5 and died five days later. Many Federalists felt cheated because they had failed to silence their greatest critic legally.

The other common law indictment for seditious libel brought by the Federalists against a Republican editor involved the New York *Time Piece* and its Irish editor, John Daly Burk. In this case, the Federalists were more successful because their efforts produced the cessation of the newspaper in question.

Burk immigrated to the United States in 1796, fleeing Ireland to avoid prosecution for sedition. He went first to Boston, but moved to New York in 1797. He became editor of the *Time Piece* on June 13, 1798. He quickly plunged into party politics by attacking the proposed Alien and Sedition Acts. The subscription list for the paper grew rapidly, with 134 new subscribers in nine days, making the *Time Piece* the second largest paper in New York. Because of this phenomenal growth, Burk and his paper became obvious targets for the Federalists. On July 6, 1798, authorities arrested Burk and his partner, Dr. James Smith, and charged them with seditious libel.[16]

Although not charged under the Sedition Act, Burk attacked the new legislation as part of his defense against the charges leveled at him. He feared that newspaper proprietors would fail to print anything about the government in order to avoid prosecution: "Of course the law will tend to the suppression of every press, however congenial with the constitution, if it be not obsequious to the will of government."[17]

As in the case of Bache, the trial of Burk for seditious libel never took place. However, the charges served to create a difference of opinion between the two partners, which resulted in the dissolution of the partnership. The *Time Piece* ceased publication at the end of August 1798. Burk reached an agreement to settle the case out of court and left New York in 1799. Thus, the Federalists succeeded in silencing one of their major critics, even without the help of the Sedition Act.

Although the Federalists silenced Bache and Burk through other means, they used the Sedition Act as the primary mechanism for attacks against the opposition press. The Federalist newspapers, particularly publications in New York and New England, led the way in encouraging the enforcement of the legislation. From the perspective of Federalist editors, just criticizing the government made opposition newspapers and their editors guilty of sedition. According to the *Albany Centinel*, sedition constituted anything that might "weaken the arm of Government, by undermining the confidence of the community in its measures."[18] The *Columbian Centinel* summed up the feelings of most Federalists: "Whatever American is a friend of the present administration of the American Government is undoubtedly a true republican, a true Patriot. . . . Whatever American opposes the Administration is an Anarchist, a Jacobin and a Traitor. . . . It is patriotism to write in favor of our government—it is sedition to write against it."[19] For the Federalist editors, the Republican press constituted a real threat to the stability of the nation that must be eliminated.

Secretary of State Timothy Pickering agreed with the opinion of the Federalist editors and sought diligently to enforce the Sedition Act. He regularly read the Republican newspapers, seeking grounds for prosecution. He also encouraged volunteer reports from others in an effort to be sure that they did not miss any seditious utterances. In the summer of 1799, Pickering sought to prosecute all the leading Republican papers that had not already been charged with sedition. The timing clearly indicated a desire to silence the opposition just as the election in 1800 approached. Pickering himself took charge of the case against William Duane and the Philadelphia *Aurora*, while instructing the district attorneys in New York, Richmond, and Baltimore to scrutinize the Republican papers of their towns and prosecute for sedition if needed.

Given this attitude, it is surprising that there were not more indictments. According to historian James Morton Smith, fourteen indictments can be verified as having been handed down under the terms of the Sedition Act, although there are references to other arrests, which apparently did not result in formal charges. The strictest enforcement of the law came in Federalist-dominated New England, New

York, and Pennsylvania. Only one sedition trial occurred outside this area, that of James T. Callender in Virginia. Designed to suppress Republican opposition, the Sedition Act operated best in areas where the Federalists already had control, thus producing a sympathetic audience for their actions.[20] Believing that their programs were the best for the nation's future, the Federalists sought to ensure their continued dominance in national politics. With the Sedition Act prosecutions, they hoped to silence the opposition and ensure victory in 1800.

Prosecutions under the Sedition Act began in October 1798. The first person charged, Representative Matthew Lyon of Vermont, had predicted during the congressional debates on the Sedition bill that he might be the first person prosecuted if the measure became law. Elected to Congress for the May 1797 session, Lyon had angered the Federalists because of his outspoken criticism of the formality of the government. Even before the Sedition Act passed, Federalist editors had denounced Lyon as a "wild Irishman"[21] who sought "to excite mobs and riots for the overthrow of the government and the constitution."[22]

Seeking reelection in 1798, Lyon used the newspapers to express his opinions to his constituents. However, his major opponent, Stanley Williams, edited the *Rutland Herald* and refused to publish any pieces that Lyon submitted. In October 1798, Lyon established his own newspaper, *The Scourge of Aristocracy and Repository of Important Political Truths*, to communicate his sentiments to the people of his district. Four days after the paper's initial publication, a jury indicted Lyon for sedition. Letters that he had published on July 31 and September 1 formed the basis for the charge. The July 31 letter, written by Lyon himself and published in the *Vermont Journal*, discussed President Adams's "continual grasp for power" and his "unbounded thirst for ridiculous pomp, foolish adulation or selfish avarice." The September 1 letter, written by Joel Barlow, appeared at Lyon's instigation to the "great scandal and infamy" of the government of the United States.[23]

Lyon defended himself at his trial, arguing that the Sedition Act was unconstitutional and that the contents of the letters were true. The presiding judge, Supreme Court Justice William Paterson, instructed the members of the jury that they could not consider the constitutionality of the legislation, stating that the only grounds for the verdict should be whether Lyon had published the letters in question and whether he had done so with "bad intent." The jury deliberated an hour and returned a guilty verdict. The judge sentenced Lyon to four months in jail and levied a fine of $1,000 and court costs of $60.96.[24]

During his months in jail, Lyon faced a runoff election for his congressional seat. The Federalists rejoiced over Lyon's conviction and urged all good citizens of his Vermont district to vote the convicted felon out of office. These pleas went unheeded, and Lyon won reelection easily, by a majority of almost 600 votes. Lyon's conviction and imprisonment made him a political martyr for the opposition, a development that the Federalists failed to anticipate. Lyon got out of prison on February 6, 1799, and immediately set off for Philadelphia to attend Congress. Crowds of supporters met him all along the route from his jail in Vergennes, Vermont, to Congress in Philadelphia. Even before his release from jail, Lyon had come to stand for those who stood up to the government. At Bridgehampton, New York, a group of men toasted "Colonel Matthew Lyon, the martyr to the cause of Liberty and the Rights of Man: may his sufferings bring good out of evil, by arousing the people to guard their rights and oppose every unconstitutional measure."[25] Although winning a temporary victory, the Federalists failed to achieve their goal of silencing their political opposition in the first prosecution under the Sedition Act.

The second Sedition Act prosecution attacked the Boston *Independent Chronicle*, the second leading Republican newspaper in the nation. Edited by Thomas Adams, the *Chronicle* had criticized the Adams administration for its stand concerning France and had attacked the Sedition Act as an attempt by the Federalists to use foreign problems "to further the work of injustice at home." Although Congress designed the act to limit the expression of political opinion, Thomas Adams promised not to let it intimidate him: "To that people we again pledge ourselves, that we will never sit quiet while their Liberties are invaded, or look in silence upon public oppression." Further, the editor promised to work "at whatever hazard to repel the invader and drag the criminal to justice, whoever may protect him in his transgression or partake of his crime."[26] A jury indicted Thomas Adams on October 23, 1798, on a charge of "sundry libellous and seditious publications . . . tending to defame the government of the United States," with the trial scheduled for June 1799.[27]

The indictment did not silence the *Chronicle*, which continued to criticize the government and the Federalist Party. As a result, government authorities instigated a second legal proceeding in February 1799. This case, brought by the state of Massachusetts, charged both Thomas Adams and his brother Abijah, the newspaper's bookkeeper, with seditious libel under the common law of England. Since Thomas Adams was severely ill, officials did not try him on this charge. They did, however, try Abijah, and he was convicted. The court sentenced him to thirty days in the county jail,[28] a sentence that he endured "with that resignation and fortitude, which becomes a man who can appeal to his conscience for the rectitude of his conduct."[29]

Still in ill health, Thomas Adams sold the *Chronicle* on May 2, 1799, less than a week after his brother's release from jail. One week later, he died. Once more, the death of the accused prevented a sedition trial from taking place. Also, the Federalists had again failed to silence the opposition press, since the *Chronicle* continued publication under its new proprietors, James White and Ebenezer Rhoades.[30]

As the election of 1800 approached, the Federalists used the Sedition Act to attack the leading Republican editors throughout the country. Among these were William Duane of Philadelphia, Thomas Cooper of Pennsylvania, and James T. Callender of Virginia.

William Duane, as Benjamin Franklin Bache's successor at the *Aurora*, quickly earned the dislike of the Federalists for his attacks on the Adams administration.

Officials first charged Duane in February 1799 with attempting to stir up a riot in opposition to the Alien Act, but a jury acquitted him for lack of evidence of any wrongdoing.

Following this incident, Duane stepped up his criticism of the Federalist-dominated government, charging that the British influenced American politics to an unacceptable degree. These charges resulted in a charge of seditious libel on August 30, 1799. By the time his case came to trial in October 1799, Duane faced a second indictment for criticizing the conduct of American troops. These indictments never came to trial because Duane had based his original charge of British influence on a letter written in 1792 by President Adams. Fearing that the president and his party would lose more than they would gain by trying Duane, authorities dropped the charges.[31]

As the election neared, the Federalists became more concerned about the need to silence the Republicans' chief newspaper, the *Aurora*, and its editor. The *Palladium* reported that one senator supposedly said that "if the *Aurora* is not blown up, Jefferson will be elected in defiance of everything."[32] The Federalists also sought to change how the electoral votes were counted in hopes of affecting the election. Federalists introduced into the Senate on January 23, 1800, a bill to create a congressional committee for the purpose of counting electoral votes. Duane received copies of the proposed legislation from several Republican senators, and he published the full text of the bill on February 19, 1800. Having been embarrassed by the publication of the bill, the Federalist-controlled Senate sought a means of punishing the editor for his actions. They created a standing committee of privileges to see if Duane had breached the Senate's rules by his actions. This committee, without ever summoning him to testify, found Duane guilty of writing a seditious libel and summoned him to appear on March 24 to explain his actions.[33]

During the proceedings of the committee, Duane defended his right to publish and discuss the proceedings of Congress. He described the actions of the Senate as an attempt to forcibly silence his criticism, an attempt that would fail. Duane vowed that he would use all legal means available to defend the freedom of the press and urged his readers to be patient: "if the enemies of our liberties should take any steps injurious to the public rights, hostile to the constitution, or dangerous to personal security and the rights of discussion, they will furnish new evidence of their views," and the people should vote them out of office at the next election.[34]

The Senate summoned Duane to appear on March 25, but he chose not to because it would do no good—the Federalists in the Senate were determined to punish him for his criticism. When he failed to appear, the Senate declared Duane guilty of contempt and ordered him arrested. Duane then went into hiding and successfully avoided arrest until after Congress adjourned. He continued to write for the *Aurora*, attacking the Senate for its actions. He also stated that the Federalists had embarked on a campaign "to terrify printers into silence or servility" through sedition trials designed to shut down Republican newspapers.[35]

The Senate failed to punish Duane for his publications, but he had not escaped trouble yet. On October 17, 1800, officials indicted him under the Sedition Act for the publication of the proposed Senate bill to change how they counted electoral votes. Authorities delayed the case until the May 1801 Circuit Court, but by then, Jefferson had replaced Adams as president and discontinued the Sedition Act prosecution, thus ending William Duane's troubles over the contents of his newspaper.[36]

Another victim of the Sedition Act, Thomas Cooper, edited the *Sunbury and Northumberland Gazette* from April 20 to June 29, 1799. In his farewell editorial, Cooper criticized the Federalist administration for measures that seemed "to stretch to the utmost the constitutional authority of our Executive, and to introduce the political evils of those European governments whose principles we have rejected."[37] This comment might have been ignored had it stopped in Northumberland, but Duane republished the entire editorial in the *Aurora* on July 12, 1799, and Cooper quickly became a target for the Federalists.[38]

Officials did not arrest Cooper for this editorial, but the Federalist press criticized him. "A True American" in the *Reading Weekly Advertiser* of October 26, 1799, accused him of attacking the administration because he failed to receive a government appointment that he had requested. Cooper responded to this attack in November 1799, stating that he had applied for a federal job, but that his editorial had not been sparked by a desire for revenge. Furthermore, the author of "A True American" could only have gotten his information from President Adams, an action that Cooper found questionable at best.[39]

The government indicted Cooper for seditious libel on April 9, 1800, with the trial commencing on April 19, 1800. The editor tried to defend his actions by acquiring copies of the correspondence concerning the government job, but the president's office refused to comply. When Cooper requested that the court order the president to release the documents, Supreme Court Justice Samuel Chase stated that the editor should have been sure of his evidence before he made any comments in the press. Cooper had little chance of winning his case because he could not gather the needed evidence. Furthermore, when Justice Chase gave his charge to the jury, he stated that the evidence clearly indicated that Cooper "intended to dare and defy the government, and to provoke them, and his subsequent conduct satisfies my mind that such was his disposition." With such a charge from the presiding judge, the jury could return no verdict but guilty. The judge sentenced Cooper to six months in federal prison and fined him $400. He fulfilled his sentence, defending his actions throughout as justified. He labeled the case a "political trial" and looked to the "solemn tribunal of the Public" for justification and retribution. Cooper saw Jefferson's victory in the election of 1800 as fulfilling this goal.[40]

The last major Republican editor indicted for sedition was James T. Callender, a pamphleteer and editorial writer in Virginia. Callender had fled Scotland in 1793 to avoid prosecution. After arriving in the United States, he continued his political writing, strongly supporting the Republican Party. In 1798, he wrote for the

Philadelphia *Aurora*. Many Federalists hoped Callender would be the first person indicted under the Sedition Act when it became law in July 1798. Fearing for his safety, Callender fled to a more hospitable location, Republican-dominated Virginia. In 1799, he joined the staff of the *Richmond Examiner*. His writings continued to criticize the administration and helped to boost the newspaper's circulation. But Callender did not face sedition charges for his newspaper comments. The basis for his indictment came from another source.[41]

In January 1800, Callender published *The Prospect Before Us*, a pamphlet supporting the election of Thomas Jefferson as president. In this piece, Callender attacked President Adams and his administration, stating that "the reign of Mr. Adams has been one continued tempest of malignant passions. As President, he has never opened his lips, or lifted his pen without threatening and scolding; the grand object of his administration has been to exasperate the rage of contending parties to calumniate and destroy every man who differs from his opinions."[42] Such statements could not go unnoticed.

At the instigation of Justice Samuel Chase, the grand jury indicted Callender under the Sedition Act on May 24, 1800. During the trial, Chase favored the prosecution in his rulings and decisions. When the jury returned a guilty verdict, Justice Chase stated that the results pleased him "because it shewed that the laws of the United States could be enforced in Virginia, the principal object of this prosecution." Chase sentenced Callender to nine months in jail and a $200 fine. Jail, however, did not silence him. The Federalist press hoped that Callender's conviction would frighten others away "from any attempts to violate the laws of our country,"[43] but its hopes failed. Callender became a martyr to the cause, and he and other Republican writers continued to criticize the administration and urge all Americans to vote for Jefferson in the approaching election.[44]

Although the indictments of Duane, Cooper, and Callender were the most widely publicized actions taken under the Sedition Law in 1800, these three men were not the only ones to face legal proceedings because of their publishing efforts. In New England, two newspaper editors became martyrs for the Republicans as they, too, faced sedition charges.

The indictment of Anthony Haswell of Vermont grew out of the Matthew Lyon case. Haswell, a strong supporter of Lyon, published in the *Vermont Gazette* on January 3, 1799, the notice for a lottery scheme to raise money for the congressman's legal expenses. This advertisement stated that Lyon had been imprisoned by "the oppressive hand of usurped power in a loathsome prison, deprived almost of the right of reason." On the same day, Haswell reprinted a piece from the *Aurora* that attacked the Adams administration for firing officeholders for their political beliefs and appointing former Tories to office. These two publications led to Haswell's indictment on October 7, 1799.[45]

The court delayed Haswell's trial until May 1800 in order to allow the defense to gather evidence. The delay did little good, and a jury convicted the editor on May 9, 1800, and sentenced him to two months in jail and a fine of $200. Haswell served his sentence, but continued to write for his paper from his jail cell. He, too, became a hero for the Republican cause, stating that the Federalist "persecution" had opened "a new era of martyrdom," as when Americans had suffered under British rule, "and although woes crowd on so fast that one treads hard upon another's heels, the whole is for the furtherance of freedom, and must eventuate in the happiness of America."[46]

Another New England editor who faced prosecution under the Sedition Act in 1800 was Samuel Holt of the *New London Bee*. First published in 1797, the *Bee* was the only Republican paper of any size published in Connecticut. At first, the Federalists paid little attention to Holt and his paper, but by 1799, the *Bee* had been branded as "a notorious Jacobin paper" by the *Connecticut Courant*.[47] Holt continued to speak out, even in the face of such criticism, because he feared that Federalism had become so strong in his state that "a man cannot vote as he pleases, read what newspapers he pleases, or hardly think as he pleases, without being denounced by the hot heads of the federal party as a Jacobin, and enemy to his country, and every attempt made to injure him."[48]

Holt got into trouble in 1799 for publishing a letter from one of his readers that criticized the creation of an army when the country was not officially at war. The letter appeared in May, but officials did not seek to indict Holt until September. Officials scheduled his trial for April 1800. Again, the verdict did not surprise because the presiding judge, Supreme Court Justice Bushrod Washington, had nullified Holt's defense in his charge to the jury. The court sentenced the editor to three months in jail and a $200 fine. While serving his prison term, Holt suspended the *Bee*. However, he resumed publication within a month of his release. He continued his attacks on the Adams administration, concentrating most of his efforts against the Sedition Act. Holt declared that the legislation would be a failure for the Federalists because it would not silence their opposition: "Punishment only hardens printers . . . they come out of jail holding their heads higher than if they had never been persecuted. Finally they assume the appearance of innocent men who have suffered wrongfully."[49]

Holt's comments ably summed up the Republican response to the Sedition Act. The Federalists believed that the Constitution provided for legislation such as the Sedition Act, particularly in situations where the safety and stability of the nation seemed threatened. Perceiving the conflict with France and the support of France by the Republicans as such a threat, the Federalists pushed the Sedition Act through Congress. They considered it essential for the continued vitality of the United States. However, they also saw a traitor in every opponent and sought to smother their opposition by forcing the Republicans to either cease publication or temper their comments. In this effort, the Federalists failed because most of the newspaper editors charged under the legislation continued to publish, both while in jail serving their sentences and after they were released. In many ways, the Sedition Act backfired, since, as Holt indicated, many editors came out of jail stronger opponents of the Federalists than they had previously been. They continually justified the right of the press to question and criticize the actions of the government, stating that such a process formed the bedrock of republican government.[50] The failure of the Federalists to silence the Republican press in the debates of 1798–1800 helped to establish the idea that disagreements and differences of opinion were part of the political system that existed in the United States. The acceptance of diversity of opinion, at least to some extent, in the political arena provided the basis for an amazing growth in the press in the early nineteenth century, as the press sought to express not only diverse political thoughts, but also a variety of ideas in areas that related to all aspects of American life.

NOTES

1. Alexander DeConde, *The Quasi-War: The Politics and Diplomacy of the Undeclared War with France, 1797–1801* (New York: Charles Scribner's Sons, 1966), 89–98; John C. Miller, *The Federalist Era, 1789–1801* (New York: Harper & Brothers, 1960), 213–17.

2. Esmond Wright, *Fabric of Freedom, 1763–1800* (New York: Hill & Wang, 1961), 226; Miller, *Federalist Era*, 212–13.

3. *Porcupine's Gazette* (Philadelphia), 27 June 1798.

4. *New York Gazette* (New York), 12 April 1798.

5. *Gazette of the United States* (Philadelphia), 7 July 1798.

6. Although severely criticized by the Republicans in Congress, the Sedition Act was relatively mild for legislation of this type in this era. In 1795, in the midst of the war with France, Great Britain adopted the Treasonable Practices Act. Under its provisions, Parliament extended treason to include any criticism, written or spoken, of the King, the government, or the constitution. Possible punishments included seven years' transportation for the second offense. This legislation, much stronger than the American Sedition Act of 1798, gave legitimacy to a policy of suppression of political dissidents, which had been adopted in 1794. The centerpiece of the policy was the suspension of the writ of habeas corpus. The British feared that the entire social order was threatened by events in France and the possible repercussions; thus, they adopted some of the most restrictive legislation possible to deal with the perceived menace. John B. Owen, *The Eighteenth Century, 1714–1815* (London: Thomas Nelson and Sons, 1974), 261; Ian R. Christie, *Wars and Revolutions: Britain, 1760–1815* (Cambridge: Harvard University Press, 1982), 228–29.

7. *Aurora* (Philadelphia), 29 June 1798.

8. Ibid., 3 July 1798.

9. *Annals of Congress*, U.S. House of Representatives, 5th Congress, 2nd Session (Washington, D.C.: Gales and Seaton, 1834), 8:2164.

10. Ibid., 8:2164. Born in Geneva, Switzerland, Gallatin immigrated to the United States in 1780. He served in Congress during most of the 1790s, becoming a leading member of the Republican Party as it developed. After Jefferson's inauguration, Gallatin served as secretary of the treasury. In later years, he served as a diplomatic representative for the United States to several European countries.

11. Ibid., 8:2108–10.

12. *Porcupine's Gazette*, 12 March 1798.

13. James Morton Smith, *Freedom's Fetters: The Alien and Sedition Laws and American Civil Liberties* (Ithaca, N.Y.: Cornell University Press, 1956), 188–93.

14. Ibid., 193–200.

15. *Aurora*, 27 June 1798.

16. Smith, *Freedom's Fetters*, 204–11.

17. *Time Piece* (New York), 25 August 1798.

18. *Albany* (N.Y.) *Centinel*, 10 August 1798.

19. *Columbian Centinel* (Boston), 5 October 1798.

20. Smith, *Freedom's Fetters*, 185–87.

21. *Porcupine's Gazette*, 23 July 1798.

22. *Albany Centinel*, 31 July 1798.

23. Quoted in Smith, *Freedom's Fetters*, 221–30.

24. Ibid., 233–35.

25. *Independent Chronicle* (Boston), 17 January 1799.

26. Reprinted in *Aurora*, 21 July 1798.

27. Quoted in Smith, *Freedom's Fetters*, 252.

28. Ibid., 253–54.

29. *Independent Chronicle*, 25 April 1799.

30. Smith, *Freedom's Fetters*, 255.

31. Ibid., 279–88.

32. *Palladium* (Frankfort, Ky.), 10 April 1800.

33. Smith, *Freedom's Fetters*, 288–95.

34. *Aurora*, 24 March 1800.

35. Ibid., 27 May 1800.

36. Smith, *Freedom's Fetters*, 295–306.

37. *Sunbury and Northumberland Gazette* (Northumberland, Pa.), 29 June 1799.

38. Smith, *Freedom's Fetters*, 308–09.

39. Ibid., 312–14.

40. Ibid., 316–32.

41. Ibid., 335–39.

42. *The Prospect Before Us*, quoted in ibid., 339–40.

43. *Virginia Gazette*, June 1800, quoted in ibid., 358.

44. Ibid., 343–56.

45. Ibid., 361–62.

46. *Albany* (N.Y.) *Register*, 23 May 1800.

47. *Connecticut Courant* (Hartford), 30 September 1799.

48. *Bee* (New London, Conn.), 21 November 1798.

49. Ibid., 3 September 1800.

50. Most Republican political leaders who protested against the Sedition Act based their opposition on the idea that prosecutions of libels should be in the state courts rather than the federal courts. The most famous protests, the Virginia and Kentucky Resolutions by James Madison and Thomas Jefferson, stated that the Constitution was a compact by which the states delegated certain powers to a central government. Under this idea, ultimate power and authority lay with the states, and, thus, prosecutions for libels should take place there. Even after he became president, Jefferson emphasized that libel prosecutions should take place at the state level. Comments by editors in the newspapers in the aftermath of the Sedition Act do not indicate that they held such a fine-tuned view of the issue. For them, libel prosecution for criticism of the government infringed the liberty of the press and thus could not be tolerated. On this issue, at least, the Republican leadership and their editors diverged in their opinions. Dumas Malone, *Jefferson and His Time*, 6 vols. (Boston: Little, Brown, 1948–1981), 3:395–409, 4:234–35, 5:8–9; Miller, *Federalist Era*, 237–41; Norman K. Risjord, *Forging the American Republic, 1760–1815* (Reading, Mass.: Addison-Wesley, 1973), 289–90.

5

The Age of Jefferson, 1800–1808

When Thomas Jefferson took the oath of office as the third president of the United States on March 3, 1801, many people hoped that the days of the strongly partisan press that had existed during the 1790s had disappeared. In some ways, these hopes were well founded because the Federalist Party slowly declined on the national level, and the national newspapers that supported that viewpoint diminished in influence. However, more localized Federalist publications continued to be influential, particularly in New England. The impact of the Federalist press continued in some parts of the country until well after the end of the War of 1812.

The press steadily grew during the first decade of the nineteenth century. In 1800, 234 newspapers were published in the United States. By the end of Jefferson's presidency, the number had reached 329. Of those 329, all but 56 were identified, at least loosely, as supporters of one of the major political parties. Most public officials of the day believed in the importance of the press in the political arena, which accounted for the continued influence of the partisan press. Although disagreeing on exactly how it should function, almost everyone perceived the newspaper as a key factor in keeping people informed and involved in the government. In 1804, Jefferson worried that the Federalists controlled the large majority of the American press. Throughout his eight years in office, he and his supporters worked to increase the number of newspapers supporting their policies. By the time Jefferson retired in 1809, the Republicans had a slight majority in the number of partisan newspapers in the United States.[1]

Besides the obvious political advantages to having a supportive press, many Republicans also believed that more newspapers meant that the people would be better informed. As much as anyone else at the beginning of the nineteenth century, Thomas Jefferson believed in the absolute necessity of a free and open press for the safe operation of a democracy. He did not, however, believe that "free and open" meant that newspapers could print anything. The limitations that he believed needed to be placed on the press have led to criticisms and concerns about how much he really wanted freedom of the press.[2]

Jefferson's writings are filled with comments about the importance of the press in the democratic process. Probably his most often quoted statement appeared in a letter to Edward Carrington in 1787 in which Jefferson stated that he would rather have "newspapers without a government" than "a government without newspapers." However, Jefferson's comment involved much more than this simple statement indicates. When read in its entirety, it reveals Jefferson's strong belief in the newspapers as the primary source of information for people in making appropriate political decisions in the democratic process:

I am persuaded that the good sense of the people will always be found to be the best army. They may be led astray for a moment, but will soon correct themselves. The people are the only censors of their governors; and even their errors will tend to keep these to the true principles of their institution. To punish these errors too severely would be to suppress the only safeguard of the public liberty. The way to prevent these irregular interpositions of the people, is to give them full information of their affairs through the channel of the public papers, and to contrive that those papers should penetrate the whole mass of the people. The basis of our government being the opinion of the people, the very first object should be to keep that right; and were it left to me to decide whether we should have a government without newspapers, or newspapers without a government, I should not hesitate a moment to prefer the latter. But I should mean that every man should receive those papers, and be capable of reading them.[3]

This comment, written before the beginnings of the partisan press era, revealed Jefferson's idealism concerning the role of newspapers in a democracy. In order for a democratic government to function, the people must remain informed. If the people received all the facts, they would automatically make right decisions. Twenty years later, however, Jefferson's opinion seems to have dimmed somewhat. After two decades of national political involvement, he lamented the current state of the American press: "Nothing can now be believed which is seen in a newspaper. Truth itself becomes suspicious by being put into that polluted vehicle." He worried about the impact of reading such newspapers on "the great body of my fellow citizens, who, reading newspapers, live and die in the belief that they have known something of what has been passing in the world of their time; whereas the accounts they have read in newspapers are just as true a history of any other period of the world as of the present, except that the real names of the day are affixed to their fables." Jefferson concluded that "the man who never looks into a newspaper is better informed than he who reads them; inasmuch as he who knows nothing is nearer to truth than he whose mind is filled with falsehoods and errors."[4]

As the years passed, Jefferson's faith in the newspapers of the United States faltered. Yet he never truly ceased believing in the importance of a free press; he just thought that American newspapers had failed to live up to their essential role in society. In 1803, before he became embittered because of numerous personal attacks in the press, Jefferson told a friend: "They [the Federalists] fill their newspapers with falsehoods, calumnies, and audacities. . . . We are going fairly through the experiment of whether freedom of discussion, unaided by coercion, is not sufficient for the propagation and protection of truth, and for the maintenance of an administration pure and upright in its actions and views." He promised to protect the press, even when they lied about him, because "a people, easy in their circumstances as ours are, are capable of conducting themselves under a government founded not in the fears and follies of man, but on his reason, on the predominance of his social over his dissocial passions, so free as to restrain him in no moral right, and so firm as to protect him from every moral wrong, which shall leave him, in short, in possession of all his natural rights."[5] Years after his retirement from public office, Jefferson once more iterated his belief in the importance of a free press. In a letter to Charles Yancey in 1816, he declared that, "where the press is free, and every man able to read, all is safe."[6]

Jefferson's support for a free and open press did not extend to personal attacks and libels. In these areas, the press should be limited. Jefferson supported an amendment to the federal Constitution to protect the liberty of the press, but "a declaration that the federal government will never restrain the presses from printing anything they please, will not take away the liability of the printers for false facts printed."[7] From Jefferson's perspective, the national government should have no control over the press at all. Rather, control of newspapers and magazines (in the sense of preventing the publication of lies and falsehoods) should remain at the state level. In 1804, he told Abigail Adams, wife of former President John Adams, "While we deny Congress has a right to control freedom of the press, we have ever asserted the right of the States and their exclusive right, to do so."[8] For Jefferson, the press should be kept true to its calling, and the states possessed the means for carrying out this task.

By the middle of his first term in office, Jefferson believed that the lying in the press had gotten out of hand. In a letter to Governor Thomas McKean of Pennsylvania, he suggested that the states exercise their power to punish seditious libel in order to get the newspapers back on track:

This is a dangerous state of things, and the press ought to be restored to its credibility if possible. The restraints provided by the laws of the states are sufficient for this if applied. And I have therefore long thought that a few prosecutions of the most prominent offenders would have a wholesome effect in restoring the integrity of the presses. Not a general prosecution, for that would look like persecution; but a selected one.[9]

Officials followed Jefferson's advice on several occasions during his second term in office. Jefferson himself did not take an active part in the state prosecutions that took place, but he did not protest the actions. The most celebrated libel case involved Harry Croswell and *The Wasp*, published in Hudson, New York. Local authorities indicted Croswell in 1803 for republishing comments from the

New York Evening Post that accused Jefferson of having paid James Callender to slander Washington and other Federalist leaders in his newspaper. Originally convicted, Croswell later lost his appeal to the New York Supreme Court, even though ably defended on appeal by Alexander Hamilton. Croswell lost primarily because of the failure of state law to protect truthful press criticism of government officials. The Croswell case, although technically a loss, helped improve the legal status of the press by convincing several states to change their laws to provide for truth as a defense in libel cases and to give the jury the authority to determine both the law and the fact of the libel.[10]

Jefferson's belief in the importance of the press in a democracy led him to support several newspapers during his public career. Philip Freneau's *National Gazette* received his encouragement during the 1790s, but it no longer existed when Jefferson became president. The leading Republican paper in 1800 was the Philadelphia *Aurora*, edited by William Duane. He had become co-editor of the *Aurora* upon the death of Benjamin Franklin Bache in 1798. Shortly thereafter, Duane married Mrs. Bache and become sole editor. Just as Bache had done, Duane continued to use the *Aurora* to support the Republican Party. The Federalists feared his voice, and they arrested him four times under the the common law of seditious libel and the Alien and Sedition Acts. By 1806, he had also been sued for libel by individuals at least sixty times. In each case, the plaintiff was a Federalist.

In 1800, Duane attacked the Federalists for attempting to change how electoral votes were counted in order to favor President Adams in the election. According to Jefferson, Duane's support for his presidential campaign proved essential in the Republican victory of 1800. Jefferson described the editor as "honest, and well intentioned, but over zealous." Duane's influence among national leaders lessened somewhat in the early 1800s, primarily because he got into arguments with James Madison and his supporters. The movement of the capital to Washington also weakened Duane's position because the *Aurora* remained in Philadelphia. However, Duane's editorials continued to appear throughout the country, and his paper continued to be a major factor in the Republican press until he retired in 1822.[11] Long after his retirement, Jefferson thanked Duane for his support: "I have not forgotten the past, nor those who were fellow-laborers in the gloomy hours of federal ascendancy, when the spirit of republicanism was beaten down, its votaries arraigned as criminals, and such threats denounced as posterity will never believe."[12]

Jefferson supported Duane's efforts as the *Aurora* continued to lead the partisan newspaper debate for the Republicans, but Jefferson apparently wanted a less volatile editor to publish a paper that would serve as his administration's official newspaper. In 1801, he persuaded Samuel Harrison Smith, a fellow member of the American Philosophical Society, to move to the capital to establish the *National Intelligencer*. Throughout his tenure as editor, Smith remained a supporter of the Republican Party. Although not blindly partisan, people correctly perceived Smith's paper as the official newspaper of Jefferson's administration. On numerous occasions, the president used the *National Intelligencer* to present the administration's position on various issues and policies. Smith broke new ground in news reporting by establishing ongoing detailed reports of the actions of Congress. By 1802, Smith had gained confirmed access to both the House and the Senate, and his knowledge of shorthand enabled him to make detailed notes concerning the debates in Congress. Both Federalist and Republican newspapers reprinted the reports published in the *National Intelligencer*. By the time Smith retired in 1810, most press outlets in the country published the doings of the national legislature on a regular basis.[13] The *National Intelligencer*, under the editorship of Joseph Gales, Jr., and William W. Seaton, remained the official government newspaper until the 1820s and continued to provide excellent coverage of the national capital and the actions of the government throughout the first half of the nineteenth century.

Jefferson also sought newspaper support in his home state of Virginia. Although popular at home, Jefferson believed a Republican journal would be useful in facing whatever opposition appeared. In May 1804, the *Richmond Enquirer* appeared for the first time. Edited by Thomas Ritchie, the *Enquirer* remained a strong supporter of President Jefferson throughout his eight years in office. Probably more than any other Republican editor at the time, Ritchie clung to a strict interpretation of the Constitution, with its emphasis on states' rights and the threat of a strong national government. A poor businessman, Ritchie remained in debt for most of his life. However, the *Enquirer* continued to succeed, primarily because its editor opened its pages to a variety of viewpoints, while still supporting, first, Jefferson and the Republicans and, later, Andrew Jackson and the Democrats. A capable journalist, Ritchie used the pages of his paper to inform and encourage his readers, primarily the political and economic elite of Virginia. From the very beginning, he included signed editorials in his paper, a regular feature by 1810. Ritchie became the friend of presidents and congressmen.[14] In particular, he and Jefferson developed a friendship and respect for one another. Jefferson praised Ritchie's journalistic abilities, declaring him capable of "culling what is good from every paper as the bee from every flower." After Jefferson's retirement from public life, he continued to read Ritchie's paper, even after he ceased subscriptions to all others.[15]

Jefferson's failure to support adequately an editor, at least from that person's perspective, produced a major press trial for the president. James Callender, convicted under the Sedition Act, grew increasingly resentful in the early 1800s because of Jefferson's failure to help pay his Sedition Act fine and to appoint him as postmaster of Richmond. Jefferson's failure to do as Callender wished pushed the editor into the Federalist Party, where he proceeded to attempt to ruin the president's reputation by accusing him of all sorts of immorality during his political career. At first, Callender said Jefferson authored the pamphlets that had resulted in his conviction under the Sedition Act. When that failed to move Jefferson to give Callender a federal job, the editor accused the president of miscegenation, the most horrible of moral crimes in the eyes of most Americans. Callender charged Jefferson with having an affair over many years with one of his slaves, Sally Hemings, and of fathering her children. The president refused to answer these allegations, but the damage to his public and private reputation was done. Callender's attacks on Jefferson were so fierce that even many Federalists opposed his actions.[16] In Pennsylvania, the *Norristown Herald*'s editor declared that "the truth is, Callender has no political honesty; no personal merit; and we are sincerely sorry to see such characters on the federal side."[17]

Other editors besides Callender opposed President Jefferson. In Boston, Benjamin Russell continued to preach the Federalist Party cause in the *Columbian Centinel*. Not long after Jefferson took office, Russell accused government officials of being absent from their posts:

If one were to ask, *Where is the government of the United States?* It would be difficult to give a direct answer.—THE PRESIDENT, we believe, is at Monticello;—the Vice-President at Washington;—The Secretary of State somewhere in Virginia;—The Secretary of War, in the District of Maine;—The Secretary of the Treasury at the seat of Government!—The Attorney General at Worcester.—The residue, the Lord only knows where.[18]

Shortly after this charge by Russell, a new Federalist newspaper appeared to join the attack. In New York, Alexander Hamilton and other Federalists hired William Coleman to edit a new party journal. On November 16, 1801, he published the first issue of the *New York Evening Post*. This first issue made it clear that Coleman's editorial stance would be in support of the Federalist Party. Furthermore, the editor hoped to "diffuse among the people correct information on all interesting subjects, to inculcate just principles in religion, morals and politics; and to cultivate a taste for sound literature." A daily, the *Evening Post* soon developed a circulation of 1,100. With the support of Alexander Hamilton, even to the point of Hamilton dictating editorials for the paper, Coleman quickly became the primary national newspaper voice for the Federalist Party during Jefferson's presidency.[19]

Throughout Jefferson's eight years in office, the newspapers discussed and debated various issues with which his administration had to deal. One of the first to receive national coverage was the issue of New Orleans and Lousiana. Louisiana had been transferred from France to Spain following the end of the Seven Years' War in 1763. In the Treaty of San Lorenzo of 1795, Spain had given Americans free navigation of the Mississippi River and the right to deposit goods in New Orleans without paying customs duties. Following the rise of Napoleon to power in the late 1790s, France sought to regain control of Louisiana. In a treaty published in March 1802, Spain returned Louisiana to France. This action produced many fears in the United States, particularly among citizens of the western states. Their concerns reached a fever pitch in the fall of 1802 when they lost their right to send trade goods through New Orleans duty-free.

The editor of Philadelphia's *American Daily Advertiser* concluded that "the impracticability of obtaining timely redress by negotiation, of this unexampled outrage on our rights, would fully and completely justify us in resorting to that expedient which is the ultimatum of aggrieved and injured nations."[20] Many westerners clearly considered war as the only option. According to the *Palladium*,

"Kentucky has the advantage of invasion; and she no doubt will use it, if unsupported by the Union; she moves alone to the combat; she is situated on the waters rapidly descending to the point of attack; she will overwhelm Orleans and West Florida with promptitude and ease."[21] Jefferson, hopeful of avoiding war, sought to negotiate with France for the purchase of New Orleans. When Napoleon offered all of Louisiana, Jefferson quickly accepted, even though he feared that he did not have the constitutional right to make such an acquisition.

The announcement of the purchase of Louisiana produced much comment in the newspapers. The *Independent Chronicle* of Boston first broke the story on June 30, 1803, under the headline "LOUISIANA CEDED TO THE UNITED STATES!"[22] Many northern papers, mostly Federalist in political outlook, opposed the acquisition as dangerous. In the *Columbian Centinel*, "Fabricus" described the territory as "a great waste, a wilderness unpeopled with any beings except wolves and wandering Indians."[23] Later the Federalist editor of the *Centinel* attacked the purchase as a big waste of money because "FRANCE COULD NOT KEEP NEW-ORLEANS and must have been glad to cede it to the U.S. that it might not fall into the hands of the English."[24] Most Federalists feared, as did the editor of the *Norristown Herald*, that Louisiana, "if ever admitted into the union, will give such a preponderance to Virginia and the South, that the northern states can never afterwards maintain any considerable consequence in the general government."[25]

Most editors, however, expressed support for the action because of the potential growth it represented for the United States. According to the *National Intelligencer*, "by the cession of Louisiana, we shall preserve peace, and acquire a territory of great extent, fertility, and local importance."[26] Buying Louisiana would prevent a war with France. Furthermore, according to William Duane, "this vast acquisition will every day unfold new advantages to the United States" such as "the prosperity and stability of the union—its internal security—its exemption from suspicious or treacherous neighbors—as an object of great importance in regard to the political influence of nations—as a check upon intrigues with the savage tribes—and various other points of view."[27]

Most Americans agreed with Jefferson when he ignored his constitutional scruples in order to double the size of the nation. Many criticized the Federalists for opposing the opportunity to enlarge the size of the country. The *Independent Chronicle*, published in Boston, the stronghold of Federalism, rejoiced that the buying of Louisiana was an event "to the utter disappointment of the factious and turbulent throughout the Union."[28] For the Federalists, such as editor Benjamin Russell, however, acquiring new territory went against their vision for the future of the United States, since it would "drain our people away from the pursuit of a better husbandry, and from manufactures and commerce."[29] For people like Alexander Hamilton, the future of America lay in an urban and industrial environment, and large amounts of territory threatened the development and growth of such areas. Thomas Jefferson and his supporters, however, viewed territorial growth as essential for the continued existence of the nation. Cities, commerce, and industry, if allowed to grow too large, only served to undermine a republic and would destroy it in the end. The Republican Party, and Jefferson in particular, believed strongly that "cultivators of the earth are the most valuable citizens" and the national government had to do all in its power to ensure their dominance in the political arena.[30] The Louisiana Purchase represented the victory of Jefferson's yeoman farmer over Federalist-inspired commercialism and urbanism as the guiding image for the American republic, at least for the bulk of the nineteenth century.

Another issue that haunted President Jefferson and elicited comment in the press involved Aaron Burr. Burr's attempt to win the contested election of 1800 in the House of Representatives[31] had ruined any chance he had of following Jefferson in office. As stated by William Duane, "[T]he vice-president, it is now well known, has not the smallest hope of a re-election: he has therefore turned all his attention to the obtaining some other office; his friends are extremely desirous of persuading he was perfectly innocent of the accusation of negociating [*sic*] for the presidential chair, although they know the public mind has been made up on the question."[32] Burr turned his attention to his home state of New York, where he lost the governor's race in 1804 through the influence of fellow New Yorker Alexander Hamilton. Burr then killed Hamilton in a duel and fled to escape prosecution for murder.

Following the duel, Burr apparently plotted to separate the western states from the nation. On trips beyond the Appalachian Mountains in 1805 and 1806, he met with various co-conspirators, including General James Wilkinson, commander of the U.S. Army in the west and governor of Louisiana. Fears of Spanish attempts to acquire the western states had abounded since the 1780s, and they continued even after the Louisiana Purchase. Burr's travels produced numerous comments in the newspapers about the potential for dangerous activities: "The latter part of his political career, fraught, perhaps, with a degree of duplicity which can never be satisfactorily defended, has made him an object of attention wherever he has traveled. His talents for intrigue are considered as unrivalled in America, and his disposition doubted by few."[33]

Fears of Burr's intentions produced many different reactions among the citizens of the western states, and the newspapers reflected all of these. Reports of Burr gathering recruits and supplies for some kind of expedition into Spanish territory became common. In December 1806, the *Palladium* reported that "it has been for some time reported and believed at Louisville that Colonel Burr was building gunboats and ships of war at Marietta and Wheeling; at those places it is understood that he is making great naval equipments at Louisville and Limestone; and some have believed that vast military preparations were making at all those places."[34] Charges of conspiracy and treason abounded, as various groups accused one another of this plan or that plot. Although few people seemed to doubt Burr's treason, they often found it hard to believe it in others. The *Orleans Gazette* questioned charges against citizens of Pittsburgh: "The first characters in Pittsburg are implicated in the Burr conspiracy. . . . [W]e cannot believe any treason is contemplated. Men of tried worth and known patriotism would never tarnish their well-earned reputations and risk their all in an enterprise in which they have nothing to gain, and where their lives would be jeopardized."[35]

Growing suspicions about Burr's activities provided a ready issue for debate between Federalists and Republicans. Federalists throughout the country increasingly believed that westerners were "ripe for revolt, and that the Kentucky papers openly advocate the idea of a separation from the Union."[36] In Frankfort, Kentucky, Federalists founded a new newspaper, the *Western World*, to report on the situation. Edited by Joseph M. Street and John Wood, the *Western World* accused Burr of conspiring to form a new nation out of the western states. Republican editors had difficulty in responding to such charges. Burr's questionable reputation made it difficult to defend him, but most editors agreed with the *National Intelligencer*, which declared "that our Western brethren are as ardently attached to the Union as the inhabitants of any section of it. We have evidence that the most remote suggestion of a separation fills their minds with alarm, justly viewing it as the most dreadful evil which could befall them."[37]

Many called on President Jefferson to take some sort of action to calm people's fears. The *Aurora*'s William Duane urged some effort to counteract fear and alarm: "It might be of some importance by some means to settle the public feeling on the subject. The whole country will be with you if there is any actual emergency. If there is not, the Administration may derive great advantage from a seasonable counteraction of the alarm."[38] Jefferson did not truly believe that most westerners would engage in a treasonable conspiracy. Eventually, however, he believed that Burr's activities had to be stopped. Authorities arrested Burr near Mobile, Alabama, on February 19, 1807.

During Burr's trial for treason in Richmond, newspapers continued to discuss his fate. The *Aurora* commented that "the 'farce at Richmond,' as the manager promised, is proceeding in as 'droll' a stile as could possibly be conceived by the most dextrous of mountebanks—the only consolation of sedate men is that scandalous as it is, yet it is better than the 'bloody tragedy' in the western country which it has superceded."[39] The jury acquitted Burr, to the horror of many who believed him guilty. Most of the blame for this outcome fell on another opponent of the president, Chief Justice John Marshall, who insisted that two witnesses be able to testify to any overt act of treason.[40] Acquiring such testimony was not possible, so the jury had no alternative but to declare Burr not guilty. Several newspaper editors expressed great disgust at this outcome, and one New York paper even accused Marshall of "being a partner in Burr's treason."[41]

Jefferson's biggest problems as president, however, developed out of growing troubles with Great Britain. As Europe erupted in war again in the face of Napoleon's imperial ambitions, the United States was caught in the middle. Although Jefferson's government had disagreements with both Britain and France, the ability of the British Royal Navy to interfere with American trade produced the greatest outcry. Throughout the first decade of the nineteenth century, the British stopped and searched American merchant vessels and often drafted, or "impressed," seamen identified as being British citizens. Because of the similarity in language, British officers had difficulty in determining who were really British citizens, and they impressed many Americans as well.

Newspapers helped lead the cry for justice in the wake of British actions. As
early as 1805, William Duane commented that "it is in vain to expect any credit
will be given to our government for its forbearance any more than respect for our
neutral rights."[42] In 1806, an American citizen was killed off the coast of New
York, and the *American Daily Advertiser* cried, "How much longer is the 'Olive
Branch' to be stained with this injustice? That some speedy measures may be
taken to punish such unprecedented aggressions cannot but be the hearty wish of
every American—who loves his country, and who reveres the sacred laws of humanity, and of JUSTICE."[43]

In June 1807, the event that almost produced war occurred—the HMS *Leopard*
attacked the USS *Chesapeake* when its captain refused to allow a search for deserters from the Royal Navy. The Americans suffered twenty-one casualties, and
the British impressed four men, one of them a deserter, but the other three were
Americans who had previously served in the British Navy. Americans all over the
country howled in protest concerning "this affair of murder and assassination."[44]

The *Washington Federalist* declared that "we have never, on any occasion, witnessed the spirit of the people excited to so great a degree of indignation, or such
a thirst for revenge, as on hearing of the late unexampled outrage on the *Chesapeake*. All parties, ranks, and professions were unanimous in their detestation of
the dastardly deed, and all cried aloud for vengeance." The editor concluded that
all Americans would support the government in whatever action it took.[45] The
New York Evening Post was not quite so supportive because its editor placed part
of the blame on President Jefferson's administration for failure to help the British
government retrieve deserters from the Royal Navy. Still, such failure to act did
not justify "the resort to force on the part of the English. On this point, we are
ready to say that we consider the national sovereignty has been attacked, the national honor tarnished, and that ample reparations and satisfaction must be given
or that war ought to be resorted to by force of arms."[46] William Duane, summing
up the opinion of many of his fellow editors, expressed pleasure with the results
of the *Chesapeake* incident because it "opened the eyes of thousands, who were
kept in delusion and ignorance by the partisans of the British government."[47]
Duane believed that such an awareness of Britain by the American people was
long overdue because, in his opinion, "there was no species of wrong that could
have been imposed, that we did not experience long before the attack on the
Chesapeake."[48]

Jefferson, harking back to the Revolution and the use of trade boycotts to
protest British actions, sought a solution short of war and instituted a policy of
"peaceful coercion." He agreed with the editor of the *Independent Chronicle*, who
declared in 1805 that "our trade is the most powerful weapon we can use in our defence."[49] The centerpiece of Jefferson's plan was the Embargo Act, passed by
Congress on December 27, 1807. Cutting off all trade with Britain and France
until they respected the rights of neutral countries, the Embargo Act served only to

ruin the American economy.[50] Particularly upset were the people of New England, and many feared that the result would be mob activity. A writer in the *Boston Gazette* wrote that "the spirit of our citizens is rising and may burst into a flame. Everything should therefore be done to calm them till the Legislature has had time to mature its plans of redress. . . . The spirit of New England is slow in rising; but when once inflamed by oppression, it will never be repressed by anything short of complete *justice.*"[51] The Republican press tried to support the measure, but most newspapers eventually came to believe that the Embargo Act was a mistake. As one of his last actions as president, Jefferson signed the repeal of the Embargo Act. Following this action, the *Federal Republican* commented that, "after depriving government of its means of support for sixteen months, and preventing the people of the United States from pursuing a lawful and profitable commerce, and reducing the whole country to a state of wretchedness and poverty, our infatuated rulers . . . have been forced to acknowledge their fatal error, and so to retrace their steps."[52]

Jefferson fled Washington in March 1809, glad to be away from the headaches of government. He spent the rest of his life in retirement at his plantations at Monticello and Poplar Grove in western Virginia. Although he continued to believe in the importance of a free press for the proper functioning of a democracy, he never believed that American newspapers fulfilled this monumental task. Following his return to his home state, he continued to keep up with current political issues, but he did not do so by reading many newspapers. In 1812, he told John Adams, "I have given up newspapers in exchange for Tacitus and Thucydides, for Newton and Euclid, and I find myself much the happier."[53] Four years later, he expressed to James Monroe his current opinion of American newspapers: "I rarely think them worth reading, and almost never worth notice."[54] For Jefferson, the press no longer mattered very much. For the rest of the country, however, that was not true. The return of war in the years following Jefferson's presidency found the newspapers in the familiar role of primary source of information concerning the military conflict.

NOTES

1. Noble E. Cunningham, Jr., *The Jeffersonian Republicans in Power: Party Operations, 1801–1809* (Chapel Hill: University of North Carolina Press for the Institute of Early American History and Culture, Williamsburg, Va., 1963), 236–39.

2. Jefferson's letters are full of comments on a variety of issues, and they do not always coincide with each other. As a result, historians and journalists have long debated Jefferson's attitude toward a free press. Two lengthy works that take opposite views are by Frank Luther Mott and Leonard Levy. Mott's *Jefferson and the Press* (Baton Rouge: Louisiana State University Press, 1943) sees Jefferson as a libertarian philosopher who led the fight to develop a free press in the United States. Levy's *Jefferson and Civil Liberties: The Darker Side* (Cambridge: Belknap Press of Harvard University Press, 1963) is more critical and concludes that Jefferson often spoke in favor of a free press, but really supported press restrictions.

3. Jefferson to Edward Carrington, 16 January 1787, *The Papers of Thomas Jefferson*, ed. Julian P. Boyd et al., 25 vols. (Princeton, N.J.: Princeton University Press, 1950–), 11:49.

4. Jefferson to John Norvell, 11 June 1807, *The Writings of Thomas Jefferson*, ed. Andrew A. Lipscomb, 20 vols. (Washington, D.C.: Thomas Jefferson Memorial Association, 1903–1904), 11:224–25.

5. Quoted in Saul K. Padover, *Jefferson* (New York: Harcourt, Brace, 1942), 329–30.

6. Jefferson to Charles Yancey, 6 January 1816, *The Writings of Thomas Jefferson*, ed. Paul Leicester Ford, 12 vols. (New York: G. P. Putnam's Sons, 1904–05), 11:497.

7. Jefferson to James Madison, 31 July 1789, *The Papers of Thomas Jefferson*, ed. Boyd, 13:442–43.

8. Jefferson to Abigail Adams, 11 September 1804, *The Writings of Thomas Jefferson*, ed. Lipscomb, 11:51.

9. Jefferson to Thomas McKean, 19 February 1803, *The Writings of Thomas Jefferson*, ed. Ford, 9:451–52.

10. James E. Pollard, *The Presidents and the Press* (New York: Macmillan, 1947), 75–76.

11. Allen Cullen Clark, "William Duane," *Records of the Columbia Historical Society* 9 (1906): 14–62. One of the few book-length studies of Duane's career is Kim Tousley Phillips, *William Duane, Radical Journalist in the Age of Jefferson* (New York: Garland, 1989).

12. *The Writings of Thomas Jefferson*, ed. Ford, 12:318.

13. William E. Ames, *A History of the National Intelligencer* (Chapel Hill: University of North Carolina Press, 1972), 3–67; Cunningham, *Jeffersonian Republicans in Power*, 259–64; Mott, *Jefferson and the Press*, 47–48; Jerry W. Knudson, "Political Journalism in the Age of Jefferson," *Journalism History* 1 (1974): 21.

14. Pollard, *Presidents and the Press*, 80, 84; Mott, *Jefferson and the Press*, 50–51; Carl R. Osthaus, *Partisans of the Southern Press* (Lexington: University Press of Kentucky, 1994), 15, 25–26.

15. Quoted in John M. Butler, "Thomas Ritchie," in *Dictionary of Literary Biography*, vol. 43, ed. Perry Ashley (Detroit: Gale Research, 1986), 394.

16. Pollard, *Presidents and the Press*, 71–72. Callender failed to get the support he desired from either political party. Both groups spread his stories and accusations at one time or another, but neither trusted him. He drowned in the James River in July 1803.

17. *Norristown* (Pa.) *Herald*, 28 October 1802.

18. *Columbian Centinel* (Boston), 12 August 1801.

19. Allan Nevins, *The Evening Post: A Century of Journalism* (New York: Boni and Liveright, 1922), 9–62.

20. *American Daily Advertiser* (Philadelphia), 20 December 1802.

21. *Palladium* (Frankfort, Ky.), 18 September 1806.

22. *Independent Chronicle* (Boston), 30 June 1803.

23. *Columbian Centinel*, 13 July 1803.

24. Ibid., 10 August 1803.

25. *Norristown Herald*, 29 June 1804. See also *Connecticut Courant* (Hartford), 6 and 20 February 1805.

26. *National Intelligencer* (Washington, D.C.), 8 July 1803.

27. *Aurora* (Philadelphia), 19 July 1803.

28. *Independent Chronicle*, 30 June 1803.

29. *Columbian Centinel*, 13 July 1803.

30. James P. Ronda, "Jefferson and the Imperial West," *Journal of the West* 31 (July 1992): 17. Ronda concludes that Americans have created a myth concerning Jefferson and the West that misses the point. Jefferson hoped to create an "empire of liberty," but slowly lost faith in it as its future became unpredictable. For Jefferson, the West was to be a sort of blank slate where life could begin anew. When that did not prove true, he turned away in disappointment.

31. When the electoral college voted in December 1800, Jefferson and Burr tied, leaving the decision of who would be president to the House. Although Burr knew he was the vice-presidential candidate, he did not step forward and urge the House to vote for Jefferson. The Federalists controlled the House, and many planned to vote for Burr because they hated Jefferson so much. The result was a series of ballots in which neither man was elected. Finally, Alexander Hamilton, disliking Jefferson, but distrusting Burr, urged the Federalists to vote for Jefferson. Hamilton's support gave the contest to Jefferson, and he was finally elected in February 1801.

32. *Aurora*, 15 February 1804.

33. *Lexington Gazette*, reprinted in *Palladium*, 9 September 1805.

34. *Palladium*, 11 December 1806.

35. *Orleans Gazette* (New Orleans), 27 January 1807.

36. *Philadelphia Gazette*, reprinted in *Palladium*, 27 November 1806.

37. *National Intelligencer*, 7 November 1806.

38. Duane to Thomas Jefferson, 4 November 1806, quoted in Walter Flavins McCaleb, *The Aaron Burr Conspiracy* (New York: Wilson-Erickson, 1936), 164.

39. *Aurora*, 12 August 1807.

40. Although it is clear that Chief Justice Marshall relished being able to thwart President Jefferson and the Republican Party in their attempts to convict Burr, more than partisanship influenced his decision. Many legal scholars believe that Marshall's narrow interpretation of the constitutional definition of treason has ensured that treason charges have not been used against one's political enemies. Without this protection, criticism of the government could have been risky because of disagreements over how to determine what is and what is not a treasonous statement. Leon Friedman and Fred L. Israel, eds., *The Justices of the United States Supreme Court, 1789–1969*, vol. 1 (New York: Chelsea House, 1969), 300; Norman K. Risjord, *Forging the American Republic, 1760–1815* (Reading, Mass.: Addison-Wesley, 1973), 329–30.

41. *Balance and Columbian Repository* (Albany, N.Y.), 6 October 1807.

42. *Aurora*, 13 December 1805.

43. *American Daily Advertiser*, 29 April 1806.

44. *Balance and Columbian Repository*, 7 July 1807.

45. *Washington Federalist* (Washington, D.C.), 3 July 1807.

46. *New York Evening Post* (New York), 24 July 1807.

47. *Aurora*, 3 August 1807.

48. Ibid., 8 August 1807.

49. Reprinted in *National Intelligencer*, 11 December 1805.

50. One can gauge the impact of the Embargo Act through the regularly published marine lists in the newspapers. During the first half of 1808, the marine lists in the *Baltimore Weekly Price Current* shrank about 50 percent, indicating that the number of ships in and out of Baltimore's harbor had dropped to half of what it had been before the embargo.

51. *Boston Gazette*, 2 February 1809.

52. *Federal Republican* (Baltimore, Md.), March 1809, quoted in Allan Nevins, ed. *American Press Opinion: Washington to Coolidge* (Boston: D. C. Heath, 1928), 40.

53. Jefferson to John Adams, 21 January 1812, *The Writings of Thomas Jefferson*, ed. Ford, 11:220–21.

54. Jefferson to James Monroe, 4 February 1816, ibid., 11:514–15.

6

The War of 1812, 1809–1815

When Thomas Jefferson left Washington for Monticello in March 1809, James Madison succeeded him as president.[1] Madison, too, tried to solve the conflict over trade with the warring European powers. He also failed because the disagreements with Britain and France involved issues other than trade. War with Great Britain resulted from the inability of President Madison and his government to negotiate settlements to these issues. During the years of argument with Britain, American newspapers, continuing to grow in size and number, discussed a whole host of subjects related to the conflict, including the reasons for and against war, the people involved in the disagreements, and the need for Americans to support the government and the military in their endeavors.

Although newspapers continued to experience growth during the War of 1812, the rapid growth of the years since the end of the Revolution ceased. As had been true during the fight for independence in the 1770s, the war with Great Britain interfered with the press and discouraged its expansion. When James Madison entered office in 1809, 329 newspapers appeared throughout the country. When peace finally came in 1815, the number had grown by fewer than a hundred, to 413.[2]

The newspaper voice of the adminstration continued to be the *National Intelligencer*, now under the control of Joseph Gales, Jr., and William Winston Seaton. Gales, son of the editor of the *Raleigh Register*, Joseph Gales, Sr., had become Samuel Harrison Smith's partner in 1807, when Smith had indicated a desire to retire. Smith spent several years teaching Gales the business and then retired in 1810. Deciding that running the *Intelligencer* constituted too big a job for one man, Gales became partners with his brother-in-law Seaton in 1812. Shortly after the beginning of the partnership, the *Intelligencer* became a daily. Throughout the presidencies of James Madison and James Monroe, editors and politicians throughout the country recognized the *National Intelligencer* as the official adminstration outlet and looked to it for the opinions of the president and his cabinet.

Gales and Seaton continued Smith's practice of detailed coverage of the actions of Congress. Both knew shorthand, a practice that helped their efforts tremendously. Gales reported on the House of Representatives, while Seaton covered the Senate. From 1812 until 1829, they held the exclusive right to report the debates in Congress and published the only lengthy records of the actions of the national legislature.

During the War of 1812, Gales and Seaton continued to provide detailed reporting on the national government as much as possible. When the British threatened an invasion of the Chesapeake Bay area in 1813, both volunteered for service in the militia. They took turns on active duty so that one of them could continue to publish the newspaper. Although smaller in size and content, the *National Intelligencer* did not miss an issue.

The following year proved less successful, and the British attack materialized this time. In the face of the real threat, the entire staff of the *Intelligencer* turned out for military service. The paper suspended publication for a short time, but resumed in a much smaller size on August 31, 1814. While burning Washington, the British destroyed all the records and much of the equipment of the newspaper office. Because of this loss, the paper appeared irregularly for several weeks. Nearly a month passed before Gales and Seaton restored their paper to its regular appearance and publication schedule. The *National Intelligencer* once more appeared in its normal size and format on September 26.[3] From that point until the 1860s, the *Intelligencer* continued its coverage of politics in the nation's capital.

The *Intelligencer*'s position as the foremost political journal of the early nineteenth century faced a challenge in 1811 with the appearance of a new political publication, *Niles's Weekly Register*. Founded in Baltimore, Maryland, in September 1811 by Hezekiah Niles, the *Register* contained documents, speeches, letters, and government papers concerning all the major political issues of the early 1800s. Departments in the periodical besides politics included history, biography, geography, manufacturing, agriculture, and a "neat summary of the news."[4]

Seeking to produce something like a twentieth-century news magazine, Niles promised political neutrality. He wanted to provide an unbiased printed record of the actions of the national government. In his prospectus, he stated that the *Register* would be open to people of all political outlooks. According to Niles, the partisan newspapers "seldom dare to '*tell the truth, the whole truth, and nothing but the truth. . . .*' [T]he dignity of the press is prostrated to the will of aspiring individuals." He promised not to get involved in "the petty disputes between the *ins* and *outs*" because "politics shall be *American*—not passive and lukewarm, but active and vigilant."[5]

Niles capably fulfilled this pledge. During the more than twenty years in which he edited the *Register*, the journal never endorsed or opposed any political candidate. Niles actively sought to present a balanced view of the various political issues of the day. By carefully selecting what he published in the *Register*, he earned the respect of most of the politicians of his day and achieved his own personal goal of being known as "an honest chronicler."[6] The pages of the *Register* still provide the best single record of the events of the early nineteenth century.

Niles and other publishers warned of the possibility of armed conflict with Great Britain, even before Congress declared war in 1812. One feared such a development as "an unnecessary, destructive war,"[7] while another asked, "How long will you continue to submit to have your commerce regulated by a foreign power?"[8] The editor of the *Balance and State Journal* of New York, a Federalist paper, concluded that war was unavoidable because "from neither belligerent have we received that justice which we had a right to expect, and which it is our duty to demand. That we shall ever receive it from either, without a resort to arms, is hardly probable."[9]

There were many reasons for gloom, at least from the perspective of most Americans. Many people, particularly those who lived west of the Appalachian Mountains, believed that the British hoped to divide the United States (both politically and physically) by encouraging the Native Americans to stir up trouble on the frontier. Beginning in 1805, two Shawnee chiefs, Tecumseh and his brother, the Prophet, began attempting to organize all the tribes into a single confederation in order to deal better with the encroachments of white settlers. After 1807, British officials in Canada became increasingly interested in the efforts of Tecumseh. Their interest did not develop into much active support because they were unwilling to risk war with the United States over the Native American issue. However, most Americans living in the Ohio Valley became convinced that the British government encouraged Tecumseh in his efforts. When conflicts occurred on the frontier, most blamed the British. For example, in August 1811, the *Kentucky Gazette* accused the British of bribing the Native Americans to attack frontier settlements, declaring that "we have in our possession information which proves beyond doubt, the late disturbances to be owing to the too successful intrigues of British emissaries with the Indians."[10]

The climactic battle occurred at the village of Tippecanoe on November 7, 1811. The forces of the Prophet lost the battle, and the Americans burned the village (Tecumseh was absent at the time). Although fighting continued for months, Tecumseh's hopes of a Native American confederation had ended. During the War of 1812, Tecumseh and his supporters fought alongside the British, an event that only further reinforced the beliefs of many Americans that the frontier troubles had been caused by British intrigues.[11] From Kentucky, the *Lexington Reporter*, echoing the feelings of many, continually stated this "fact," declaring that "the war on the Wabash is purely BRITISH" and "the SCALPING KNIFE and TOMAHAWK of *British savages, is now, again devastating our frontiers.*"[12]

Following the Battle of Tippecanoe, William Duane accused the British of having a "bloody and assassinating policy."[13] Most Republican editors, in full agreement with these statements, believed that the options available to the United States seemed clear. The *Lexington Reporter*'s editor declared that, since "the blood of our fellow-citizens murdered on the Wabash by British intrigue calls aloud for vengeance," war provided the only answer.[14] *Niles's Weekly Register* summed up the beliefs of many Americans: "We have had but one opinion as to the cause of the depredations of the Indians; they are instigated and supported by the British in Canada."[15]

Canada seemed to be the source of many of the frontier's problems, so many people came to support a call for war in order to take Canada and remove it as a source of trouble. In discussing the raising of the militia in Kentucky, one editor declared that "this is all preparatory to the invasion of Canada, now more than ever necessary, as presenting whilst in the possession of Britain, a never failing source of Indian hostility. Until those civilized allies of our Savage neighbors, are expelled from our continent, we must expect the frequent recurrence of the late scenes on the Wabash."[16] The *Lexington Reporter* proposed that the acquisition of Canada would solve the Native American problem by placing "the American arm between the hands of the English and their savage allies. This done, the occupation of the Canadas, New Brunswick and Nova-Scotia, would give us perpetual concord with the Indians; who would be obliged *to depend upon us* for supplies of Blankets, knives, gun-powder, etc."[17] Thus, not only would the Native Americans be pacified, but also trade would grow as new markets became available in the newly acquired territories.

Everyone, however, did not support desires to acquire Canada. Most Federalists believed that such an attempt was foolhardy, dangerous, and a waste of money. An editorial in the *New York Evening Post* summed up such opposition: "[W]ill you spend thousands of millions in conquering a province, which, were it made a present to us, would not be worth accepting? Our territories are already too large." Furthermore, "what benefit will it ever be to the great body of the people, after their wealth is exhausted, and their best blood is shed in its reduction? . . . Canada, if annexed to the United States, will furnish offices to a set of hungry villains, grown quite too numerous for our present wide limits; and that is *all* the benefit we ever shall derive from it."[18] Federalists throughout the country opposed the approach of war, but for the most part, their complaints went unnoticed.

Even with the fear of the Native Americans and the desire to acquire Canada, most newspapers still emphasized British interference with American trade as the primary reason for going to war. As 1811 came to a close and the calls for war increased, the *Lexington Reporter* commented that "it appears that our government will at last make war, to produce a market for our Tobacco, Flour, and Cotton."[19] In Philadelphia, William Duane considered that Great Britain's use of impressment constituted the major issue: "The impressment of American seamen by foreign nations, to fight their battles, and to plunder their countrymen, is the most degrading of all the wrongs we suffer—our submission to it, the foulest stain on the national character."[20] Duane and many others increasingly believed that "the 'opprobrium' of America, like others of its sufferings, is approaching to a point at which it must find a corrective."[21] When one considered the long list of British wrongs committed against the United States, no other option seemed available:

The actual situation of the country arising out of the oppression of our commerce on the high seas—the piratical seizure and the unprecedented code of piracy established in the British admiralty courts—the manstealing outrages on our citizens—the letting loose of the savages with arms—new rifles, new scalping knives, new tomahawks, and all the apparatus of perfidious savage war; these facts, and the feelings of the nation under them, leave no doubt of certain war.[22]

Hezekiah Niles also believed that offenses on the high seas, particularly impressment, constituted the major complaint against the British. He strongly urged American leaders to settle for nothing less than retribution for these wrongs: "Accursed be the American government, and every individual of it, who by the omission or commission of any thing, shall agree to make peace with Great Britain, until ample provision shall be made for our impressed seamen, and security shall be given for the prevention of such abominable outrages in future."[23]

The decision of whether to go to war with Great Britain or not lay in the hands of the Twelfth Congress, which assembled in Washington, D.C., on November 4, 1811. Later, the *Independent Chronicle* expressed the awareness of most Americans as the new session began: "Never did the American Congress assemble under circumstances of greater interest and responsibility."[24] A group of new congressmen, who became known as the "War Hawks," quickly took leadership of the House of Representatives. Primarily from the South and the West and led by Henry Clay of Kentucky and John C. Calhoun of South Carolina, these young men believed that American pride and honor had suffered enough at the hands of European powers, and they insisted that the United States refuse to back down again. Too young to remember the Revolution, they believed that war provided the only solution to disagreements, particularly those with Great Britain.[25] They began preparing for an armed conflict almost immediately and encouraged President Madison to ask for a declaration of war. He agreed during the summer of 1812, and Congress declared war on Great Britain on June 18. Even with all the many grievances that Americans believed they had against Great Britain, most who supported the war also saw it as a second war for independence, another attempt to establish national honor and win the respect of Europe. Editors filled their newspapers with comparisons between the heroes of 1776 and the leaders of 1812. In July, the *National Intelligencer* explicitly compared the Continental Congress and the Twelfth U.S. Congress: "Under the auspices of the one this nation sprung into existence; under those of the other it will have been preserved from disgraceful recolonization."[26]

Nevertheless, some newspaper editors expressed concern over the approach of war, fearing that the United States could not win. As the vote in Congress took place, the editor of Philadelphia's *American Daily Advertiser* prayed that "it now remains with the Senate to decide the fate of their country—to snatch it from the dreadful calamity into which it is about to be plunged by the mad ambition of a few self-styled republicans. It is to be hoped there is in that body discernment enough to judge of the ill consequences attendant on a declaration of war at this time against Great Britain."[27] The editor of another Philadelphia paper, the *True American,* concluded that "as a prelude to their approaching fall, God in his mercy has deprived our rulers of their senses."[28] These editors reflected the opinion of many Americans, particularly in New England, that war with Britain was not a good idea.

Other editors criticized such comments. The *Balance and State Journal* declared that "on subjects of national interest, unity of sentiment ought to prevail."[29] Following the congressional declaration of war, one editor stated that "Congress have declared war against Great Britain. The step has been taken, and it is not now the time to debate, whether wisely or imprudently. It is sufficient for us to know, that the fact exists, and it calls upon every one to unite in support of the government, or deserve to be branded as a Traitor." Furthermore, "editors of all political complexions are loud in their appeals for a suspension of party animosities, and a general concurrence in supporting our government."[30] The leading Republican paper, the *National Intelligencer*, summed up the feelings of many: "This is not time for debating the propriety of war. WAR IS DECLARED, and every patriot heart must unite in its support."[31]

Once Congress actually declared war and Americans braced for armed conflict, the press tried to keep readers informed about battles and other related events. News reports about victories and defeats appeared on a regular basis. During most of the war, the news was not good because the American military lost more than it won. By and large, the Federalist press used losses to criticize the war, while the Republican newspapers sought to put as good a face as possible on the efforts of the U.S. military forces.

The American navy received great praise from all the newspapers throughout the war because it succeeded very well. During the fighting in 1812, the navy was the only branch of the military that won. Described by William Duane as "the gallant little fleet,"[32] American naval forces provided the only hope in the midst of losses in Canada and elsewhere on land. Rejoicing over the victories of the USS *Constitution* and other ships, another Philadelphia editor praised the "valor and skill"[33] of American sailors. Others laughed over the supposed "supremacy of the British navy,"[34] declaring that "man to man and gun to gun, even the veteran British tars can get no advantage over the Americans."[35] Others criticized the government for wasting money and effort on the militia, which could not win, while failing to truly reward "the heroes of the OCEAN," who continually won.[36]

When covering land engagements, many of which the United States lost, Republican newspaper editors sought to emphasize success and downplay defeat. They reported every victory, no matter how small. Blame for defeats, such as the loss of Detroit in 1812, fell on the generals in command.[37] In 1813, New York's *The War* described the lifting of the seige of Fort Meigs in Ohio as an indication that "OUR MILITARY PROSPECTS are daily brightening."[38]

Such news stories served as propaganda, and Republican editors continually used them to urge Americans to fight until the United States achieved victory. When news of the victory at New Orleans and the Treaty of Ghent reached the cities of the Atlantic Coast, newspaper editors rejoiced over the confirmation of their earlier predictions of military success and victory. Triumph at New Orleans made Andrew Jackson a national hero. Even the Federalist papers joined in the celebration of the victory. One editor declared that "the more we contemplate the glorious victory achieved by Gen. Jackson, the more we are wont to applaud and admire his heroic ardour, and the steady valor of his faithful soldiers."[39] Success at New Orleans convinced many Americans that the United States had won the war because American forces had won this battle. Many believed this, even though the battle actually occurred two weeks after the signing of the peace treaty in Europe. The Boston *Yankee* rejoiced: "We have unqueened the self-stiled Queen of the Ocean," and "we have beaten at every opportunity, 'Wellington's Veterans!' "[40]

News of the war's end and the signing of the Treaty of Ghent also elicited much comment in the newspapers. The *National Intelligencer* declared, "The Peace. Americans! Rejoice! Republicans, rejoice! Federalists, rejoice! Rejoice, all men, of whatever party ye be!"[41] Many Americans agreed with these comments, for public celebrations took place throughout the country. People stopped working and joined together to rejoice over the success of the soldiers and the diplomats. William Duane, in celebrating American success, declared that "from a state of humiliation in the eyes of the world, we stand on an elevation which now commands the respect of all the world."[42] In New York, the *National Advocate* asserted that "this second war of independence has been illustrated by more splendid achievements than the war of the revolution."[43] For many Americans, success in the War of 1812 only confirmed the rightness of the republican experiment that had begun in 1776, and no country, Great Britain or any other, could stand in the way of American triumph.

Even before the declaration of war, many newspapers stated that the United States could not lose in a contest with Great Britain. In calling for war, the *National Intelligencer* declared that "our wrongs have been great; our cause is just; and, if we are decided and firm, success is inevitable."[44] Shortly before Congress declared war, one editor issued a call to battle: "Let every arm be nerved for the glorious contest; every voice prepared to bid it welcome!—England we can punish."[45]

Many pro-war editors sought to increase public support for the war by increasing American hatred of England. The destruction of the capitol, the White House, and several other government buildings in Washington, D.C., in 1814 provided numerous occasions for criticisms of the British. The British justified the destruction because American forces had burned government buildings in York, Canada, in 1813. Most Americans, however, did not agree with this view, primarily because they perceived the British damage to be worse than that done earlier by American forces. Newspaper editors attacked the British for the severity of their actions. They described Admiral Sir George Cockburn, commander of the invading forces, as a "Great Bandit"[46] and "quite a mountebank, exhibiting in the streets a gross levity of manner, displaying sundry articles of trifling value of which he had robbed the president's house."[47] One report of the death of British General Robert Ross at Baltimore urged the building of a monument dedicated to "THE LEADER

OF A HOST OF BARBARIANS, who destroyed the capitol . . . and devoted . . .
Baltimore, to rape, robbery and conflagration."[48]

Hezekiah Niles, in particular, hated the British. In 1813, he described England as

the common robber, the man-stealer, the scalper of women and children and prisoners, the
incendiary and the ravisher . . . the enemy of our fathers, and our present unprincipled foe
. . . the cause of every war that has afflicted the civilized world for fifty years past, the common pest of society and plague of the earth . . . the cold-calculating assassin of thirty millions of people in *India,* the ferocious murderer in Ireland, the minister of famine and
pestillence [*sic*] in America . . . the most profligate and corrupt government in the universe
. . . a government so polluted, so gangrened with every abomination, that it must perish of
its own action, sooner or later. . . . [A] nation red to her arm-pits in the blood of innocents.[49]

Niles also believed that during a military conflict was not the time for partisan
wrangling and disagreement. Generally separated from political allegiances even
before the war, Niles urged his fellow editors to avoid political entanglements because it was impossible to take sides when the nation was in danger: "But—in regard to the war against *Great Britain*—though we would not knowingly insinuate
a falsehood, or distort a fact, we cannot, dare not, will not, stand with our arms
folded, *neutral* and *insensible.*"[50]

Editors did not heed such calls for unity in the press, and disagreements about
the wisdom of the war continued throughout the conflict. Some perceived the war
as unavoidable because, as William Duane said, "[N]ational honor and character
has obliged the government" to forcefully oppose "a nation which has so shame-
fully trampled on our rights."[51] But Federalists who disliked the conflict saw it
"originating in folly and infatuation (or something worse)."[52] The editor of the
Amercan Daily Advertiser concluded that "THE WAR in which we are engaged is
the most hopeless of any ever undertaken by any nation.—It is the fortune of our
administration to involve us in a war, in which our success and our defeat would
be equally ruinous. If we are defeated, we are overwhelmed with disgrace, if we
are victorious, we are victorious over that power which stands between us and the
despotism of Imperial France."[53]

Federalists expressed their opposition to the war in a variety of ways. Most believed that the war was totally unjustified, no matter what the reason given. Benjamin Russell criticized the war as a "waste of blood, property, and money"
designed to "afford encouragement to . . . runaway sailors, to enter on board
American vessels, and then to be PROTECTED, while they are underworking the
native born American Seamen and Navigators, and thereby taking the bread from
the mouths of their wives and children!"[54]

Such comments reflected the nativism that members of the Federalist Party increasingly expressed. In discussing Albert Gallatin's appointment as one of the
peace commissioners, Thomas C. Cushing, editor of the *Salem Gazette,* declared
that "native born citizens are excluded from office and honor, and this War is a
Foreign War on account of Foreigners only."[55] Throughout the war, Federalist ed-

itors argued that it was being fought over meaningless issues and that it was a waste of money.

When news of the Treaty of Ghent reached the United States in early 1815, many of them felt vindicated, since the peace agreement did not deal directly with any of the issues referred to in the declaration of war in 1812: "Let it not be supposed that federalists are dissatisfied with the treaty of peace, because they remind the people who elected the 'war makers', that not one of the professed objects for which the war was declared has been accomplished. Peace has been made on full as good terms as the Federalists often predicted it would be."[56]

Several leading Federalist newspapers came out openly against the war with Britain. Included in this group were the *Federal Republican* in Baltimore, the *United States' Gazette* in Philadelphia, the *Alexandria Gazette*, and the *New York Evening Post*. As these papers became more vocal in their opposition to the war, the issue arose of how much press criticism could be allowed during times of crisis. Madison, as author of the First Amendment and a supporter of a free press, could not sanction government action against such critics, even when they seemed to undermine the success of the government's war effort. Many people, however, did not agree with the president, and in some parts of the country, opposition became increasingly dangerous. Mobs drove both the *American Patriot* (Savannah, Georgia) and the *Norristown Herald* (Pennsylvania) out of business in 1812. Crowds threatened other Federalist editors with bodily harm if they did not end their opposition.[57]

The worst example of mob violence against a Federalist editor occurred in Baltimore in June 1812 when a mob destroyed the office and equipment of the *Federal Republican*. Editor Alexander Hanson had criticized the growing conflict with Great Britain for several years, and his comments did not cease once hostilities commenced. Two days after the official declaration of war, Hanson attacked the conflict as "unnecessary, inexpedient, and entered into from a partial, personal, and as we believe, motives bearing upon their front marks of undisguised foreign influence."[58] Two days following the appearance of this editorial, a riot broke out, and thirty to forty men destroyed the newspaper's office while a crowd of 400 watched and cheered. Following this incident, rioting occurred throughout Baltimore during June and July, as crowds attacked British sympathizers and anyone suspected of secretly trading with the British. Hanson attempted to revive his paper in Baltimore on two occasions, but mob violence prevented the paper's reappearance each time. The editor of the *American Watchman and Delaware Republican* praised the action, declaring that the editors of the *Federal Republican* deserved to be driven out of town because "they have labored assiduously in abusing, vilifying and calumniating the men whom the people have delighted to honor—can it then be a matter of astonishment, that the forbearance of the people should be exhausted, and that they should break to atoms the Trumpet of Sedition?"[59]

In some areas at least, opposition to the war was unacceptable. Although national leaders discussed the question, government authorities never took any form

of action against the dissident press during the War of 1812. As a result, the issue
of how much press criticism could be allowed in wartime did not receive serious
debate until the Civil War.[60]

The strongest opposition to the war found expression in New England, where
many people believed the impact on the commercial economy was too great. By
the time of the War of 1812, the Federalists had most of their support centered in
New England, and their traditional support for Britain over France made the conflict distasteful to them. Feeling that the war was a big mistake, the Federalists in
New England finally decided to meet and formally protest the war in progress. The
result was the Hartford Convention, which met in late 1814 and received considerable press coverage, particularly north of Washington, D.C. The *Boston Gazette*
declared that "the hope of millions rest on their decisions,"[61] while a Philadelphia
editor declared that "the people are anxiously waiting, and are fully prepared for
an effort to save themselves, to save the country from impending ruin."[62] Benjamin
Russell, one of the boldest of the Federalist editors, even urged New Englanders to
consider the possibility of a division in the United States: "Suffer yourselves not
to be entangled by the *cobwebs* of a compact which has long since ceased to
exist."[63] For many Federalists in New England, the War of 1812 indicated that they
no longer influenced the national government in any effective manner. Those who
supported the Hartford Convention hoped that they could propose changes in the
national structure that would prevent a catastrophe like the war with Britain from
ever happening again. News of the signing of the peace treaty on December 24,
1814, and the American victory at New Orleans on January 8, 1815, dashed these
hopes to pieces.

Most Republican editors accused the Federalists of plotting against the government. William Duane, responding to the Hartford Convention with sarcasm, stated
that "the mountain has terminated its labor, and (as we predicted) the mouse has
come forth, in the shape of a report."[64] Following the announcement of peace, he
concluded that "the nations of Europe see in the result of this war of only three
years, that the resistance of a popular government . . . has been able to repel and
defeat and triumph over the nation which has been successively marshalling them
against each other for more than 20 years past.—From a state of humiliation in the
eyes of the world, we stand on an elevation which now commands the respect of
all the world."[65]

The newspaper debates over the war with Great Britain reflect that throughout
the early 1800s the party press of the 1790s could still be found operating in many
parts of the United States. For editors such as William Duane, the political role of
the newspaper was most important and dictated almost every action taken by an
editor. Partisan newspaper operators continued to attack the political opposition as
dangerous to the country's welfare. In 1803, the *Aurora* castigated the Federalist
papers in Pennsylvania for attempting "to sow division among the democratic
party, and thereby to destroy it."[66] The Federalist editor of the *Norristown Herald*
described his party members as "the only true friends of the constitution and the
union"[67] and urged his readers to vote "in order to secure the triumph of sound

principles over the disorganizing scheme of foreign renegadoes and deluded natives."[68] Such participation would produce benefits, according to one New York
editor, because "the spirits of Washington and Hamilton will smile upon you, if, at
this time, you make an united effort to save a republic which they defended and
loved."[69] Even during the War of 1812, both sides claimed preeminence by declaring that forces under the leadership of members of their party gained all the important American victories.[70]

However, the press also expressed a growing awareness that the power and influence of the Federalists was declining. As early as 1808, the editor of Albany's
Balance, in discussing the upcoming presidential election, declared that "in the
choice, 'the still small voice' of federalism will not be heard. We cannot view the
contest with indifference; and though we can have no influence in the affair, yet
we shall, when the candidates are known, speak our sentiments with candor and
freedom."[71] Following the end of the War of 1812 and the Federalist debacle of the
Hartford Convention, many Republicans rejoiced with the editor of the *American
Watchman and Delaware Republican* that "the enemies of the country shrunk into
their native insignificance before the appalling ranks of republican freemen. They
have sunk, never more to rise."[72] The Republicans believed that partisanship had
ended and that with the Federalists out of the way the country could now enter into
an "Era of Good Feelings,"[73] when all would be in general agreement. For a while,
during the early years of the presidency of James Monroe, this goal seemed to
reach fruition, but a new era of partisanship soon came into existence.

NOTES

1. James Madison's primary biographer in recent years has been Irving Brant [*James
Madison*, 6 vols. (Indianapolis: Bobbs-Merrill, 1941–1961)]. He also produced a one-vol-
ume condensed version, *The Fourth President: The Life of James Madison* (Indianapolis:
Bobbs-Merrill, 1970). Another useful one-volume work is Robert A. Rutland's *James
Madison: The Founding Father* (New York: Macmillan, 1987).

2. Numbers for 1810 are from Alfred McClung Lee, *The Daily Newspaper in America*
(New York: Macmillan, 1937), 711; numbers for 1815 are based on Clarence S. Brigham,
History and Bibliography of American Newspapers, 1690–1820, 2 vols. (Worcester, Mass.:
American Antiquarian Society, 1947).

3. William E. Ames, *A History of the National Intelligencer* (Chapel Hill: University
of North Carolina Press, 1972), 68–103.

4. Norval Neil Luxon, *Niles's Weekly Register: News Magazine of the Nineteenth Century* (Baton Rouge: Louisiana State University Press, 1947), 2, 37.

5. Quoted in ibid., 125.

6. Quotation from *Henry VIII* 4.2.69–72 by William Shakespeare—part of the masthead of the *Register* during its first year of publication. See *Niles's Weekly Register* (Baltimore, Md.), 7 September 1811.

7. *True American* (Philadelphia), 11 January 1809.

8. *Aurora* (Philadelphia), 22 July 1809.

9. *Balance and State Journal* (Albany, N.Y.), 12 November 1811.

10. *Kentucky Gazette* (Lexington), 27 August 1811.

11. Growing interest in Native American heritage has resulted in several studies of famous Indian leaders, including Tecumseh and the Prophet. R. David Edmunds has produced valuable biographies of both of these men: *Tecumseh and the Quest for Indian Leadership* (Boston: Little, Brown, 1984) and *The Shawnee Prophet* (Lincoln: University of Nebraska Press, 1983).

12. *Lexington* (Ky.) *Reporter*, 23 November, 10 December 1811.

13. *Aurora*, 29 November 1811.

14. *Lexington Reporter*, 14 March 1812.

15. *Niles's Weekly Register*, 7 March 1812.

16. *Kentucky Gazette*, quoted in Julius Pratt, "The Bargain Between South and West," in Bradford Perkins, ed., *The Causes of the War of 1812* (New York: Holt, Rinehart & Winston, 1961), 62.

17. *Lexington Reporter*, 21 January 1812.

18. *New York Evening Post* (New York), 21 April 1812.

19. *Lexington Reporter*, 10 December 1811.

20. *Aurora*, 16 November 1811.

21. Ibid.

22. Ibid., 31 December 1811.

23. *Niles's Weekly Register*, 18 April 1812.

24. *Independent Chronicle* (Boston), 30 September 1812.

25. For more detailed discussions of the War Hawks and their ideas concerning the conflict with Great Britain, see Reginald Horsman, *The Causes of the War of 1812* (Philadelphia: University of Pennsylvania Press, 1962), Chap. 13, and Donald R. Hickey, *The War of 1812: A Forgotten Conflict* (Urbana: University of Illinois Press, 1989), Chap. 2.

26. *National Intelligencer* (Washington, D.C.), 8 July 1812.

27. *American Daily Advertiser* (Philadelphia), 11 June 1812.

28. *True American*, 19 June 1812.

29. *Balance and State Journal*, 7 May 1811.

30. *War* (New York), 11 July 1812.

31. *National Intelligencer*, 27 June 1812.

32. *Aurora*, 1 July 1812.

33. *Relf's Philadelphia Gazette and Daily Advertiser*, 29 February 1813.

34. *American Watchman and Delaware Republican* (Wilmington), 19 June 1813.

35. *New York Evening Post*, 2 September 1812.

36. *True American*, 20 February 1813.

37. *National Intelligencer*, 3 September 1812. For another example, see *War*, 16 February 1813.

38. *War*, 25 May 1813.

39. *Federal Republican* (Georgetown, Va.), 7 February 1815.

40. *Yankee* (Boston), 3 March 1815.

41. *National Intelligencer*, 16 February 1815.

42. *Aurora*, 20 February 1815.

43. *National Advocate* (New York), 20 February 1815.

44. *National Intelligencer*, 14 April 1812.

45. *Lexington Reporter*, 6 June 1812.

46. *Niles's Weekly Register*, 27 October 1814.

47. *National Intelligencer*, 30 August 1814.

48. *Niles's Weekly Register*, 27 October 1814.

49. *Niles's Weekly Register*, 30 October 1813, quoted in Norval Neil Luxon, *Niles's Weekly Register: News Magazine of the Nineteenth Century*, 166.

50. *Niles's Weekly Register*, 6 March 1813.

51. *Aurora*, 17 August 1813.

52. *Relf's Philadelphia Gazette and Daily Advertiser*, 29 November 1813.

53. *American Daily Advertiser*, 10 February 1813.

54. *Columbian Centinel* (Boston), quoted in Joseph T. Buckingham, *Specimens of Newspaper Literature*, 2 vols. (Boston: Charles C. Little and James Brown, 1850), 2:93.

55. *Salem* (Mass.) *Gazette*, 10 April 1813.

56. *Federal Gazette, Engine of Liberty* (Baltimore, Md.), 2 March 1815. Even before seeing the treaty, William Coleman, editor of the *New York Evening Post*, predicted that, "when the terms are disclosed, it will be found that the government have not by this negotiation obtained one single avowed object for which they involved the country in this bloody and expensive war." 13 February 1815.

57. For a discussion of attempts to limit the press during the War of 1812, see Donna Lee Dickerson, *The Course of Tolerance: Freedom of the Press in Nineteenth-Century America* (Westport, Conn.: Greenwood Press, 1990), 39–54.

58. *Federal Republican* (Baltimore, Md.), 20 June 1812.

59. *American Watchman and Delaware Republican*, 26 June 1812. For a discussion of the Baltimore riots and the attempted suppression of the *Federal Republican*, see Hickey, *The War of 1812*, Chap. 3. Hickey concludes that, rather than stifling dissent, mob violence increased the circulation of the *Federal Republican*, making it one of the most widely read newspapers in the country.

60. For a discussion of the issue of press criticism during the War of 1812, see John Tebbell and Sarah Miles Watts, *The Press and the Presidency: From George Washington to Ronald Reagan* (New York: Oxford University Press, 1985), 48–53.

61. *Boston Gazette*, 15 December 1814.

62. *Relf's Philadelphia Gazette and Daily Advertiser*, 19 December 1814.

63. *Columbian Centinel*, 21 December 1814.

64. *Aurora*, 10 January 1815.

65. Ibid., 10 February 1815.

66. Ibid., 13 April 1803.

67. *Norristown* (Pa.) *Herald*, 29 June 1804.

68. Ibid., 25 September 1807.

69. *Balance and Columbian Repository* (Albany, N.Y.), 19 April 1808.

70. See, for example, *Oracle of Dauphin* (Harrisburg, Pa.), 2 October 1813, and *Democratic Press* (Philadelphia), 28 March 1815.

71. *Balance and Columbian Repository*, 5 January 1808.

72. *American Watchman and Delaware Republican*, 21 October 1815.

73. Ironically, Benjamin Russell, a Federalist editor, coined this phrase.

7

The Era of Good
Feelings, 1815–1824

The inauguration of James Monroe on March 4, 1817, appeared to herald the beginning of a new era, one without the rabid partisanship that had dominated the political scene since the mid-1790s. For all intents and purposes, Monroe ran for president basically unopposed in 1816.[1] Although the Federalists nominated Rufus King, he did not have enough national recognition to launch a successful campaign. When the electoral college voted, Monroe won by the sizeable margin of 183 to 34. The circumstances of the inaugural ceremony itself, however, indicated that all was not as peaceful and happy as many people hoped. Still in the midst of reconstruction following the destruction of the War of 1812, the House and the Senate could not reach an agreement on holding the inauguration as usual in the House chambers. At the last minute, they agreed on an outdoor ceremony. The inauguration went well, but many blamed the conflict over the site on Henry Clay, Speaker of the House. Clay, apparently resentful over not being appointed secretary of state by the new president, seemed to confirm these rumors when he failed to attend the inaugural ceremony.[2] Such animosities and arguments did not bode well for the future.

For a while, at least, all went well, and many believed that the nation had truly entered into "an era of good feelings." With the Federalist Party basically no longer in existence, people asserted that partisanship would now disappear and that the country could concentrate on the more important issues of growth and development. The newspapers expressed these hopes and beliefs as they continued to inform their readers about the various news and events of Washington and elsewhere. The War of 1812 had slowed the spread of the press somewhat, but peace allowed it once more to grow throughout the country. In 1815, the first year after the end of the war, 413 newspapers appeared in the United States. By 1820, the year of Monroe's reelection, the number had grown to 512. And in 1828, when

Andrew Jackson became the first president from beyond the Appalachian Mountains, 863 newspapers were published throughout the nation. The majority of these productions appeared weekly, but the number of more frequent publications, particularly dailies, continued to increase.[3]

Although the number of newspapers increased, no new major publications appeared. The major press voices of this supposed nonpartisan period continued to be the same as during Madison's presidency and the War of 1812. Benjamin Russell, editor of Boston's *Columbian Centinel*, coined the term "era of good feelings," which has come to represent the years of Monroe's presidency.[4] Russell, a Federalist, continued to preach the cause of his party even though it had almost ceased to exist. Other Federalist newspapers continued to publish, but few had a national audience. In Baltimore, Hezekiah Niles continued the *Weekly Register*, seeking to provide a true record of the happenings of the national government. On the Republican side, William Duane still edited the *Aurora* in Philadelphia, but national leaders increasingly overlooked him as his influence with them waned. In Richmond, the *Enquirer* still supported the Republican cause, but its editor, Thomas Ritchie, became increasingly disillusioned as Monroe apparently led the party toward a more nationalistic perspective. Ritchie's growing concern over the protective tariff and slavery provided an early indication of the growing disagreements that would lead to a new party alignment, which would ultimately be more sectional than ideological in division.

The *National Intelligencer* under the editorship of Joseph Gales and William Seaton continued as the semi-official paper of the administration. The two editors did not get along with Monroe as well as they had with James Madison, but they still had access to members of the administration for information. Although never writing anything for publication himself, Monroe did occasionally ask cabinet members to write editorials on important controversial issues. In 1819, for example, Attorney General William Wirt wrote to defend the government's action in not condemning Andrew Jackson for his seizure of Spanish territory in Florida.[5]

James Monroe liked the term "era of good feelings" and hoped to fulfill that dream while in office. He believed that party strife was dangerous for the nation's health and sought to eliminate it as much as possible. In his first message to Congress in 1817, he declared that "local jealousies are rapidly yielding to more generous, enlarged, and enlightened views of national policy."[6] One editor stated that Monroe's tenure promised to be a successful one: "It is really believed that no president has commenced his career under more favourable circumstances. Mr. Monroe has lived through the terms of all his predecessors in office, and has the advantage of their experiments."[7] Hopes were high for the end of partisanship as Monroe took office.

In order to encourage such an attitude among all Americans, he decided to go on a presidential tour to the northern states, particularly New England, the heart of Federalism. Officially, Monroe went to inspect coastal and frontier fortifications, but he also clearly sought to heal old wounds and eliminate any remaining party strife by reaching out as much as possible to the political opposition. Throughout the country, newspapers covered the president's trip, discussing in detail his itinerary and how warmly people welcomed him everywhere he went. According to the *National Intelligencer*, "the unanimity of sentiment" indicated that "[n]ever before, perhaps, since the institution of civil government, did the same harmony, the same absence of party spirit, the same national feeling, pervade a community."[8] For many, party strife had completely disappeared.

Partisanship faded primarily because the Federalist Party faded. Its opposition to the War of 1812 weakened its national influence, but the change in outlook on the part of many Republicans constituted the primary factor in its decline. The war with Great Britain had been difficult to conduct under the loose style of government established by Jefferson and continued by Madison. Many Republicans came out of the War of 1812 convinced that the national government had to be strengthened. As a result, even before Madison left office, the party in power in Washington began to call for a national bank, a protective tariff, and support for manufacturing and internal improvements. To many Federalists, these ideas sounded familiar, and the Federalist press did not hesitate to point this out. As early as late 1815, the *Boston Palladium* declared that the Republicans "are now, good souls, heartily in love with a national bank. A lover never sighed half so much for his absent fair-one, as they have within the year for the establishment for a national bank."[9] Three years later, the *Norristown Herald* praised President Monroe for his support of nationalistic policies and assumed that the Federalists would offer little opposition to his reelection bid.[10] The *Federal Republican* agreed, declaring that "the nearer the Democratic administration and party come up to the old federal principles and measures, the better they act and the more we prosper—that is the reason that every body is contented with President Monroe's administration, which is in system and effect strictly federal."[11]

The Federalists had expressed particular interest and concern about the need for a protective tariff. Lack of goods during the War of 1812 had convinced many that American manufacturing needed encouragement in order to grow in the face of European imports. *Niles's Weekly Register* reported speeches in Parliament following the war that indicated the British willingness to dump goods at a loss in the United States in order to regain control of the American market. For example, one English lord stated that it would be "well worthwhile to incur a loss upon the first exportation, in order, by the glut, to stifle in the cradle those rising manufacturers in the United States, which the war had forced into existence, *contrary to the natural course of things.*"[12]

Congress first passed a protective tariff in 1816, and its existence formed a major political issue until the Civil War and beyond. Many newspaper editors supported a stronger tariff throughout Monroe's presidency, convinced that the only sure way to encourage the growth of the American economy lay in ensuring that a home market existed for American products.[13] During Monroe's northern tour, the *True American* criticized him for not properly supporting American business: "It is to be regretted that President MONROE, did not make his appearance in a suit of 'American Manufactures.' We would respectfully recommend to him the propriety of setting the example, and thereby show to the citizens of the United States, the reality of his professions."[14] One pro-business editor even launched campaigns to encourage their readers to "Buy American": "Let our ladies and gentlemen inquire for AMERICAN GOODS only, when they enter a retail shop, and the retailers will soon have good assortments of them, and will reap a better profit than they now make on the imported trumpery which they buy in Boston."[15]

The tariff did not constitute a major issue during Monroe's tenure—that would come later. Other issues, however, produced arguments and divisions within the Republican Party in particular and the American public in general. One of the most volatile disputes arose over the issue of slavery expansion. Missouri's application for statehood in 1818 sparked a major debate over the status of slavery in the United States, and the press provided a major mechanism for communicating the various arguments.

The question of whether slavery should be legal in the United States had been discussed by some people since before the Revolutionary War, but it received little attention from most people. After 1800, however, several newspaper editors came out in opposition to the institution, saying that Americans were not living up to their ideals by allowing the continued existence of African bondage.[16] For example, in 1810, the *Rural Visiter* of Burlington, New Jersey, in reporting the smuggling of Africans by American ships, decried that "WE, who prate so much about 'liberty' and the 'rights of man,' should be so regardless of those rights."[17] By 1818, one Philadelphia editor called for the adoption of some plan for gradual emancipation in order to bring slavery to an end.[18]

The growth of such attitudes among many Northerners helped set the stage for the conflict over Missouri in 1818–1820.[19] When Missouri applied for statehood in 1818 with a constitution legalizing slavery, many opposed it because they hoped to prevent the expansion of the South's "peculiar institution." In Philadelphia, the center of Quaker opposition to slavery, public meetings took place to petition Congress to prevent the admission of any new states that allowed African bondage.[20] In reporting these and other efforts against the addition of new slave states, the editor of the *American Daily Advertiser* expressed great concern over the whole issue because slavery "is a practice repugnant to the spirit of liberty which effected our revolution, and was the basis of our national fabric." He declared that Congress should not settle the issue. Rather, "it ought to be settled 'by the constitution itself,' and an amendment now made, agreeable to the common sense and feeling and principle of the country, that no new State should be formed or admitted without an express prohibition of slavery. At the present period, we trust, there would be no difficulty in affecting such an amendment."[21]

The concern expressed in the *American Daily Advertiser* reflected the attitudes of many people. The balance of power between the North and the South in the national government and the domination of the presidency by the South, specifically Virginia, since the founding of the nation formed a key factor in many of the debates. Increasingly, many Northerners believed that the South had too much influence, given its total population, and they hoped to reduce that influence by restricting the expansion of slavery. In New York, Representative James Tallmadge, author of the original amendment to restrict slavery in Missouri, received praise because he "dared to oppose that aristocratical southern influence, which, like the inundation of Gothic and Vandal power, threatens to overrun the Union."[22] Some editors, desiring the restriction of slavery, called on Congress to reject the proposed Missouri constitution because its toleration of slavery made it antirepublican.[23] The *New York Daily Advertiser* opposed any extension of slavery, declaring that "this question involves not only the future character of our nation, but the future weight and influence of the Free States. If now lost—it is lost forever."[24]

Many Southerners had similar thoughts, believing that they were slowly losing their influence in the government as the population of the North increased. One editor called for a strong southern stand in the Missouri controversy, declaring that "the slave-holding states will not brook an invasion of their rights. They will not be driven by compulsion to the emancipation, even gradually, of their slaves."[25] The *Lexington Gazette* concluded that whatever happened in Missouri "must affect the interests, power, political weight and destinies of the southern and western states; and either make us, as we have too long been, dependents on Atlantic or Yankee notions and views—or the Independent members of Independent governments. In this subject the die is cast—and we must win or lose by the event."[26]

Many people in both sections, however, called for some sort of compromise as necessary for the preservation of the nation. Congressman Bernard Smith of New Jersey called for some sort of agreement as "necessary to prevent a dissolution of the Union."[27] Congressman Joshua Cushman of Maine, the state eventually admitted in conjunction with Missouri, stated that "the safety of our republic" depends on "the balance of power."[28] The editor of the *American Watchman* feared the rise of sectionalism because of the conflict over Missouri: "Those are seeds of dissention, which, if continued to be sown, will, like the fabled dragon's teeth, produce, in North and South, Men of Blood! I wash my hands of the consequences. I wish not to be for the North or the South alone. I wish to be for my country."[29]

Members of Congress struggled with the decision concerning the admission of Missouri for well over a year. Finally, in early 1820, Congress reached a compromise whereby Missouri and Maine both entered simultaneously, while slavery was prohibited north of 36°30', the southern boundary of Missouri, except in the new state of Missouri itself. Many believed that this compromise had settled the issue of slavery in the territories forever. Nearly thirty years passed before people discovered otherwise.

Press reaction to the settlement was mixed. Many editors rejoiced to see the issue settled, believing that too much time had been spent on it. In Cincinnati, the *Inquisitor Advertiser* described the Missouri controversy as "the black question with which they have been so long agitated, and with which the country had become much disgusted."[30] During the debates, the *New York Columbian* bemoaned that "the important business of the session should be suspended to give place to this unprofitable and angry discussion."[31] And the *Clarksville Gazette* in Tennessee lamented that "Congress has already taken up so much time, on this, as we conceived, unimportant subject, that we fear objects of great interest to the community will be laid over—or at least that that attention will not be paid to them which they merit."[32]

Most editors cautiously supported the compromise, hoping that it represented a final settlement of this volatile issue. A few had stronger opinions, either strongly for the settlement or strongly opposed to it. The *Village Record*, a Federalist paper in Pennsylvania, praised the effort as a victory for the North in the face of the "Virginia dynasty": "For once the South has been completely out generaled; and forced to do right, in spite of all their pride and prejudices, and all their preconceived opinions and resolutions."[33] The *Providence Gazette*, however, complained that duly elected representatives had not kept their promises to their constituents: "The astonishing course which it took in the House of Representatives, after a long and lucid debate, has, we believe, never been accounted for by the deserters, to the satisfaction of those who continued steadfast to the end."[34]

The comments of Hezekiah Niles, generally shrewd in his analyses of political situations, ably expressed the feelings of many people concerning the Missouri conflict: "Collectively, the latter [Southerners] deprecate slavery as severely as the former [Northerners], and deprecate its increase; but individual cupidity and rashness acts against the common sentiment, in the hope that an event which everybody believes must happen, will not happen in their day." Furthermore, people of African descent could never be part of the United States because "their difference of color is an insuperable barrier to their incorporation within the society; and the mixture of free blacks with slaves is detrimental to the happiness of both, the cause of uncounted crimes." Finally, "the harmony of the Union, and the peace and prosperity of the white population, most excited our sympathies." Niles did not like the compromise, but he hoped "the contest was at an end, and that things would settle down, and adapt themselves to the agreement which necessity imposed."[35] His fears of "the worst of calamities" proved true in years to come, as the compromise worked out in 1820 unraveled in the face of new controversies over slavery. For now, however, it served to quiet the sectional animosities and allowed Monroe and his administration to deal with other issues of concern.

Foreign affairs also proved of great concern and interest during the years of Monroe's presidency. From the actions of Andrew Jackson in Florida in 1818 until the issuance of the Monroe Doctrine in 1823, many Americans debated what the role of Europe in the New World should be and what the United States should do in response to that role. Throughout the period, newspapers followed the events and the discussions related to these issues, taking a greater interest in some than in others.

The activities of General Andrew Jackson in Florida in 1818 drew great attention from many people. In attempting to eliminate raids into American territory by Seminole Indians and runaway slaves, Jackson invaded Spanish territory. He captured two Spanish forts and arrested and executed two British citizens as spies. Most Americans praised his successes, believing that he had addressed a growing problem along the southern border of the United States. Some people, however, severely criticized Jackson, fearing that his actions would result in more problems.

Henry Clay and William Crawford led the critics in Congress, urging that Jackson be reprimanded for the invasion of Florida without congressional approval. Although probably looking toward the 1824 election when President Monroe would step down from office, Clay and Crawford also believed that Jackson's activities would probably precipitate war with Spain and Great Britain.[36] In the end, Secretary of State John Quincy Adams used the problems that produced Jackson's invasion to force Spain to sell Florida to the United States, but such an outcome was not a foregone conclusion.

Many newspaper editors did not seem too concerned about the potential results of the invasion of Florida, apparently believing that the elimination of the problem with the Seminole Indians and their allies was worth the risk. William Duane praised Jackson as "defender of his country" and criticized both those who attacked Jackson and the government for failing to actively defend him.[37] Several editors, however, began to attack Jackson severely. One grieved that Jackson "should do any thing to tarnish the glory he has so nobly earned" and declared that, no matter his previous successes, no one should "draw a veil over the arbitrary exercise of power by any man."[38] Thomas Ritchie, editor of the *Richmond Enquirer*, led the press critics. He believed that Jackson had gone too far and had totally disregarded constitutional restrictions on the executive placed in the hands of Congress.[39] Once more, Hezekiah Niles ably stated the political concerns involved in the controversy: "General Jackson . . . does not sufficiently reflect how intimately the character of the country is connected with his own, now that he is an officer."[40] Most editors, however, did not reciprocate Niles's concerns, and the Florida controversy faded once Spain sold the territory to the United States in 1819.

Of more ongoing interest to most Americans was the future of Latin America. Many people had long been interested in the Spanish colonies in the New World, hoping that the spirit of independence that had started in 1776 would spread southward. In 1811, the *Rural Visiter* declared that "one general impulse in favour of liberty seems to pervade the whole southern hemisphere."[41] As revolts spread throughout Latin America, some joined with the editor of the *Norristown Herald* in believing that "the disturbances in South America will terminate in a compleat revolution in the Spanish provinces, and in the establishment of a free and liberal government."[42] During the late 1810s and the early 1820s, newspapers throughout the United States published numerous stories about the attempts of the Spanish colonies to gain independence. As colony after colony declared independence, the issue became whether the United States would grant the new countries diplomatic recognition.[43] Many editors urged the president to do just that. In March 1822, one announced that "no nation has yet recognized their independence, and there are undoubtedly good reasons why the U. States should be the first to adopt that measure."[44] By the end of the year, the editor saw his wish fulfilled as the United States recognized all of the newly formed republics in Latin America.

This action potentially put the United States on a collision course with much of Europe and provided the background for the issuance of the Monroe Doctrine. In 1822, the Holy Alliance decided to aid Spain in an attempt to regain the Latin

American colonies. Both Great Britain and the United States opposed such an action. The British foreign minister, George Canning, suggested a joint declaration of opposition to European interference in Latin America, but President Monroe, at the urging of John Quincy Adams, chose to issue a separate statement as part of his annual message to Congress in December 1823. The result was the Monroe Doctrine, which stated that the United States would consider any attempt by a European power to interfere in the affairs of the independent American nations or to recolonize the New World as a threat to its national "peace and safety."[45]

Press reaction to the president's message was generally positive. Some editors expressed concern about whether the United States could truly follow through with the promise to guarantee republican governments to the new countries of Latin America.[46] Most, however, agreed with Monroe's concern about potential European interference and praised his efforts to prevent such an occurrence. Hezekiah Niles, while applauding the president's message, called for the increased efficiency of military defenses in case the powers of Europe followed through on their plans.[47] The *New York Spectator* summed up the feelings of most editors, declaring that "the principle assumed appears to be a broad one at first, but no one on reflection will doubt its justice, or hesitate to commend the President for the intrepidity of its annunciation."[48] As in the case of the War of 1812, the United States had once more defended its honor by standing up to Europe.

Another issue of great interest to the press during Monroe's tenure in office revolved around the need for internal improvements and who would pay for them. This issue had come up for debate in Congress on several occasions. Immediately after the War of 1812, Henry Clay pushed the need for federal support of road and canal construction as part of his American System designed to unify the various sections and interests of the country.[49] Clay's proposals never reached full fruition, primarily because of some constitutional scruples and disagreements over where to build the federally funded transportation routes. Because of the failure of the national government to act in this area, several states undertook internal improvement efforts on their own. New York's construction of the Erie Canal provided the leading example. The move to build the canal and the slow progress toward its creation provided great copy for the newspapers for almost a decade.

Political leaders in New York had discussed the need to improve internal water transportation in the state as early as the American Revolution. Prior to the War of 1812, the state legislature passed a resolution supporting the construction of a canal to connect the Hudson River either to Lake Ontario or to Lake Erie. In 1810, the state legislature appointed a commission to survey the best route. Reporting in March 1811, the commission favored the Lake Erie terminus. Whatever the route chosen, many people believed the canal would be important because it would provide, as described by one New York editor, "the means of retaining the affections of our western brethren, who are now trading principally with their Canadian neighbors, and from continued intercourse they may soon fancy their interest inseparable."[50]

The war with Great Britain had slowed the move to build a canal, but once peace returned, many began urging the continuation and completion of this ambitious project. Newspaper editors, particularly in the western part of New York, urged the legislature to fund the project, calling the canal "the great, all important object."[51] Construction of the canal began in 1817, and people throughout the state rejoiced over the benefits it would bring to their state. An Albany editor affirmed that "we believe the commencement of this splendid project will be hailed by the great body of the people of this state, as the dawning of an era which will be productive of more durable renown and glory to New York, than has been imparted to her by anything she has accomplished since the first settlement of the country."[52]

By 1819, enough of the canal was completed so that part of it opened to navigation. On October 23, 1819, the first boat traveled from Utica to Rome. Reports of this event spread throughout the United States, as people from everywhere took an avid interest in the events in upstate New York. One correspondent, describing the event, declared: "To see the first boat launched, to be among the first that were borne on the waters of a canal which is to connect the great chain of western lakes with the Hudson, and which will be one of the most stupendous works the world has ever known . . . produced emotions which those only who felt them can conceive."[53] As construction on the canal continued, the press continued to provide coverage of its progress. The editor of the *Lyons* (New York) *Advertiser* summed up the reactions of many, stating that the canal constituted "more than any thing else occupying the thoughts of a great community."[54]

Once the work was done, editors throughout New York rejoiced over the successful completion of such a large construction project. The *Rochester Telegraph* rejoiced that "the work is finished! Our brightest, highest hopes, are all consummated. Let the shouts of triumph be heard from Erie to the Atlantic, and from the Atlantic resound back to Erie. Let the air itself be made vocal with our paeans of exultation and gratitude."[55] Plans quickly took shape for the formal opening of the entire canal and for statewide celebrations of the event. The *Buffalo Emporium* affirmed that "it will be a proud day in the history of New-York, such as has not occurred since the Declaration of our country's Independence. Well may New-York rejoice in an achievement that would add glory to the most powerful nation on earth."[56] Newspapers throughout the country described the opening of the Erie Canal in 1822. The editor of the *New York Commercial Advertiser* called on all Americans to rejoice, since the event was national in scope and effect: "Wednesday of the present week was not only a proud day for New York, but for the Union" because, although New York had built the canal, "the stupendous object is not the less important in a national point of view." Because of the Erie Canal, the eastern and western regions of the nation "will become neighbors, and a close community of interests will induce them to cling together with a degree of tenaciousness and constancy which even a daily recollection of their consanguinity would not otherwise have produced."[57]

People celebrated and rejoiced throughout New York at the completion of the Erie Canal, but it had not all been easy to accomplish. Although most people had supported the project, funding it had developed into a partisan issue between factions within the state Republican Party. A primary proponent of the canal, Dewitt Clinton served as governor during most of its construction, but found himself forced out of office from 1823 to 1825 because of partisan wrangling. Clinton's opponents the Bucktails, under the leadership of Martin Van Buren, accused him of stealing money from the people through the canal project, while they themselves faced accusations of trying to destroy the canal altogether.

Several newspaper editors, normally partisan in their political outlook, urged state officials to avoid such arguments because the canal project was too important for the future of New York. The editor of a Buffalo paper declared that, "as the canal is obviously a work of the first importance to the state, and will need, in its progress, our united energies to prosecute it effectually, it should be kept perfectly distinct from any political question that may arise, in the present unsettled state of parties in this state."[58] The *Buffalo Patriot*, in reporting on a ceremony to mark the termination point of the canal, summed up the feelings of many concerning the party conflicts related to the canal: "Political feuds and personal animosities were lost in the greatness of the scene, and nothing was heard but one universal expression of heartfelt approbation. And here we cannot but indulge the animating hope, that as this great work may be the source of our wealth and greatness, so may it prove the grave of those local feuds which have so long disturbed our repose, and impeded our prosperity."[59] The editorial referred directly to conflicts between Buffalo and neighboring Black Rock over where the canal should end, but his opinion reflected that of most people—the canal project was just too important to let it get bogged down in partisan wrangling.

The politicians of New York managed to avoid severe partisan conflict, at least long enough to allow the completion of the canal. However, the existence of such infighting within the ranks of the Republican Party existed throughout the nation and indicated that the partisanship of the 1790s had not completely disappeared as had been hoped by President Monroe and others.

After 1816, the Federalist Party was gone, at least on the national level. The *New York American* declared that the names Republican and Federalist were now "obsolete."[60] Throughout Monroe's presidency, more and more active politicians sought to avoid being identified as Federalists in order to remain involved. Some, like Daniel Webster and John Quincy Adams, recognized that Federalism was dead and sought other options.

The Republicans rejoiced that they had finally succeeded in eliminating party strife in the national political arena. As the Federalists continued to decrease in number and influence, more and more people commented on the decline in partisanship throughout the country. "From all quarters we are advised," said the *True American*, "that party feuds are fast disappearing; the interest of the country every where claims precedence; and divisions among politicians are no longer likely to prejudice the publick good."[61] One editor, however, in reporting about politics in

Ohio, declared that divisions still existed there: "The political divisions of Federal and Democratic, seem here to be unknown. Yet parties exist, and as much zeal is exhibited, as in any state where the old party names still prevail."[62]

What was happening, unbeknownst to editors and politicians alike, was the beginning of the new party system, which appeared during the presidency of Andrew Jackson. With the Federalists no longer a real threat, the Republicans increasingly argued among themselves. This process began almost as soon as the War of 1812 ended. The editor of the *American Watchman* deplored this development: "It is a subject of regret, that at a time when the crisis demands all the energy and united exertions of the republican party in the country, the most trifling cause of discontent should assume the 'form and pressure' of importance, and that men possessing republican principles, should endeavor to counteract the will of the majority of the party." He assumed that these disagreements were temporary because "the interests of republicans are mutual, and their endeavors should not be variant."[63] With the Federalists no longer a threat, political unity should be easily achieved.

This editor, and many others, quickly found that such unity seemed difficult to obtain. Increasingly, after the War of 1812, state and local parties witnessed divisions within their own ranks, and the press was unsure how to address this issue. The *Democratic Press* expressed the concerns of many in 1815 when it worried about the "communion and friendship existing between the disappointed Democrats and the Federalists." The editor urged "those who call themselves real democrats . . . to shake them off" because "men who are thus destitute of principle, men who thus mix and compound federalism and what they call democracy, into a base alloy, cannot, ought not to be denominated democrats."[64] Another editor urged everyone to be wary of men "whose speech and actions have a tendency to create doubts to what party they really belong" and to hold such men "up to public detestation and contempt."[65] One discussion of Pennsylvania politics in 1819 declared that five parties existed in local politics.[66] By this time, as had been true in the 1790s, each group accused all others of betraying the principles on which the nation had been founded. The *Aurora* stated that "the independent republicans, [are] all those who are devoted to the principles of the declaration of independence, in theory and in practice, and who are consequently adverse to the all corrupting policy which hath brought this country and state to the present deplorable condition of suffering."[67]

The apparent lack of conflict on the national level somewhat masked the existence of such infighting . As the 1820 election approached, no serious opposition appeared against President Monroe. The apparent lack of party strife made most people apathetic about the presidential election. News reports declared that voting turnout was almost nonexistent. For example, in Philadelphia, 2,000 people voted in the national election, where 4,700 had voted in the earlier governor's race, and in Richmond, Virginia, apparently only seventeen people voted.[68] In the entire state of Virginia, out of a population of 600,000 whites, only 4,321 bothered to go and vote. Many people assumed that no one could really oppose Monroe because of the two-term tradition established by George Washington, so going to the polls seemed a waste of time.[69]

Also because of the two-term tradition, many people already had their attention focused on the 1824 election, when Monroe would obviously step down. As early as 1821, some newspapers actively discussed and debated the next election in anticipation of the conflict it would produce.[70] With no party rivalry to shape the arguments, politicians and newspapers took sides based on either personalities or sectional issues. Political warfare quickly became personal and consisted primarily of personal attacks on one's opponents.[71] These developments only encouraged further disagreements within the Republican Party, and the press reflected these divisions. Such infighting would continue until finally, during the presidency of Andrew Jackson, a new party division of Democrat and Whig would emerge to dominate the national scene for another generation of politicians.

NOTES

1. James Monroe has really been overshadowed by his more famous contemporaries, so he has few substantial biographies. One good work is Harry Ammon, *James Monroe: The Quest for National Identity* (New York: McGraw-Hill, 1971).

2. Ibid., 368–69.

3. Numbers for 1815 are based on Clarence S. Brigham, *History and Bibliography of American Newspapers, 1690–1820*, 2 vols. (Worcester, Mass.: American Antiquarian Society, 1947); numbers for 1820, from Alfred McClung Lee, *The Daily Newspaper in America* (New York: Macmillan, 1937), 711; numbers for 1828, from S. N. D. North, *History and Present Conditions of the Newspaper and Periodical Press of the United States* (Washington, D.C.: U.S. Government Printing Office, 1884), 47.

4. *Columbian Centinel* (Boston), 12 July 1817. While using this term in his book title, George Dangerfield pointed out that all was not "good" during the presidency of James Monroe. George Dangerfield, *The Era of Good Feelings* (London: Methuen, 1953).

5. Harry Ammon, "The Fifth President and the Press: Monroe," *Media History Digest* 3 (1983): 27; William E. Ames, *A History of the National Intelligencer* (Chapel Hill: University of North Carolina Press, 1972), 104–26.

6. Quoted in S. Putnam Waldo, *The Tour of James Monroe, President of the United States, Through the Northern and Eastern States, in 1817* (Hartford, Conn.: F. D. Bolles, 1818), 273.

7. *Norristown* (Pa.) *Herald*, 12 March 1817.

8. *National Intelligencer* (Washington, D.C.), 24 July 1817.

9. *Boston Palladium*, 10 November 1815.

10. *Norristown Herald*, 25 March 1818.

11. *Federal Republican* (Baltimore, Md.), 25 June 1819.

12. Quoted in Norris W. Preyer, "Southern Support of the Tariff of 1816: A Reappraisal," in *Essays on Jacksonian America*, ed. Frank Otto Gatell (New York: Holt, Rinehart & Winston, 1970), 15.

13. See, for example, *Manufacturers' & Farmers' Journal* (Providence, R.I.), 25 September 1820; *Patron of Industry* (New York), 23 and 27 December 1820; *Niles's Weekly Register* (Baltimore, Md.), 23 June 1821.

14. *True American* (Philadelphia), 6 June 1817.

15. *Manufacturers' & Farmers' Journal*, 18 May 1820.

16. One reflection of the change of attitude concerning slavery by many Americans in the northern states was the beginnings of the abolitionist press. The first antislavery newspaper, *Genius of Universal Emancipation*, began in 1821 under the editorship of Benjamin Lundy. See Chapter 9 for further information.

17. *Rural Visiter* (Burlington, N.J.), 22 October 1810.

18. *American Daily Advertiser* (Philadelphia), 23 October 1818.

19. The Missouri controversy has long been seen as one of the precursors of the Civil War. Two substantial studies of the conflict are Glover Moore, *The Missouri Controversy, 1819–1821* (Lexington: University of Kentucky Press, 1953) and Don Edward Fehrenbacher, *The South and Three Sectional Crises* (Baton Rouge: Louisiana State University Press, 1980).

20. *American Daily Advertiser*, 23 and 25 November 1819.

21. Ibid., 29 November 1819, reprinted from *Salem* (Mass.) *Gazette*.

22. *Dutchess Observer* (Poughkeepsie, N.Y.), 21 April 1819.

23. *American Daily Advertiser*, 23 March and 17 April 1820; *Aurora* (Philadelphia), 25 March 1820; *New York Daily Advertiser* (New York), 28 March 1820.

24. *New York Daily Advertiser*, 4 December 1819.

25. *Western Monitor* (Lexington, Ky.), 20 March 1821.

26. *Lexington* (Ky.) *Gazette*, 10 March 1820.

27. *Centinel of Freedom* (Newark, N.J.), 2 May 1820.

28. *Portland* (Me.) *Eastern Argus*, 9 January 1821.

29. *American Watchman and Delaware Republican* (Wilmington), 2 February 1821.

30. *Inquisitor Advertiser* (Cincinnati, Ohio), 21 March 1820.

31. *New York Columbian* (New York), 3 February 1820.

32. *Clarksville* (Tenn.) *Gazette*, 18 March 1820.

33. *Village Record* (West Chester, Pa.), 7 March 1821.

34. Reprinted in *American Daily Advertiser*, 30 June 1820.

35. *Niles's Weekly Register*, 23 December 1820.

36. Dangerfield, *Era of Good Feelings*, 122–36; Ammon, *James Monroe*, 430.

37. *Aurora*, 25 July 1818.

38. *Norristown Herald*, 20 December 1818.

39. Dangerfield, *Era of Good Feelings*, 136; Ammon, *James Monroe*, 430.

40. Quoted in Dangerfield, *Era of Good Feelings*, 136.

41. *Rural Visiter*, 25 March 1811.

42. *Norristown Herald*, 4 September 1816.

43. The history of the revolutions in Latin America has often been overshadowed by the Monroe Doctrine. One study, however, that looks at the entire issue is Arthur Preston Whitaker, *The United States and the Independence of Latin America, 1800–1830* (Baltimore, Md.: Johns Hopkins University Press, 1941).

44. *Old Colony Reporter* (Taunton, Mass.), 20 March 1822.

45. The Monroe Doctrine has produced much work by historians in the area of foreign policy. Some of the best-known work is by Dexter Perkins. Both *The Monroe Doctrine, 1823–1826* (Cambridge: Harvard University Press, 1932) and *A History of the Monroe*

Doctrine (Boston: Little, Brown, 1955) review the adoption of the new policy. Also useful is Ernest R. May's *The Making of the Monroe Doctrine* (Cambridge: Belknap Press of Harvard University Press, 1975).

46. See, for example, *New York Advertiser* (New York), 6 December 1823; *Salem Gazette*, 9 and 16 December 1823.

47. *Niles's Weekly Register*, 6 December 1823.

48. *New York Spectator* (New York), 6 December 1823.

49. Henry Clay ran for president three times and lost. As a major political figure in the United States from the War of 1812 until the early 1850s, he played an important role in trying to avoid sectional conflict over slavery and the tariff. Valuable studies of his political career and his efforts to cement the nation closely together are Robert V. Remini, *Henry Clay: Statesman for the Union* (New York: W. W. Norton, 1991) and Merrill D. Peterson, *The Great Triumvirate: Webster, Clay, and Calhoun* (New York: Oxford University Press, 1987).

50. *New York Evening Post* (New York), 1 February 1811.

51. *Buffalo* (N.Y.) *Gazette*, 28 January 1817.

52. *Albany* (N.Y.) *Gazette*, 15 May 1817.

53. *Rochester* (N.Y.) *Telegraph*, 2 November 1819.

54. *Lyons* (N.Y.) *Advertiser*, quoted in *Rochester Telegraph*, 22 June 1822.

55. *Rochester Telegraph*, 18 October 1825.

56. *Buffalo* (N.Y.) *Emporium*, 8 October 1825.

57. *New York Commercial Advertiser* (New York), 11 October 1822.

58. *Niagara Patriot* (Buffalo, N.Y.), 16 February 1819.

59. *Buffalo* (N.Y.) *Patriot*, 13 August 1822.

60. *New York American* (New York), 24 July 1819.

61. *True American*, 8 December 1817.

62. *Village Record*, 10 November 1819.

63. *American Watchman and Delaware Republican*, 23 September 1815.

64. *Democratic Press* (Philadelphia), 13 May 1815.

65. *American Watchman and Delaware Republican*, 3 October 1815.

66. *Village Record*, 11 August 1819.

67. *Aurora*, 31 August 1819.

68. *American Daily Advertiser*, 4 November 1820.

69. Ammon, *James Monroe*, 458–59.

70. See *Norristown Herald*, 5 December 1821.

71. Ammon, "The Fifth President," 28.

8

The Age of Jackson,
1824–1833

With the entrance of Andrew Jackson into the national political arena, the party press revived as new divisions appeared between those who supported Jackson and those who opposed him. Jackson's rise to power resulted in a new political party system in the United States, one that was once more strongly supported by partisan publications throughout the country. The return of partisanship to the press encouraged growth. When Jackson finally won election as president in 1828, 863 newspapers existed in the United States. Five years later, as Jackson entered his second term in office in 1833, the number of publications stood at approximately 1,200.[1]

Jackson first became a nationally known figure during the War of 1812. As a general in the American army, he successfully defended New Orleans in 1815 and defeated the British army. Although this military action actually took place after the signing of the peace treaty at Ghent, news of the war's end had not yet crossed the Atlantic. Thus, Jackson became "the Hero of New Orleans," a beloved figure who won the only major military victory of the war. Following the War of 1812, Jackson remained in the army, primarily fighting Indians throughout the southeastern United States. As noted earlier, in 1818, he got into trouble for following a group of renegade Seminole Indians into Florida and, while there, executing two British subjects as spies. Jackson escaped court martial for this incident, primarily because it helped give the U.S. government reason to pressure Spain into selling Florida. Jackson's image, however, was tarnished, and it appeared that his public career might be over.

Nevertheless, by 1823, his reputation had revived, and he embarked on a national political career. When the Tennessee state legislature nominated him for president as a "favorite son" in 1822, many expressed surprise to find out that Jackson had a real chance to win the 1824 election.[2]

Newspapers made it clear that many people sought something new and different in the political arena. The terminology of the party system of the 1790s still existed, but seemed meaningless following the disintegration of the national Federalist Party after the War of 1812. According to the *National Gazette*, "Federalists and Democrats are so intermingled as the advocates of each of the candidates that neither of them can deem himself specially obliged to one denomination more than another."[3] For many like William Duane, Jackson provided the means of reviving the political system in a more democratic direction: "[T]he election of the Hero of New Orleans, will give rise to a purely American party, and become a rallying point for those who have retired from the political ranks, disgusted with party zeal."[4] According to Duane, Jackson himself favored such a change because he wished "that the bane of free government, 'Party Animosity' should be destroyed, and that the question 'is he honest, is he capable, is he a friend to his country,' when affirmatively answered should be a passport to office."[5]

The subsequent campaign did not contain the name-calling and accusatory rhetoric between Federalists and Republicans that occurred in the 1790s, but it was a strenuous campaign nonetheless. In many ways, the campaign for the 1824 nomination began shortly after James Monroe was reelected for his second term in 1820. Everyone assumed that he would follow the two-term tradition established by George Washington, so those considered possible successors jockeyed eagerly for position. A writer in the *Richmond Enquirer* labeled the coming battle "the war of the giants,"[6] an apt name for a campaign that revolved more around personalities than issues.

Originally, five candidates entered the race. The congressional caucus nominated Secretary of State William Crawford of Georgia in the traditional manner. However, only a minority of the members of Congress participated, so many people did not consider the nomination valid. Monroe privately favored Secretary of State John Quincy Adams of Massachusetts, but the president refused to take a public stand, so Adams did not receive much benefit from Monroe's support. Some in Congress backed Secretary of War John C. Calhoun of South Carolina, but he withdrew to run unopposed for vice-president. Speaker of the House Henry Clay of Kentucky also had some support from congressional members, but proved unable to translate that support into victory. The most popular candidate appeared to be General Jackson, who had little political experience.

Most of the newspapers lined up in favor of one of the candidates and used their pages to attack the record, character, and reputation of the others in the race. By 1822, the press outlets of Washington, D.C., were generally identified as supporters of one candidate or the other. The *Washington Gazette* supported William Crawford, while the *Washington Republican and Congressional Examiner* came out for John C. Calhoun. Although hesitant to take too strong a stand because of its dependence on government printing contracts, the *National Intelligencer* generally supported Crawford and occasionally John Quincy Adams. The *National Journal* also supported Adams until it absorbed the *Washington Republican*, after which it supported both Adams and Calhoun. Clay and Jackson did not have a newspaper in the capital, but had strong support from other parts of the country. Clay's primary newspaper outlets were the *Argus of Western America* in Kentucky and the *Liberty Hall and Cincinnati Gazette* in Ohio. Jackson's candidacy found favor in the *Columbian Observer* and the *Franklin Gazette* of Philadelphia and the *National Republican* in Cincinnati.[7] The result was a campaign "too often disfigured by passion and disgraced by violence."[8]

Crawford, while seen by some as a continuation of the good southern leadership of previous administrations, was attacked as a minority candidate. He also lost momentum in his campaign after he suffered a stroke in the fall of 1823. Many Republicans saw Adams, a former Federalist, as a person who could not be trusted and who proved unable to gain a national following. Clay lacked enough national recognition for victory. The newspapers that supported Crawford, Adams, and Clay failed to overcome these deficiencies. Andrew Jackson was popular and well known, but had few qualifications for national office. Many feared that his military background would make him a dictator of sorts once in office.[9]

In many ways, the 1824 election was problematic because the contest was judged more on personalities than on issues. With no national two-party system, the campaign revolved around men because there seemed no compelling questions about which to argue. A Federalist editor worried that "self-interest seems to be the ruling principle of too many politicians."[10] The editor of the *Columbian Reporter* better understood the situation. He declared that the present political parties did not resemble those of the past in any way because "the present differences grow out of a preference for men—all probably agreeing essentially in their political faith. In the past periods of our history, it has been a difference of opinion in regard to the measures and policy of the government which have chiefly created political divisions among us." Now, politicians "advocate the claims of their favorite chiefly, if not exclusively, upon the ground that he is 'more honest' and 'more capable' than his competitors."[11] The consequence of the lack of partisan organization was a hard-fought campaign with little of substance involved.

The vigorous contest produced a close vote, with no clear winner in the electoral college. The result was something that no one wanted, an election that had to be decided by the House of Representatives.[12] When they finally elected John Quincy Adams in February 1825, the *Christian Gazette and Youth's Herald* in Philadelphia concluded that "the Presidential contest having closed, it is sincerely to be desired that the disagreements and broils, the vituperations and accusations which it has occasioned may be heard of no more. The notoriety, frequency and apparent malignity of these, have been disgraceful to a nation which claims to be civilized, as well as free."[13]

The election of John Quincy Adams produced a storm of protest from the press supporters of Jackson, who had assumed that the House would elect their candidate because he had received a plurality of the popular votes. Shortly before the vote in Congress, the editor of the *Aurora* stated "that public opinion will eventually be respected by the election of the General."[14] But such was not to be the case because, "contrary to the wishes and expectations of a very large portion of the cit-

izens of the United States," John Quincy Adams won on the first ballot.[15] Adams
succeeded because he received the support of Henry Clay of Kentucky, whom
Adams subsequently appointed as secretary of state. Cries of corruption filled the
Jacksonian press. Even the newspapers such as *Democratic Press*, which expressed neutrality or supported someone other than Jackson, realized that "Mr.
Adams will enter upon the duties of his high station, under peculiar and not very
cheering circumstances. A powerful political opposition, powerful in every sense
of the word, will watch his every movement."[16]

Because of the cloud that hung over his administration, Adams had little chance
of success as president.[17] He knew that his personality, being one of reserve and
apparent coldness, would not endear him to the people. He believed that he could
be a good president, but realized that carrying out his duties would not be easy because he could not cater to public opinion in the way that seemed increasingly important for politicians in the 1820s. Adams, a strong nationalist, hoped to continue
the policies of his predecessor. In his inaugural address, he called for a national
bankruptcy law, a national university, and national efforts to explore the earth and
to observe the heavens. In urging even more government involvement in so many
areas, Adams frightened people who were not already strongly opposed to him.
His inability to use the press to explain his reasons for his policies doomed Adams
to failure and resulted in his being branded an aristocrat by his opponents.[18]

Jacksonian editors spent the entire four years of the Adams presidency attacking his personal character and spreading all sorts of stories through the pages of
their publications. Many of these stories, based on little, if any, fact, still circulate
as truth. Probably the most famous legend declared that Anne Royall, editor of
Paul Pry, got the first personal interview with any president by sitting on his
clothes on the bank of the Potomac while Adams was swimming. Less dramatic,
but still personally painful for Adams and his family, were accusations that Louisa
Adams was actually English, rather than American, and that the president attended
church barefoot on a regular basis. Because of his reticence, Adams seldom answered these charges, and many people came to believe them.[19]

Because of Adams's unpopularity and Jackson's frustration over losing, plans
began for the 1828 election as soon as the 1824 contest ended. The editor of the
Aurora remarked in February 1825 that "when the time again arrives for the exercise of their suffrages upon the question of chief magistrate, the rights of the
people, the purity of republican principles, grossly violated against General
JACKSON, may be triumphantly vindicated in his person and in his favor."[20]

As personalities had been the focus of the 1824 election, it appeared that the
same would be true in the 1828 campaign. All the discussions revolved around
Adams and Jackson and their respective supporters. In the midst of all the disagreements, something happened that startled and frightened many people, raising
concerns that the United States had lost its direction. In 1826, the nation celebrated its fiftieth birthday on July 4. Following all of the celebrations, word slowly
spread throughout the country that John Adams and Thomas Jefferson had both
died on that day. The freakishness of the event struck many people. Boston's *In-*

dependent Chronicle stated that, "without being superstitious, we cannot but think it was so ordered, that their race on earth should be completed on the day of the Jubilee, that the run of their existence might set in a blaze of splendid glory."[21] Others joined the *Aurora* in praising their records of service to their country: "The mind is crowded with reflections in contemplating the termination, on the same day, and that day the fiftieth anniversary of their country's freedom, of two of the most able, efficient and illustrious statesmen that the world ever produced."[22]

The reaction to the deaths of Adams and Jefferson provides interesting insights into how the press shapes public perceptions concerning history and historical figures. Throughout the first quarter of the nineteenth century, Thomas Jefferson had been the hero of the age, while John Adams had been the villain of the Sedition Act. Adams's public reputation had been totally ruined because of the problems of the late 1790s, and his efforts for independence during the Revolutionary War had been almost forgotten. Jefferson, on the other hand, was the author of the Declaration of Independence and the great president who had ensured future American growth by purchasing Louisiana. In commenting on the two deaths, Adams's grandson, Charles Francis Adams, swore to do all in his power to restore the public reputation of his grandfather.[23] John Adams's position in history did improve following his death, but the press, rather than the members of the Adams family, played the important role in the process. Because of the common death date for Jefferson and Adams, the newspapers talked of their passing together. As a result, Jefferson's popularity rubbed off and helped restore Adams to a place of renown as one of the heroes of the Revolution. Letters and statements from family members, such as John Quincy Adams and Charles Francis Adams, could not have accomplished this goal, for personal bias would have been involved. The newspapers, in commenting on the unusualness of both men's deaths, forever linked their activities together in a manner that had not occurred since the 1780s.

Hezekiah Niles, in commenting on the loss of the two Revolutionary leaders, summed up the feelings of many, full of praise for past efforts and fears for the future:

It was a fearful time. But "there were giants in those days." And none were more conspicuous for ardent devotion and unlimited zeal, fixed resolution and steady perseverance, than John Adams of Massachusetts and Thomas Jefferson of Virginia. They both lived to grow old, if we may be allowed the expression, in the glories of the nation which they labored so faithfully to establish; they both died on the same day, and that was the jubilee-anniversary of the nation's existence! What a torrent of thought rushes on the mind when these things are mentioned—recollections of the past seemingly overwhelm us by the importance of events that have happened—we greatly wonder at what has taken place and endeavor to look into futurity; saying to ourselves, what will the next fifty years produce?—will anyone now living behold such mighty marches of mind and power as Adams and Jefferson witnessed?[24]

Many people worried that the days of American glory were gone. For them, neither John Quincy Adams nor Andrew Jackson represented greatness for the future.[25]

Andrew Jackson did not have any such qualms, and he believed that he had been cheated out of the presidency by John Quincy Adams. In reality, he began running for the election of 1828 in 1825. The editor of the *Connecticut Mirror* expressed surprise that a presidential campaign could be sustained for that length of time: "Surely the good people of these States must be marvelously fond of political squabbles that they can so soon be excited to discuss and quarrel about another Presidential election. . . . [W]as not the last quarrel of the ring, the last 'knock down and drag out' riot enough to sicken the people for four years at least of Presidential electioneering?"[26] The answer to this question was clearly no, and newspapers played a major role in keeping things stirred up.

Even before the election of 1824, many politicians recognized the potential impact of newspapers. One editor, a supporter of Jackson, stated that the press kept William Crawford's candidacy alive: "He has but a few papers to support his cause, but they are clamorous and vigilent in his services. If half as much were done for either of the other candidates, as has been for this 'progeny of the Caucus,' he would before this, have been abandoned by his most strenuous advocates."[27] Other editors who hoped to stay neutral until shortly before the election found it impossible to do so. In June 1827, the editors of the *Norristown Herald* stated that "two or three months is in all conscience long enough to wage a war of abusive words,"[28] but by August, they felt impelled to change their minds, since "to remain longer 'neutral' would be doing injustice to our numerous readers; because we cannot make our paper satisfactorily interesting without engaging in the contest."[29] The reality was probably complaints from customers at the very least and a decline in subscriptions at the very worst. But whatever the reason, most newspapers of the mid-1820s found it impossible to stay out of the political fray going on around them.[30]

What was happening was the beginnings of a new two-party system in the United States. The Republicans and Federalists of the 1790s were gone, and new divisions began to appear. Since politicians conducted the campaigns of the 1820s primarily on the basis of personality, the growing partisan conflicts originally revolved around people rather than issues. With the rise of Andrew Jackson to a place of prominence in national politics, people began to divide along the lines of whether they were for or against Jackson. Jackson's party became the Democrats, a group pledged to individualism and as little government involvement in people's lives as possible. For many Democrats, the national government's primary purpose was to provide a central focus in times of international crisis. Beyond dealing with other countries, there was little that leaders in Washington needed to do. Those opposed to Jackson, including John Quincy Adams and Henry Clay, slowly evolved into the Whig Party, believing that the nation prospered when the government took action that benefited the whole in a variety of areas. They supported government construction of transportation networks, protective tariffs to encourage manufacturing, and a national bank to provide a sound financial basis for the economy. It took over a decade for the Whig Party to completely evolve. In 1828 and 1832, these men primarily coalesced into an anti-Jackson clique. By 1836, they were organized well enough to field a national ticket of sorts, although they could not agree on one candidate. By 1840, they mimicked the Jackson organizations of 1828 and 1832 well enough to put their candidate, William Henry Harrison, into the White House.[31]

In all of these electoral victories, the press played an important role. Looking toward the election in 1828, Jackson and his supporters sought to organize in a manner that would improve their chances of success. They sought to simplify the campaign issues by attacking the reputation and record of John Quincy Adams, describing him as a patrician who had little in common with the majority of Americans. According to the *Natchez Gazette*, "John Quincy Adams has passed the principal part of his life in Europe, amid the luxury and splendor of regal governments. . . . It was there that he learned the superiority of a monarchical over a democratic or federative government—that the people were not calculated to govern themselves—that [a] republic wanted energy."[32]

Adams's purchase of an ivory chess set and a billiard table for the White House, described in the newspapers as a "gaming table and gambling furniture," provided further proof of his aristocratic leanings.[33] In a nutshell, "the parties are Jackson and Adams, democracy and aristocracy."[34] Jackson's people established committees throughout the country and sought to gain newspaper support wherever needed. For example, in Philadelphia, a new paper appeared in 1826, "having for its primary Political object the elevation of General Andrew Jackson to the Presidency."[35] When the campaign was in full swing, a newspaper supportive of Adams, fearing the final outcome, declared that "organization is the secret of victory. By the want of it we have been overthrown."[36]

Those opposed to Jackson's candidacy tried to undermine his position by describing him as a "military chieftain" and an "ignorant and ferocious 'slave-dealer,'" terms they hoped would sway voters against Jackson.[37] Charles Hammond, in a pamphlet entitled *Truth's Advocate,* described the General as "a rash, vain, and presumptuous ignoramus: . . . it is to a good portion of animal courage, and to an uncommon share of vindictive fury, united to an impetuous temper, that he has made an impression on those around him."[38] The *National Intelligencer* warned Americans about the possible results if Jackson were elected president: "Of the seductiveness of military fame in popular governments, if we had ever doubted it, the last Presidential election has given us instructive illustration." The United States had almost tried "the experiment . . . which we have been taught by all history to deprecate, of a successful general arriving, by means solely of a military achievement, at the highest station of the republic." Electing a military leader to high office would be dangerous because, "having once tasted of the pleasure of absolute command, as on the field of battle, he may retain the relish for it, and is too likely, in the exercise of public duties, to substitute for the injunctions of law, or the suggestions of policy, his own sovereign will and pleasure."[39]

Some editors even got more personal, attacking Rachel Jackson because of the problems of her marriage. When she and Andrew Jackson got married, they believed her first husband, Lewis Robards, had divorced her. They later discovered that he had not. Rachel was forced to acquire a divorce, and then she and Jackson quietly remarried. Jackson's opponents in 1828 used this incident to question Jackson's morals and fitness for public office: "Ought a convicted adulteress and her paramour husband to be placed in the highest office of this free and Christian land?"[40]

Jackson himself summed up the press campaign against him: "The whole object of the coalition is to calumniate me, cartloads of coffin handbills, forgeries, and pamphlets of the most base calumnies are circulated by the franking privilege of members of Congress & Mr. Clay's men. . . . I am branded with every crime. . . . The day of retribution must come."[41] For Jackson, the day of retribution came on election day in 1828, when he defeated John Quincy Adams for the presidency. However, Jackson never forgave the newspaper producers who attacked him and his family during the campaign, and throughout his eight years in office, he sought to ensure that he continued to have influential newspaper people supporting him.

Jackson's primary journalistic support came from three newspapers: Amos Kendall's *Argus of Western America* in Frankfort, Kentucky; Duff Green's *United States Telegraph* in Washington, D.C.; and Francis P. Blair's *Washington Globe*. In turn, each of these journals bolstered Jackson's campaigns for president and promoted his legislative agenda once he got elected. Other newspapers that supported Jackson looked to these three for guidance on the official stance of the pro-Jackson forces.

The most influential of these editors was Amos Kendall. Originally from New England, Kendall graduated from Dartmouth College in 1811. In 1814, he moved to Kentucky to seek his fortune. He quickly became involved in local politics and took over the editorship of the political organ *Argus of Western America* in 1816. Originally a friend and supporter of Henry Clay, Kendall broke with him in the mid-1820s and thereafter promoted Andrew Jackson for president. More than any other individual, Kendall organized Jackson's ideas into a viable platform for the 1828 campaign. The *Argus* became Jackson's first official newspaper outlet, and he used its pages in 1825 to discuss his views on government and his political platform for the first time. Kendall developed the public image of Jackson as a "farmer soldier," which appealed to many of the voters. Following Jackson's victory in the 1828 election, Kendall followed him to Washington, where he continued as a close adviser throughout Jackson's presidency.[42]

Also important in Jackson's election victory was Duff Green's *United States Telegraph*, founded in Washington, D.C., in 1826. Supporters of this new journal determined to use its pages to help prevent the theft of the presidency from Jackson again in 1828. The *Telegraph* adopted the motto "Power is always stealing from the many to the few" and continually attacked the Adams administration as being Federalist in disguise. But Green's efforts on behalf of Jackson went beyond just attacking President John Quincy Adams. Where Amos Kendall gave the campaign ideological substance, Green gave it physical substance. He used individual contacts, both in person and through the mail, as well as his newspaper to create an organization for Jackson's budding political party, the Democrats. Green directed the Washington Central Committee of twenty-four top Democratic politicians from across the nation, which essentially made him the national coordinator of Jackson's 1828 campaign. Following Jackson's election, Green's paper continued as the official party organ. Green also served as printer for Congress and several executive departments, contracts that earned him $50,000 a year from 1829 to 1833. In 1830, however, Green fell out of favor when he supported John C. Calhoun in his growing argument with President Jackson over the tariff. After 1820, the *Telegraph* became a vocal supporter of states' rights and slavery.[43]

Following Green's defection to Calhoun, Jackson and Kendall sought to establish another party paper in Washington, D.C. The result was Francis P. Blair's *Washington Globe*, founded in 1830. Blair had succeeded Kendall as editor of the *Argus* following the 1828 election and zealously supported Jackson and his policies. Blair continued the work of Green's *Telegraph*, using the pages of his newspaper to present Jackson's program and urge widespread support for it. The *Globe* became Jackson's voice around the country. Eventually, more than 400 newspapers throughout the nation drew information and opinion about the administration from the pages of Blair's paper. But Blair's influence went beyond that of Green because Blair also became a personal adviser of Jackson, like Kendall, and these two journalists helped shape official policy as well as presenting it in the pages of their publications.[44]

Although these three newspapers provided the leadership for the Jacksonian press, other important Democratic papers appeared throughout the country. During the 1820s, supporters of Jackson founded journals everywhere. Because of the growing cohesion in the budding Democratic Party, state organizations usually sponsored these newspapers, which then served as official organs for state party leaders. These publications cooperated in disseminating the party platform and helped in developing party cohesion and consensus throughout the country. Most important among these regional papers were the *Albany Argus* and the *Richmond Enquirer*.

The *Argus* represented the Albany Regency, the political machine in New York headed by future president Martin Van Buren. Edited by Edwin Croswell, the *Argus* played an important role in maintaining the political power of the Regency by clearly presenting its position on various issues. Croswell strongly believed in party politics and used his newspaper to support the Democratic Party. He became one of the directors of the Regency, the most influential political organization at the time. When the Regency decided to support Andrew Jackson in 1828, several other states followed its lead. As a result of the importance of the Albany Regency during the Jacksonian era, its newspaper, the *Argus*, was generally seen as the most important newspaper published north of Washington, D.C.[45]

The *Richmond Enquirer* represented the Richmond Junto, the Virginia political machine headed by the *Enquirer*'s editor, Thomas Ritchie. Founded in 1804, the *Enquirer* always considered the interests of the state of Virginia in choosing its political stance. Originally an ardent supporter of Thomas Jefferson, Ritchie came out strongly in favor of Andrew Jackson in 1825 after Ritchie and Henry Clay split over the issues of the tariff and the national bank. Many believed that Ritchie would replace Duff Green after Green defected to Calhoun in 1830. However, Ritchie had opposed Andrew Jackson's actions in Florida in 1818–1820, and Jackson's long-smoldering resentment over such criticism apparently prevented the appointment. Also, Ritchie never hesitated to oppose Jackson if a policy seemed dangerous. Even with such disagreements, the *Enquirer* continued to support Jackson and his policies because they seemed best for Virginia. Although a strong advocate of states' rights, Ritchie opposed South Carolina and the attempt to prevent the enforcement of the federal tariff through nullification as taking the issue too far, but he also opposed the tariff as bad for the southern economy.[46]

Along with the national party paper and these two regional publications, other state party organs played an important role in pronouncing Democratic ideas. Influential state newspapers in the South included the *Charleston Mercury* and the *Nashville Republican*. In Massachusetts, the *Boston Statesman* (later the *Boston Morning Post*) served as a mouthpiece for the state party. In New Hampshire, the editor of the *New Hampshire Patriot*, Isaac Hill, headed the state political machine. Hill used his paper to speak for the state Democratic Party, and it was generally considered to be New England's leading Democratic paper. Altogether, these state, regional, and national newspapers formed a cohesive organization that provided constant communication for Andrew Jackson and his supporters during his successful political career.[47]

Jackson's opponents, the Whigs, never duplicated the success of the Democrats in organizing the press. However, they maintained a majority in the number of newspapers. The growing number of Jacksonian publications during the presidency of John Quincy Adams led many to believe that future political battles would have to be fought, at least partially, in the newspapers. Henry Clay stated that "the course adopted by the Opposition, in the dissemination of Newspapers and publications against the administration and supporting presses, leaves to its friends no other alternative than that of following their example, so far at least as to circulate information among the people."[48]

In Washington, the Whigs had two publications, primarily by default. The *National Intelligencer*, published by Joseph Gates and William Seaton, had supported Crawford in 1824 and Adams in 1828. They attacked Jackson in their paper, and he never forgave them. They lost the Senate printing contract even before Jackson was elected, and the House gave its printing business to someone else in 1829. Financially, the opposition of Gales and Seaton to Andrew Jackson proved costly, but they continued to support the tariff and the Bank of the United States as good, sound economic policy.[49] The *National Journal*, published by Peter Force, reached a place of some prominence primarily because it became a semi-official organ for John Quincy Adams. However, Force was too independent to follow Henry Clay's guidance, and he sold the paper in 1830.[50]

A group of newspapers scattered through the states supported these two national papers. The leading regional Whig newspapers were the *Springfield Republican*, the *Albany Evening Journal*, and the New York *Courier and Enquirer*. Together, these anti-Jackson publications reached readers all across the nation.

Samuel Bowles II founded the *Springfield Republican* in 1824 as an advocate of John Quincy Adams and his adminstration. Following Adams's defeat in 1828, Bowles continued his opposition to Jackson, slowly moving into the newly forming Whig Party. Throughout most of the nineteenth century, a member of the Bowles family continued to edit the *Springfield Republican*, and most people considered it the best small-town paper in the United States at the time.[51]

Thurlow Weed edited the *Evening Journal* following its establishment in 1830 as a Whig newspaper. Weed had originally gotten his political start in the anti-Masonry movement in western New York in the 1820s, but he moved to strongly oppose Andrew Jackson in the 1830s. Weed quickly became one of the Whig Party's leading political strategists, and he joined with William Seward and Horace Greeley to form a successful political machine to rival the Albany Regency.[52]

The *Courier and Enquirer*, founded in 1827 by James Watson Webb, first appeared as a publication intended for the merchants of New York. Webb also supported Jackson at first, but began to turn against him when the Albany Regency leadership failed to consult him concerning state political decisions. With a circulation of 4,500 by 1830, Webb's paper had great potential impact. He became increasingly disenchanted with the New York political machine and began to use his newspaper to challenge its leadership. The final split with the Democratic Party came in the early 1830s, primarily over the issue of the rechartering of the Second Bank of the United States. The switch in political allegiance seemed sudden to many, who accused Webb of accepting bribes from Nicholas Biddle, president of the bank.[53] Webb declared that he found he had more in common with the anti-Jackson forces. Whatever the reason, Webb and his paper became strong advocates of the opposition by the election of 1832. In making this move, Webb suggested that the new party assume the name "Whig," a suggestion that was quickly followed.[54]

During Jackson's two terms in office, the press continued to discuss many of the various current issues in Washington. Some controversies received more coverage than others in the newspapers, even when the impact on the government seemed the same. The scandal involving Secretary of the Treasury John Eaton and his new wife, Peggy, did not receive much press coverage until after it ended, even though the event produced the mass resignation of most of Jackson's cabinet. The controversy arose because Eaton married Margaret "Peggy" O'Neal Timberlake, the daughter of a Washington innkeeper. Peggy's first husband, John Timberlake, had apparently committed suicide. Some said the death occurred because Eaton and Mrs. Timberlake were already romantically involved. Whatever the truth of the case, John and Peggy Eaton began their marriage under a cloud. Because she was not of the Washington elite, Peggy's position as the wife of a cabinet official proved problematic for many. The questions about her personal character only worsened the situation. The rest of the cabinet wives, led by Floride Calhoun, wife of Vice-President John C. Calhoun, refused to receive Mrs. Eaton into Washington society. The final result was a disaster in which President Jackson sought to defend the wife of his friend. In the end, most of Jackson's cabinet resigned, and he created a new council of advisers who were less likely to challenge his authority in any area.[55]

All of this activity received little attention in the press until the cabinet members resigned. Clearly, the propriety of the issues involved did not explain why editors failed to discuss the crisis, since many had been very ready to accuse Rachel Jackson of adultery during the 1828 campaign. More possible is the fact that little apparent political gain could be made at the time from the disagreements, so newspapers concentrated on other, apparently more important, issues. Also, the conflict originated with the wives of Jackson's cabinet members. Since women in the nineteenth century were generally seen as totally uninvolved in the political arena, newspaper editors could easily have considered any argument they precipitated as unimportant to the big picture, even when it involved the president's closest advisers and associates.

The issue of the Native Americans also proved to be of importance with the passage of the Indian Removal Bill in 1830, but newspapers provided little discussion of the issue, apparently because few white Americans disagreed with the policy. The *Cherokee Phoenix*, one of the new kind of newspapers appearing in the 1820s, protested the actions of the government with little effect.[56] It stated that, "as long as they [the Cherokee] are conscious of the justice of their cause, and the unjust proceedings of the State, they cannot tamely agree to have their rights wrested from them, rights which they have always possessed and exercised, and which have been from time to time secured and guaranteed by the faith of the United States."[57] As the Removal Bill approached final passage in 1830, the editor concluded: "[L]et both Houses of Congress decide as they may, we confidently think justice will be done, even if the Cherokees are not in the land of the living to receive it—posterity will give a correct verdict."[58]

Other political issues received more attention from the newspapers than did Peggy Eaton and the Native Americans. The most important issues during Jackson's eight years in office were the conflict with South Carolina over the tariff and the fight over the renewal of the charter of the Bank of the United States. Both produced great controversy, and both resulted in much discussion in the press.

The tariff conflict actually developed several years before Jackson became president. The United States had adopted its first protective tariff in 1816,[59] designed to slow the importation of British goods and encourage the development of American manufactures. Increasingly opposed by Southerners who depended on British markets to sell their cotton, more and more Northerners supported the tariff as a means to stabilize the American economy. Beginning in the 1820s, several northern business papers began to actively support an increase in the tariff in order to encourage economic growth. One editor, in reporting a meeting of importers hoping to stop the adoption of a new tariff, complained that "we have been kept in a state of vassallage to our step mother England, and subjected to the payment of 'tribute' to an immense amount, in the balance of trade."[60] Another editor summed up the opposition to the tariff: "The principal objection urged against the policy which we vindicate is, that it tends to benefit a few, at the expense of the great mass of the community; that it will have the effect of a tax on the great body of the people, for the pecuniary advantage of a few manufacturers."[61] Strongly disagreeing with this outlook, he argued that a higher tariff "would set the springs of every kind of industry in motion, and make the inexhaustible raw materials of the country valuable."[62]

Several newspapers supporting the tariff complained that sectional desires were winning out over the interests of the nation at large. One editor accused the merchants who opposed the tariff of being "tools of designing Virginia politicians, who dread nothing else so much as the growth and prosperity of New-England."[63] The tariff was necessary because "Commerce, Agriculture and Manufactures, are mutually dependent, and . . . the policy which goes to depress either of these important branches of industry, must, in the end, be equally inimical to all."[64] The government must act in the interests of the entire nation: "It is for the interests of the whole, that legislators are bound to vigilance; and he who, disregarding this great truth acts upon sectional or partial views, and sacrifices or foregoes the good of his country, in conformity to the petty rivalships or jealousies of districts or classes, is unworthy of the name of American."[65] In 1821, the editor of the *Patron of Industry* concluded that "the question of 'protecting' the industry of the country is likely at no distant period to enter into all the judgments of the people in reference to public men, as well as public measures. It will, we have no doubt, become the criterion by which men and measures will be judged."[66]

By the time Jackson became president in 1829, this editor's prediction had come true because the tariff became a major issue that threatened to divide the nation in half. Virginia continued its opposition, led by Thomas Ritchie's *Richmond Enquirer*. He declared in 1831 that "it is impossible that the people of the oppressed sections of the United States *can submit much longer to so oppressive a system. . . .* But we cannot tolerate oppression—a subjection to a system so absurd, so much at war with every principle of our Federal system, the unfettering institutions of a young and a free people, and with the very spirit of the age itself."[67] South Carolina, however, had become the leading opponent. With the passage of a new tariff in 1828, South Carolina, led by Vice-President John C. Calhoun, stated categorically that a state could oppose, or "nullify," a federal law that it thought unconstitutional. Newspapers throughout the country joined in the debate. One South Carolina editor summed up the feelings of many of the Nullifiers when he stated that the Constitution "has been perverted from its legitimate purposes, and made an instrument of legislation, partial, unjust and tyrannical."[68] Jackson generally supported states' rights, but he found the doctrine of nullification too dangerous to the stability of the Union.

Pro-Jackson newspapers joined Ritchie in opposing the actions of South Carolina. Francis P. Blair's *Washington Globe* led this group. Blair denounced nullification as "unconstitutional and revolutionary." Furthermore, the Nullifiers presumed too much by trying to be "the keepers and preservers of the Constitution. The first act they propose is not only the most flagitious violation of the Constitution ever attempted in America, but is, at once, a dissolution of the Gov-

ernment, by a total withdrawal of its revenue."[69] Blair called on all Americans to
stand up and prevent the dissolution of the Union:

Let the whole country rise up as one man and denounce them. Let the whole people out of
the limits of South Carolina, and the true hearts within, form themselves at once into a great
UNION PARTY, and say to them, in a language which they shall understand, THIS UNION
SHALL NOT BE DISSOLVED. Let them resolve, one and all, that while they will make
every concession to remove all just causes of complaint, they will rally round the government in support of the Union which *must be preserved at every hazard.*[70]

President Jackson threatened the use of military force to enforce the laws of the
United States, and the state of South Carolina backed down. But the conflict
helped outline the growing division between the two geographic sections of the
country, a problem that would grow worse in the future. One South Carolina editor summed up the feelings of many Southerners: "[T]he Tariff is only one of the
subjects of complaint. . . . The Internal Improvements, the general bribery system,
and the interference with our domestic policy—most particularly the latter—are
things which . . . will, if necessary be met with more than words."[71]

The controversy over the Bank of the United States grew out of the presidential
election of 1832. The bank's charter expired in 1836, and some people expressed
concern that President Jackson would oppose renewal because he did not trust
large commercial banks. Senator Henry Clay and Nicholas Biddle, president of
the bank, sought renewal of the charter in 1832 in an attempt either to force Jackson to agree or to provide a good campaign issue for the upcoming election. The
recharter bill passed Congress in July 1832. Jackson promptly vetoed it, describing the bank as a dangerous monopoly, which should be eliminated.

The press immediately got involved in this conflict. Approximately two-thirds
of the newspapers published in the country supported the bank.[72] They quickly attacked Jackson for his actions, which, according to the editor of the Cincinnati
Daily Advertiser, went against the will of the people by abrogating the actions of
"two houses of Congress, the Supreme Court and the Constitution of the United
States."[73] Gales and Seaton had earlier declared that the bank had been important
in "giving internal commerce, exchange and intercourse their present unequalled
facilities."[74] They warned that the disappearance of the bank would result in "universal ruin and widespread desolation over the face of our smiling land" as the
people "face depreciation in the value of every species of property, devouring
usury, ruinous sacrifices, bankruptcy, overwhelming gloom and deep dismay."[75]
Gales and Seaton concluded that the "Constitution is gone! It is a dead letter, and
the will of a DICTATOR is the Supreme Law!"[76] They urged the American people
to save their nation by not reelecting Andrew Jackson as president because, "during the short period that he has been in power, he has put his veto upon more laws
than all the other presidents, since the adoption of the constitution—laws, too,
some of them, which had passed both branches of the national legislature by
strong majorities."[77]

Pro-Jackson editors responded with attacks on the various newspapers that supported the bank, accusing them of misleading the public and of giving in to bribery. Nicholas Biddle gave numerous contributions and loans to various newspaper outlets, actions that produced criticism, even from his allies. Records indicate that between late 1829 and 1832, Biddle spent approximately $50,000 to disseminate pro-bank materials. He paid for the publication of speeches from Henry Clay and other leading politicians who opposed Jackson and supported the recharter of the bank.[78] Biddle justified his actions as appropriate business behavior: "If a grocer wishes to apprize the public that he had a fresh supply of figs, the printer whom he employed, for that purpose, never thinks of giving his labor for nothing, but charges him for his trouble in inserting the advertisement. If the Bank, in like manner, wishes a printer to insert information about its concerns, why should it not pay him for his trouble?"[79] Such activities only increased the criticism heaped on Biddle and his allies by Jackson and his supporters. Even the *Saturday Evening Post*, technically a nonpolitical family publication, received criticism from Francis P. Blair for trying to send "its stealthy political influence into the bosom of such 'families' as avoided the contests of politics."[80]

Blair, as Jackson's leading newspaper editor, led the attack against the bank. He argued that the bank was un-American because it favored a small group of wealthy men and that it had too much power over the economy. Being from Kentucky, Blair aimed most of his ire at problems that he saw the bank creating for the western states: "The history of the operations of the Bank of the United States in the West, proves one great and prominent fact. . . . If a human heart could be committed to the group of the Board of Directors at Philadelphia, it could not have a more absolute control over the circulation of the blood in the body, than they have over the currency of the West." As a result, "its market, therefore, may be said to be entirely subject to the power of the merchants who manage the Bank at Philadelphia."[81]

But Blair and Jackson broadened the attack on the bank into a much larger battle, a fight against special privilege in a society based on egalitarian ideals. "The Jackson cause is the cause of democracy and the people, against a corrupt and abandoned aristocracy."[82] Such ideas proved popular among the American people, and Jackson easily won reelection in 1832. Once more, Jackson's use of the press had helped him win an important political battle.

More than any president prior to him, and more than most of his successors until well into the twentieth century, Jackson depended extensively on the press and its producers to fight his political battles. While in office, he personally subscribed to twenty newspapers.[83] Throughout his eight years in Washington, he had a local newspaper serve as his official news organ, first Duff Green's *Telegraph* and then Francis Blair's *Globe*. Jackson's personal correspondence shows clearly his use of the press to publicize his intentions and ideas. On several occasions, he told friends and colleagues that "the *Globe* of tomorrow will inform you" or "the *Globe* of tomorrow will give my views on. . . ."[84] The election of 1832 probably witnessed the height of the *Globe*'s influence. During that contest, the *Globe* became a major producer of campaign propaganda as Blair produced thirty issues of the *Globe Extra* in the final six months prior to the election. These publications were designed "to throw this paper into every neighborhood of the United States," and they were sent "into every town where a Jackson man can be found to distribute them." Even government officials and congressmen were enlisted to help with the distribution. That these publications proved effective is best shown by the massive amount of criticism that they received from Jackson's opponents.[85]

Jackson also involved journalists in public office more than ever before. He gave fifty-seven journalists jobs in the federal government.[86] Even some of Jackson's supporters criticized these appointments,[87] but he saw no problem with this practice. In 1831, he wrote:

I was never sensible of the justness of the exceptions stated to the employment of Printers in the public service. The press is the Palladium of our liberties. Disfranchise those who conduct it: or what is the same thing make the calling of an editor a qualification for the possession of those rewards which are calculated to enlarge the sphere of talent and merit, and which are accessible to other callings in life, and you necessarily degrade it. . . . I refused to consider the editorial calling as unfit to offer a candidate for office; and accordingly appointed them on a few occasions when they were deemed honest and capable.[88]

Jackson believed in providing offices to those who agreed with him politically and had supported him, and journalists were no exception to this practice.

Finally, not only did Jackson use newspapers to advance the causes he favored and not only did he reward those who supported him with government jobs, but also he turned to journalists for advice concerning a variety of issues. The Jackson administration directly involved newspapermen more than at any other time in American history to date. Duff Green, Amos Kendall, and Francis Blair all wielded influence in the national Democratic Party, and all worked as organizers of campaigns. They also all served at one time or another in Jackson's unofficial group of advisers, which became known as his "kitchen cabinet." Blair, in particular, became very influential, as he came to function almost as a press secretary for President Jackson. Blair's paper, the *Washington Globe*, clearly functioned as the administration paper, and everyone considered the ideas published in its pages as Jackson's own. Blair met with Jackson almost every day and then proceeded to publish the president's ideas on the major issues confronting the administration.[89] Party regulars perceived Blair as an important member of Jackson's support team, and they wrote directly to him to ask for political appointments, jobs, and advice.[90]

Jackson and Blair worked well together, in a manner never duplicated by another president and publisher. Jackson's ability to use the press enabled him to bypass the more traditional political mechanisms and appeal directly to the people for support. In doing so, he made effective use of the press, but he also sowed the seeds of the final dissolution of the partisan press. The growing involvement of the middle and working classes in politics and the growing availability of newspapers and magazines in the wake of industrialization increased the variety of voices being published. Variety often results in fragmentation, and the American press experienced fragmentation in the wake of Andrew Jackson's presidency. Politics remained an important part of the press's role in the nineteenth century, but it played other roles as well. The mass publications that appeared in the 1830s sought to do more than discuss political issues, and that desire eventually helped lead to a distancing of newspapers from the political arena, a distancing that encouraged the more recent idea of the press as "the fourth estate" or watchdog of the government. President Jackson, and most of his political contemporaries, would have found this concept bewildering because they perceived the press as the ally of politicians rather than the opposition.

NOTES

1. Numbers are from S. N. D. North, *History and Present Conditions of the Newspaper and Periodical Press of the United States* (Washington, D.C.: U.S. Government Printing Office, 1884), 47.

2. There are many biographies of Andrew Jackson. He was one of the first presidential candidates to have official campaign biographies [both by his good friend, John Eaton—*The Life of Andrew Jackson* (Cincinnati: Hatch & Nichols, 1827) and *Memoirs of Andrew Jackson* (Boston: C. Ewer, 1828)]. Although containing many apocryphal stories, one of the best discussions of Jackson's life is still James A. Parton, *Life of Andrew Jackson*, 3 vols. (Boston: Houghton Mifflin, 1885 [1861]). The best recent treatment is the three-volume work by Robert V. Remini: *Andrew Jackson and the Course of American Empire, 1767–1821* (New York: Harper & Row, 1977), *Andrew Jackson and the Course of American Freedom, 1822–1832* (New York: Harper & Row, 1981), and *Andrew Jackson and the Course of American Democracy, 1832–1845* (New York: Harper & Row, 1984). Remini also produced a good single-volume biography, *The Life of Andrew Jackson* (New York: Harper & Row, 1988).

3. *National Gazette* (Philadelphia), 16 June 1824.

4. *Aurora* (Philadelphia), 13 April 1824.

5. Ibid., 20 July 1824.

6. *Richmond* (Va.) *Enquirer*, 7 November 1820.

7. James E. Pollard, *The Presidents and the Press* (New York: Macmillan, 1947), 122; Culver H. Smith, *The Press, Politics, and Patronage: The American Government's Use of Newspapers, 1789–1875* (Athens: University of Georgia Press, 1977), 57–58.

8. *Democratic Press* (Philadelphia), 12 February 1825.

9. For a good discussion of the various problems of the candidates from the perspective of a Clay supporter, see *Aurora*, 29 October 1824.

10. *Norristown* (Pa.) *Herald*, 23 April 1823.

11. *Columbian Reporter* (Taunton, Mass.), 3 March 1824.

12. *Aurora*, 8 October 1824; *Norristown Herald*, 24 November 1824; *Democratic Press*, 3 February 1825.

13. *Christian Gazette and Youth's Herald* (Philadelphia), 19 February 1825.

14. *Aurora*, 2 February 1825.

15. *Norristown Herald*, 16 February 1825.

16. *Democratic Press*, 12 February 1825.

17. This cloud seems to have extended to historical consideration of Adams as well, for few scholars have studied Adams's career in any detail, and those who have concentrate on

his diplomatic career prior to becoming president. A recent consideration of Adams's polit-ical thought is Greg Russell's *John Quincy Adams and the Public Virtues of Diplomacy* (Columbia: University of Missouri Press, 1995).

18. John Tebbel and Sarah Miles Watts, *The Press and the Presidency: From George Washington to Ronald Reagan* (New York: Oxford University Press, 1985), 63–73.

19. Ibid., 68.

20. *Aurora*, 16 February 1825.

21. *Independent Chronicle and Boston Patriot*, 11 July 1826.

22. *Aurora and Franklin Gazette*, 10 July 1826.

23. Page Smith, *The Shaping of America*, vol. 3 (New York: McGraw-Hill, 1980), 822–23.

24. *Niles's Weekly Register* (Baltimore, Md.), 15 July 1826.

25. John William Ward has stated that the people of the Jacksonian era turned Andrew Jackson into a symbol of their hopes and dreams for the future. *Andrew Jackson: Symbol for an Age* (New York: Oxford University Press, 1955). This was true for those who sup-ported Jackson and believed that he represented a good change for the nation. For those who disagreed, the Founding Fathers, particularly John Adams and Thomas Jefferson, rep-resented the past and what was being lost. Their deaths on the same day only accentuated these fears and emphasized the differences between these "enlightened patricians" and "Old Hickory" from the frontier of Tennessee. This fear of decline also did not fade quickly. Sixteen years after the deaths of Adams and Jefferson, Charles Dickens, on a tour of the United States, commented on the decline perceived by many: "[Y]ear by year, the memory of the Great Fathers of the Revolution must be outraged more and more in the bad life of their degenerate child." Quoted in John Nerone, *The Culture of the Press in the Early Re-public: Cincinnati, 1793–1848* (New York: Garland, 1989), 18. See also 157–58 for a dis-cussion of the fears of the passing of the Revolutionary generation.

26. *Connecticut Mirror* (Hartford), 14 August 1826.

27. *Aurora*, 16 July 1824.

28. *Norristown Herald*, 27 June 1827.

29. Ibid., 15 August 1827.

30. In *The Press and the Presidency*, Tebbel and Watts concluded the results of the 1824 election indicate that the press really had little impact on the outcome. Neither of the front-runners, Adams and Jackson, had a well-organized newspaper campaign. Adams apparently got a large number of votes because he represented a continuation of the satisfactory poli-cies of President Monroe, while Jackson's personal popularity as a national hero garnered him the largest number of votes. Tebbel and Watts, *The Press and the Presidency*, 62.

31. Primarily because of the dominating personality of Andrew Jackson and because it is still in existence, the Democratic Party has received much more attention than has the Whig Party. Daniel Walker Howe's *The Political Culture of the American Whigs* (Chicago: University of Chicago Press, 1979) tries to adjust this inequality. He concludes that the Whigs became much more than just an anti-Jackson clique and that their ideas became an important part of the American political milieu of ideas.

32. *Natchez* (Miss.) *Gazette*, 1 November 1827.

33. Quoted in Tebbel and Watts, *The Press and the Presidency*, 72.

34. *United States Telegraph* (Washington, D.C.), 24 January 1828.

35. *Democratic Press*, 1 December 1826.

36. *New York American* (New York), 9 November 1827.

37. *Norristown Herald*, 24 October 1827; *Genius of Universal Emancipation* (Balti-more, Md.), 13 September 1828.

38. *Truth's Advocate*, October 1828, quoted in Nerone, *Culture of the Press*, 149.

39. *National Intelligencer* (Washington, D.C.), 4 August 1827.

40. Quoted in Tebbel and Watts, *The Press and the Presidency*, 72. Rachel Jackson died in late December 1828. Jackson always blamed her death on the viciousness of the newspaper attacks on her personal character during the presidential campaign.

41. Jackson to Colonel Richard Keith Call, 14 August 1828, Virginia Historical Society, Richmond, Virginia.

42. "Kendall, Amos," in *Dictionary of American Biography* (New York: Charles Scribner's Sons, 1937), 10:325–26.

43. Gretchen Garst Ewing, "Duff Green, Independent Editor of a Party Press," *Journalism Quarterly* 54 (Winter 1977): 733–39; Fletcher M. Green, "Duff Green, Militant Journalist of the Old School," *American Historical Review* 52 (January 1947): 247–64.

44. William E. Smith, "Francis P. Blair, Pen-Executive of Andrew Jackson," *Mississippi Valley Historical Review* 17 (1931): 543–56; William E. Smith, *The Francis Preston Blair Family in Politics* (New York: Macmillan, 1933), 56–95; Elbert B. Smith, *Francis Preston Blair* (New York: Free Press, 1980), 27–97.

45. Gerald J. Baldasty, "The Press and Politics in the Age of Jackson," *Journalism Monographs* 89 (1984): 11.

46. Charles Henry Ambler, *Thomas Ritchie: A Study in Virginia Politics* (Richmond, Va.: Bell Book & Stationery Co., 1913), 85–154.

47. Baldasty, "The Press and Politics in the Age of Jackson," 12, 14.

48. Quoted in Robert V. Remini, *The Election of Andrew Jackson* (Philadelphia: Lippincott, 1963), 128.

49. William E. Ames, *A History of the National Intelligencer* (Chapel Hill: University of North Carolina Press, 1972), 127–231.

50. David Alan Lincove, "Peter Force," in *Dictionary of Literary Biography*, vol. 30, ed. Clyde N. Wilson (Detroit: Gale Research, 1984), 90.

51. "Bowles, Samuel," in *Dictionary of American Biography* (New York: Charles Scribner's Sons, 1937), 2:513.

52. Glyndon G. Van Deusen, *Thurlow Weed: Wizard of the Lobby* (Boston: Little, Brown, 1947), 53–85.

53. A congressional investigation uncovered evidence of large loans from the Bank of the United States to the *Courier*, but declared that evidence of wrongdoing by the editor was circumstantial. James L. Crouthamel, *James Watson Webb: A Biography* (Middletown, Conn.: Wesleyan University Press, 1969), 39–43.

54. Ibid., 12–66.

55. Remini, *Life of Andrew Jackson*, 173–74, 190–95, 204–205.

56. For example, see *Cherokee Phoenix* (New Echota, Ga.), 24 June, 26 August, 30 September, 30 December 1829, 27 January, 29 May 1830.

57. *Cherokee Phoenix*, 21 October 1829.

58. Ibid., 15 May 1830.

59. The United States adopted its first tariff in 1789, shortly after the inauguration of the new government under the Constitution. However, unlike the measure of 1816, this original tariff served as a revenue measure rather than a protection for industry. When Alexander Hamilton proposed supporting domestic manufacturing, through either a protective tariff or some other mechanism, as part of his financial plan, the Congress soundly defeated the idea.

60. *Manufacturers' & Farmers' Journal, and Providence and Pawtucket Advertiser* (Providence, R.I.), 9 November 1820.

61. *Patron of Industry: Agricultural, Manufacturing, Commercial* (New York), 16 September 1820.

62. Ibid., 23 September 1820.

63. *Manufacturers'& Farmers' Journal*, 4 September 1820.

64. Ibid.

65. Ibid., 25 December 1820.

66. *Patron of Industry*, 10 January 1821.

67. *Richmond Enquirer*, 15 March 1831.

68. *Banner* (Yorkville, S.C.), quoted in *Patriot* (Greensboro, N.C.), 4 December 1830.

69. *Washington* (D.C.) *Globe*, 25 August 1832.

70. Ibid., 29 November 1832.

71. *Winyaw Intelligencer* (Georgetown, S.C.), 12 May 1830.

72. Arthur M. Schlesinger, Jr., *The Age of Jackson* (Boston: Little, Brown, 1945), 92.

73. Quoted in *National Intelligencer*, 6 September 1832.

74. *National Intelligencer*, 12 March 1831.

75. Ibid.

76. Ibid., 6 September 1832.

77. Ibid., 7 August 1832.

78. Ralph C. H. Catterall, "The Bank at Bay," in *Jackson v. Biddle's Bank*, ed. George Rogers Taylor (Lexington, Mass.: D. C. Heath, 1972), 76–85. For a negative contemporary discussion of Biddle's spending on newspaper coverage, see the *Washington Globe*, 4 July 1833.

79. Biddle to J. Hunter, 4 May 1831, Biddle Letterbooks, pp. 514–15, Biddle Papers, Library of Congress, Washington, D.C.

80. *Washington Globe*, 7 November 1833.

81. Ibid., 6 June 1832.

82. Ibid., 5 September 1832.

83. M. L. Stein, *When Presidents Meet the Press* (New York: Julian Messner, 1969), 24.

84. Jackson to Martin Van Buren, 19 and 22 September 1833, *Correspondence of Andrew Jackson*, ed. John Spencer Bassett, 6 vols. (Washington, D.C.: Carnegie Institution of Washington, 1926–1933), 5:203, 205.

85. *Niles's Weekly Register*, 14 March 1832; *Washington Globe*, 10 April 1832.

86. Stein, *When Presidents Meet the Press*, 24.

87. See, for example, the *Richmond Enquirer*, quoted in the *National Journal* (Washington, D.C.), 18 August 1829.

88. Jackson to John Randolph, 11 November 1831, *Correspondence of Andrew Jackson*, ed. Bassett, 4:371–72.

89. Herbert Ershkowitz, "Andrew Jackson: Seventh President and the Press," *Media History Digest* 5 (1985): 15–16.

90. Gerald J. Baldasty, "The Washington, D.C., Political Press in the Age of Jackson," *Journalism History* 10 (Autumn/Winter 1983): 68.

9

Changes in Journalism, 1800–1833

Journalism in the United States experienced a variety of changes during the early decades of the nineteenth century. The most obvious development was the large growth in the number of newspapers being published. In 1800, 234 newspapers were published in the United States; by 1833, that number had grown to 1,200.[1]

Along with the growth in numbers came geographical expansion. Following the end of the Revolution, Americans began to move in greater numbers into the areas west of the Appalachian Mountains. Printers joined this caravan, and many established newspapers wherever they went. In 1786, John Scull produced the first paper printed west of the mountains, the *Pittsburgh Gazette*. The next year John Bradford published the *Kentucky Gazette* in Lexington. By 1800, twenty-one newspapers appeared in towns west of the mountains, and in 1808, the press crossed the Mississippi River as the *Missouri Gazette* appeared in St. Louis. Further growth in western publishing found encouragement from the national government in 1814 with the requirement that all federal laws be published in at least two newspapers in each state and territory. By 1819, areas as far west as Arkansas and Texas had local newspapers. By the time the penny papers first appeared in New York in 1833, newspapers were published throughout the United States and its adjacent territories, providing a means of communication for almost everyone throughout the young Republic.[2]

As was true with every other aspect of life in the United States during the nineteenth century, the Industrial Revolution produced changes in the field of journalism. The most readily visible change appeared in output, as the number of copies per issue expanded as a result of improved presses and other machines related to the printing business that had been developed to satisfy growing demand. Prior to the early 1800s, the printing industry had changed little since the days of Gutenberg. Printing was a slow process that involved thirteen steps just to produce one page. The hourly output of a good two-man crew on such a press was 200 to 250 sheets, or about 2,000 to 2,500 pages during a ten-hour day.[3] Such a production level did not encourage speedy publication of the news.

Attempts to improve the printing press had occurred in the eighteenth century, but had resulted in few major advancements. In the 1820s and 1830s, however, several changes occurred that revolutionized the publishing business. The flatbed press was limited in output because of the necessity of continuously taking the paper in and out of the press. In the 1820s, R. Hoe & Company, printing-press makers in New York, introduced the first cylinder press. Not having to change paper so often speeded up production to 2,000 four-page papers per hour. The *New York Daily Advertiser* became the first newspaper to use the Hoe cylinder press, installing one in 1825. Still, the presses had to be operated completely by hand, the cylinder being turned by a crank. By 1832, Hoe & Company had developed the double cylinder press, which could print both sides of the page at once, and, using previous press models developed in Europe by Friedrich Koenig and David Napier, had applied steam power to the printing press, raising the production level to 4,000 copies an hour.[4]

Other changes occurred as part of industrialization that helped mechanize publishing. Stereotype printing, which is the casting of a mold from pages composed of moveable type, developed in New York after 1810.[5] This method made it easier for publishers to do mass productions without having to leave type standing for long periods of time. Another important development was the use of machinery to speed up the papermaking process. Prior to 1817, all paper in America was made by hand. However, in that year, Thomas Gilpin of Delaware introduced the first papermaking machine. Over the next decade, machine-made paper became common in all areas of publishing in the United States.[6]

Such mechanical improvements eventually would help increase newspaper circulation and produce the penny press of the 1830s–1840s. But even before the printing press improvements came, the development of the United States in other ways encouraged newspaper expansion throughout the country. Physical growth sparked increases in the number of news sheets because the spread of population into new territory encouraged the establishment of new newspapers and the expanded circulation of well-established publications. Although the most famous, the Erie Canal was not the only transportation improvement built during this era. Canals, roads, and river improvements appeared throughout the country, making access to previously isolated areas easier. Improved methods of transportation helped broaden and interweave the American economy into a market economy that increasingly intertwined. Interdependence produced a need to know about the other ends of the economic trail, and newspapers provided the necessary information. This material also reached people more quickly, since transportation improvements shortened the time necessary to spread news throughout the United States from several weeks to a matter of days. By 1830, news could travel from New York to Washington, D.C., in thirty-six hours, and in 1832, the *Journal of Commerce* rejoiced that its special twenty-four-hour delivery system could get a story from the White House to its New York City office in twenty hours.[7] Physical expansion made the world seem larger, but such transportation and communication developments made it seem much smaller.

The growth of reading also encouraged the expansion of the press. The British colonies in North America had always been one of the more literate societies in the world, with the Puritan colonies in New England leading the way. Estimates vary, depending on what material the measure of literacy is based on,[8] but most figures indicate that over half of the adult white men could read in the early 1700s. By 1800, literacy was widespread, reaching over 90 percent in New England. Also by 1800, the gap between male and female literacy had almost disappeared.[9]

Such high literacy rates encouraged reading by the large majority of Americans. During the first half of the nineteenth century, reading became "a necessity of life," no matter one's profession or one's address. Americans became increasingly aware of the larger world, and printed materials provided the easiest avenue for gaining additional information about that world. And newspaper readership went far beyond subscriptions because many people (possibly as many as twenty) read most individual copies of a newspaper.[10]

Although knowledge of the world came through a variety of printed channels, the newspaper, with its sense of immediacy, became an increasingly important source as it became more readily available. As Alden Spooner stated in the masthead of the *Vermont Journal*: "From realms far distant and from Climes unknown, we make the Knowledge of Mankind your own." More and more people clearly agreed with this idea, and by 1830, over half of all families in the United States subscribed to a newspaper.[11]

The *Salem Literary & Commercial Observer* commented on the growth of newspapers during the country's early history: "There were but seven papers in the United States in 1730, in 1810 there were 359, (including 25 published daily) which circulated 20,200,000 copies in the year. In 1823 they had increased to 578, and at present they are about 640. The number of copies circulated in the year by these journals, exceeds 30 millions." In comparison, "in the British Isles in 1821, with twenty millions of people, the number of newspapers was estimated to be 234, and the copies printed 28 millions" and "the whole of continental Europe, containing 110 millions of inhabitants, where the press is chained down by royal and priestly jealousy, certainly does not support half the number of journals which exist in the U. States."[12] Records from the 1800s indicate that not only was the number of newspapers published growing, but also the circulation of individual papers increased. During the eighteenth century, the average subscription list of a profitable paper was 500. By the 1820s, most successful papers issued in runs of 1,500–2,000 and circulated through the mails far beyond the town or city of publication.[13]

Ideas about politics also influenced the growth of literacy and reading in the United States. The Revolution produced a strong belief that a literate population was essential if a republican government was to survive. Mass literacy became the mechanism for creating good productive citizens.[14] By 1825, Daniel Webster praised the growth of literacy as the creation of a "community of opinions and knowledge amongst men in different nations existing in a degree heretofore unknown."[15]

Also by this time, the nation had moved toward democracy and equal participation by all men in government through the vote, a development that many believed only increased the need for knowledge, particularly information about ongoing political questions. Newspapers provided ready access to such information, and, thus, people should read them as often as possible. Editors, supporting such encouragements and slowly beginning to realize the potential market these statements represented, sought to democratize their publications through the elimination of all forms of social division, such as elitist essays and the use of educated language. Even the national government encouraged the reading of newspapers by setting postal rates low enough to encourage broader circulation and by allowing free exchanges of newspapers between publishers to help spread the news.[16]

Comments by foreign visitors indicated that Americans took the advice to read seriously. In 1828, Karl Anton Postl[17] declared that Americans took an avid interest in their government, an interest "which would in some countries be deemed arrogance, in others a crime [yet it] is with him a point of duty. . . . The newspapers, therefore comprehend the whole life, public and private, of the Union."[18] In 1832, Frances Trollope[19] referred to "the universal reading of newspapers."[20] Alexis de Tocqueville, one of the most observant of foreigners to visit the United States in the early nineteenth century, also commented on the impact and importance of newspapers. First, such publications were useful, since "nothing but a newspaper can drop the same thought into a thousand minds at the same moment . . . without distracting you from your private affairs." And "in America there is scarcely a hamlet that has not its newspaper." In some ways, the large numbers diluted the impact of the press, but Tocqueville ultimately concluded that the influence of the press in the United States was "immense":

It causes political life to circulate through all the parts of that vast territory. Its eye is constantly open to detect the secret springs of political designs and to summon the leaders of all parties in turn to the bar of public opinion. It rallies the interests of the community round certain principles and draws up the creed of every party; for it affords a means of intercourse between those who hear and address each other without ever coming into immediate contact. When many organs of the press adopt the same line of conduct, their influence in the long run becomes irresistible, and public opinion, perpetually assailed from the same side, eventually yields to the attack. In the United States each separate journal exercises but little authority; but the power of the periodical press is second only to that of the people.

Furthermore, newspapers "become more necessary in proportion as men become more equal and individualism more to be feared. To suppose that they only serve to protect freedom would be to diminish their importance: they maintain civilization."[21]

The increase in the numbers of voters, as well as the expansion of the press and its readership, encouraged the growth of political groups and helped foster the development of the first third party in American history. Centered in upstate New York, the anti-Masonry movement began in 1826 and continued as a force in New York, New England, Pennsylvania, and Ohio until the mid-1830s. The death of William Morgan, a man who threatened to publish details about the practices of the Freemasons, sparked the movement. Newspapers provided the impetus for the anti-Masonic Party, as they reached to an ever-increasing number of potential readers in the growing electorate.

In an age of growing democracy, Freemasonry proved a ready target because it seemed an elitist organization that encouraged aristocratic ideas.[22] Many who hoped to undermine aristocratic control in the United States, particularly in New York, used the press to publicize their ideas. Between the time of Morgan's death and the 1832 presidential election, seventy anti-Masonic papers appeared, primarily in western New York. Thurlow Weed, editor of the *Rochester Telegraph*, led the many people who became involved in this movement. In 1830, he moved to Albany to run the *Evening Journal*, the leading anti-Masonic newspaper.[23]

Weed immediately went on the attack, urging all citizens to vote Freemasons out of office whenever they had the chance. He declared that the "aims of the Masonic institution . . . will soon be unfolded, and found to be utterly inconsistent with private rights, and fraught with manifold dangers to the public welfare." He called on all Freemasons to give up their special position: "[I]ts opponents, having clearly proved it to be *dangerous,* call upon its thousand virtuous members to renounce it and place themselves upon an equality with their fellow-citizens."[24]

That year, 1830, the anti-Masonic Party almost won the governorship of New York. After that, it slowly faded into obscurity, and most of the leading members gravitated into the Whig Party and became strong opponents of Andrew Jackson. Ultimately, the anti-Masonry movement failed, but it showed the potential for a newspaper-driven campaign and for a single-issue party. Most third parties in American history have followed the pattern established in the late 1820s, relying heavily on the press and concentrating primarily on one issue to provide focus for group activities and efforts.

Growth and expansion encouraged competition and forced many publishers to seek out ways to maintain and attract customers. Continued success often called for money not easily available. For example, the editor of the *Norristown Herald*, competing with the Philadelphia press, sought further support through the expansion of his printing office and the purchase of a second press. His efforts, however, almost failed because of his inability to collect past-due subscriptions in order to have the cash for the changes he wanted to undertake.[25] The problems of this editor indicated that some concerns had not changed for newspaper producers from the 1700s to the 1800s. Collection of subscriptions continued to be a big problem.

Prior to the 1830s, most newspapers could be purchased only through a subscription, generally for a year. Such a policy limited access somewhat to newspapers, but sought to ensure a set amount of income for the publishers. But the many pleas for payment and the increasing threats of lawsuits in the pages of the early nineteenth-century press[26] showed that this problem, at least, had changed little since the days of John Campbell's *Boston News-Letter*. William Duane complained that "a man who devotes himself to conduct a daily paper with any industry or capacity, and with fidelity to the public interests, ought not to be forced into the humiliating condition of a pauper begging alms, when he is only, in fact, requiring the compensation of an important, and when faithfully performed, an honorable public service."[27] Many editors believed that Duane sold the *Aurora* in 1822 because of unpaid subscriptions amounting to nearly $80,000.[28]

In 1825, the editor of the *Norristown Herald* summed up the feelings of many of his colleagues when they considered their situation: "Perhaps it may not be amiss to remember the Printer in many discourses. He is in a very difficult and disagreeable situation. He trusts every body, he knows not whom: his money is scattered every where, he hardly knows where to look for it. His paper, his ink, his presses and his types, his labor and his living, all must punctually be paid for." At the same time, "you, and your wives and your children and your neighbors have been amused and informed, and I hope improved by it." But "have you ever complied with the conditions of subscription? Have you taken as much pains to furnish the printer with his money as he has to furnish you with your paper? Have you contributed your might [*sic*] to repay him for his ink, his paper, his types, his presses, his handwork and headwork?—If you have not, go pay him off, 'and sin no more.'"[29] Mechanical improvements brought the potential of increased circulations, but could not force people to pay their debts. Financial problems because of unpaid subscriptions continued to face many newspaper publishers throughout this period.

Other problems common during the 1700s continued to exist during the nineteenth century. The weather, as always, played havoc with access to news. Most news still came through the exchange system developed during the colonial period, and bad weather often cut this outlet off, sometimes for weeks at a time.[30] In 1792, Congress had adopted the Post Office Act, which provided for the free mailing of newspapers between publishers. For many small papers, particularly in the western part of the country, such access provided a major source of information and enabled them to produce a more comprehensive coverage of national and foreign news for their customers.[31]

But the growth of newspaper publishing even produced problems in this area. As the number of papers printed grew, many publishers felt overwhelmed by the number of exchanges that they received. This proved particularly true for the large-city daily papers, which received little of direct use from the rural papers who sought to participate in the exchange system. William Duane emphasized this problem when he dealt with the problem of exchanging newspapers. At first, he insisted that the rural papers pay the difference in subscription prices between their publication and the *Aurora*, even though, "from the great majority of those papers, no manner of editorial advantage had been derived."[32] Finally, he decided to reduce the number of exchanges for the *Aurora*, stating that the number had grown so much "without yielding any sort of advantage in return, that we are under the necessity of limiting our exchanges to those papers which contribute, by their freedom of discussion, their talent, or their ability to the public benefit."[33] As indicated by Duane's earlier remarks, trying to ascertain the differences in costs between dailies and weeklies created headaches for many editors. John Carter, editor of the *Providence Gazette*, recognized this problem and sought to address it in desiring to receive the *Port Folio*: "I am well aware that mine is not an Equivalent for yours, be pleased therefore to forward as many as you may judge to be equal."[34] The growing problems with the exchange system would help encourage the development of new methods of news gathering in the future.

Along with the changes in production methods, the early 1800s witnessed developments in the structure of printing offices. As newspaper ventures grew larger, the staff became more complicated. The Industrial Revolution intensified class divisions in the United States, as owners and workers became distinct groups that did not generally labor together under the same circumstances, as had been true during the preindustrial age. The publishing field experienced similar developments during the early 1800s. During the 1700s, a printer and one or two journeymen or apprentices produced most newspapers. By the early 1800s, most newspaper offices contained an editor, a master printer, and several journeymen and apprentices, and the divisions among these various groups became more defined. The appearance of labor disagreements and strikes exemplified the hardening of such class lines.[35] In 1810, the journeymen printers of Philadelphia struck for higher wages. The newspapers carried little about the actual strike, but announcements of meetings of the "Master Printers of the City of Philadelphia" indicated a desire to deal with the problem and an awareness of differences between the two groups of printers. This labor issue crossed political lines, since, of the three publications that paid the most attention to the strike, one paper was Republican and the other two were Federalist.[36] The journeymen hoped to standardize wages, but failed in their attempt.[37]

Newspaper content also changed during the early 1800s in a variety of ways. The first change to occur came as a result of the changes in the makeup of the newspaper staff. During the colonial era, much of the material for a newspaper came from other papers, or someone in the community wrote it for publication. Beginning during the 1780s, comments from newspaper operators became more common. By the 1790s, editors became commonplace as the newspaper business became more complicated and as the national political situation encouraged comments from the press. Increasingly, the editor was recognized as the person who directed the content of the paper. As ably stated in the *Balance and State Journal*: "An editor is, and ought to be, alone responsible for the contents of his paper. His own opinion, therefore, ought always to be the guide of his conduct. He may take advice; but should never submit to dictation. He may make 'the public good his aim;' but 'the public will' should never be 'his guide.'"[38] Although not adopted by everyone, this attitude clearly indicated that the neutral printer of the colonial era had faded away.

The appearance of editors resulted in the development of clear-cut editorials. Eighteenth-century editorial comments generally appeared in long essays, but the 1780s saw the development of brief comments related to specific issues. By 1810, editorials appeared in most papers as separate columns that were clearly written by

the editor of the paper.[39] During the political struggles of the 1820s, many came to
see the influence of such writings on the general populace. The editor of the *Norristown Herald* declared: "Newspapers and literary journals owe a great portion of their
popularity to the merits of their original writings, both from editors and correspondents. The opinion of an Editor has often a greater influence than he is himself probably aware of. His sentiments are always adopted by a majority of his readers."[40]

Along with the further development of the position of editor, the early 1800s also
saw the appearance of the first recognizable correspondents. During the presidencies of Thomas Jefferson and James Madison, partisan newspapers desired to get
accurate coverage of happenings in Washington, D.C. The best information appeared in the Republican *National Intelligencer*. Federalist printers hated to depend
on the Republican press for information, so in 1808 the *United States Gazette* and
the *Freeman's Journal* in Philadelphia employed Federalists to provide reports on
the actions of the national government. The War of 1812 interrupted these reports,
but several newspapers developed the practice anew during the 1820s.[41]

Another major change in content developed with a shifting emphasis on the
types of news covered. Prior to 1800, foreign news had predominated in American
newspapers. Particularly prior to the American Revolution, the colonies, as part of
the British Empire, perceived Europe, particularly Great Britain, as the center of
important events. This attitude changed somewhat after independence, but communication problems slowed down the increasing awareness of happenings in
neighboring states. Growing interest in national politics helped produce growing
interest in domestic news. The trend toward emphasizing American events over
European happenings was obvious by 1810, and the War of 1812 and the fighting
within the boundaries of the United States itself cemented it in place.[42]

Changes in mechanics, office structure, and news emphasis contributed to other
developments in the press of the early nineteenth century. Prior to 1800, most
newspapers had been "miscellanies," conglomerations of a variety of materials with
an emphasis on foreign news and essays. By the 1790s, many people recognized
the important role of the press in the political arena, but the emphasis continued on
traditional news. A Delaware paper emphasized the growing role of newspapers in
American society: "They have become the vehicles of discussion in which the principles of government, the interests of nations, the spirit and tendency of public measures, and the public and private characters of individuals are all arraigned, tried
and decided. . . . They have become immense moral and political engines, closely
connected with the welfare of the state, and deeply involving both its peace and
prosperity."[43] After 1800, however, and particularly after the War of 1812, newspapers increasingly varied their content far beyond the traditional international and
political news to include an extensive variety of new and different topics. One editor, recognizing the growing diversity, described a newspaper as

a bill of fare, containing a variety of dishes, suited to the different tastes and appetites of
those who sit down at the entertainment. Politics are beef steaks, palatable to almost every
one. Those who prefer them rare done, choose those from France. Electioneering is veni-

son. Congress news is stuffed meats. Essays, humorous, speculative, moral, and divine, are a fine boiled dish, where, by a happy commixture in the use of bread, meat, and vegetables, a diet is obtained, nutritive, pleasant, and healthy. Ship news is a glass of grog at eleven. Poetry is custard. Marriages are sweet meats. Ballads and love ditties, plum pudding. Anecdotes, conundrums, and epigrams are spice and mustard. Sometimes here comes along a printer's dun—that is sour crust or cranberry tart.[44]

Another editor declared that newspapers provided the best means of communicating information to the most people because, "from their uncommon cheapness, their pages are made accessible to every individual, however humble and indigent: thousands of worthy freeman are consequently instructed and benefitted by this means, who would otherwise be doomed to a life of perpetual ignorance."[45]

More and more editors, such as the publisher of the *Rural Visiter*, hoped to avoid the political entanglements that had characterized the press of the 1790s by operating "independent of the passions or the patronage of a party." Rather, "notwithstanding the temper of the times, and the 'habit' of the press in this particular, the editor cannot but hope a more favourable result from his attempt to cultivate 'another taste', by making *The Rural Visiter* a vehicle of useful and agreeable information to country people."[46] Although publishers were not always successful in avoiding politics, the partisan emphasis of the entirety of the press started to decline during this era. Although revived during the years of Andrew Jackson's presidency, the partisan press that had dominated during the 1790s and early 1800s had passed its zenith and slowly faded from the journalistic scene.

Growing diversity in content resulted in the consideration of new subjects by the press. Increasingly, moral and social issues became objects of discussion in the newspapers. The appearance of the revival movement known as the Second Great Awakening helped produce this development. Sparking increased religious activity throughout the nation, the revival received considerable attention in the press. Many sought to further their spiritual efforts through the use of newspapers, a source of information that Americans already turned to in large numbers.[47] In 1825, David Roper, in proposing a new religious newspaper in Richmond, stated that "the press is now generally admitted to be one of the most efficient instruments of supporting any cause to which it may be enlisted. . . . A thirst for newspaper reading prevails among all ranks of society throughout our country, and therefore opens an easy medium of access to many whose reading is almost exclusively confined to these fugitive productions."[48]

Most of the religious newspapers that appeared between 1800 and 1830 seemed to differ little from those produced by the secular press, at least on the surface. They mixed religious and secular material together. The earliest religious newspapers were generally nonsectarian because most editors realized that the needed audience would not be found in only one denomination. The first religious paper published in the United States was the *Herald of Gospel Liberty*, established in Portsmouth, New Hampshire, in 1808 by Elias Smith, a Baptist minister.[49] Seven years later, John W. Scott established the ecumenical *Religious Remembrancer* in

Philadelphia. By the 1830s, however, religious newspapers had become common enough in the United States to be produced by both numerous denominations and individuals.[50] In 1823, New York's *Methodist Magazine* declared that "a religious newspaper would have been a phenomenon not many years since, but now the groaning press throws them out in almost every direction."[51] David Benedict declared that in 1800 no one seriously considered the publication of a religious newspaper, but by 1830 the press had become the major mechanism for uniting believers and spreading the message around the country.[52] Publications, particularly newspapers, expanded because "the power of the printed word [served] to reinforce the spoken word and to extend the message beyond the local audience."[53]

The editors of these religious newspapers had seldom trained for the business of journalism. Almost all of them were clergymen who perceived a newspaper as a useful tool for carrying on their work of reaching out to people and improving society. When he founded the *Georgia Analytical Repository* in Savannah in 1802, Henry Holcombe hoped to help fight crime and sin by providing moral support to those fighting against them. Because of this desire, these editors were dedicated to their newspapers, but they also often found their publication a daunting task. Not only were they unfamiliar with the mechanics of the business, but also many found it difficult to remain solvent. Many proprietors poured all their money into their publications in hopes of stabilizing them economically. However, this goal generally proved elusive. Prior to the 1840s, religious journals seldom were truly successful. One exception to this trend was the *Christian Journal and Advocate*, published in New York, which circulated to 26,000 homes in 1826.[54]

As noted above, many religious newspapers seemed little different from the ones put out by the secular press. Much of the content came from other journals, which the editor received as exchanges. However, several distinctions become obvious upon a closer examination. One variation related to money. Most of the religious publications used their profits to support some sort of religious work. For example, the *Religious Remembrancer* supported missionary work, while the *Christian Gazette and Youth's Herald* provided aid to men in training for the gospel ministry.[55]

Another variance between the religious and the secular presses related to content and issues of importance to the editors. One editor stated that his paper would "embrace every subject relative to the Redeemer's Kingdom."[56] For most editors, the list of relevant subjects was a long one. Religious newspapers sought to advertise and support the work of tract and Bible societies and Sabbath schools, as well as less clearly religious reform efforts such as helping orphans, establishing an institution for the deaf, and furthering the work of the American Colonization Society.[57] For example, in 1826, the New York *Religious Chronicle* praised the work of several Christian benevolent societies, which "aim at nothing more or less than the greatest good of our country. . . . With what gratitude then should every Christian and every patriot regard these noble institutions which work together in diffusing the light of the gospel. . . . This is not the benevolence which exhausts itself in sighs and tears and sentiments. . . . But it is the benevolence of action."[58]

The early efforts to promote world peace received praise from John W. Scott: "If there be any meaning in the song of the celestial messengers who announced the advent of Christ, doubtless a field is open for cultivation by such institutions extensive as that occupied by 'Bible societies'; and HE who has blessed the exertions of these benevolent agents, has also said, 'Blessed are the peace-makers, for they shall be called the children of God.' "[59] Social ills also produced concern. The editor of the *Christian Gazette and Youth's Herald* bemoaned the appearance of "symptoms of moral desolation" in New York City because 300 families in the Tenth Ward did not have Bibles in their homes[60] and expressed concern that people would "mock the Redeemer" by getting drunk on Christmas Day, thus choosing "this season of solemnity for the orgies of debauchery and guilt."[61] For an ever-growing number of religious organizations, newspapers became an increasingly important part of their outreach and efforts to produce change and reform in the United States.

The topic of slavery became a major issue that grew out of political controversy, but evolved into much more. The widespread existence of slavery in the South and not in the North had been a problem since the days of the Revolution, but major conflict had been avoided. This situation changed in the years following the War of 1812, and the issue soon divided the nation and transcended traditional political boundaries and identities. For example, the debate over the admission of Missouri as a slave state during 1819–1820 produced agreement between the Federalist and the Republican papers of Philadelphia. The editor of the *American Daily Advertiser* stated that the Missouri decision would clearly reflect "the character of this country" because "if, in the face of the very nature of a free government, the door should be opened for the spreading of this evil, it would be difficult to avoid the conclusion, that the profession and practice of this country are pointedly at variance."[62] William Duane basically agreed, declaring that "on the foundation of independence, the country found itself burdened with an evil, which admitted of no immediate, adequate, and safe remedy." By 1820, however, the time had come to end slavery "as contrary to the laws of God and man."[63]

Throughout the early 1800s, an ever-growing number of people saw slavery as a blight on the United States that had to be eliminated. The editor of the *Columbian Reporter* declared that "slavery has been, and ever will continue to be the curse of every land in which it has been tolerated. Exempting as it does the white population from labor, enterprise of every species is palsied, and even the labor of learning requires too great a sacrifice of ease and of habits of idleness. It blights, indeed, every thing which falls within the pale of its influence—is a pestilence whose bane no precaution or providence can avoid."[64] He could not accept the contradiction between the United States as the land of liberty and the existence of slavery, and he asked "[W]ho is there, who knows the sweets of liberty, and is willing to adopt the rule of our Saviour, and do to others as he would have others do to him, who would not gladly abolish slavery."[65] Also growing was the number of Christians who saw slavery as a national sin. The *Religious Remembrancer* declared: "Christians, ought not something to be done? Christians, 'by the mercies of God, I beseech you,' awake, and from your guilty country, wipe off the stain of slavery,—avert the wrath of God. Christians, by all that is sacred, by all that is dear—by all that is dreadful—I conjure you, purge your nation."[66] For all of these people, the press provided a mechanism for expressing their concerns and communicating their ideas to a wider audience.

Most opponents of slavery prior to the 1830s used the pages of regular newspapers to express their ideas. However, the growing American population and press diversification encouraged specialized publications and antislavery advocates took early advantage of this development. Beginning in 1821, Benjamin Lundy published the *Genius of Universal Emancipation* from a variety of locations. Finally settling in Baltimore, Lundy used his paper to advocate the end of slavery by implementing the plans of the American Colonization Society. Lundy became an early example of a one-issue campaigner for, to him, nothing else mattered but the issue of slavery.[67] In the election of 1828, Lundy opposed Andrew Jackson because he owned slaves: "His private practice, connected with his local situation, uncontradicted by any of his public conduct, leaves sufficient evidence to authorize a very 'strong presumption' that he would 'not' exert his influence very powerfully in wiping off this foul stain from our annals!"[68] Lundy represented a new breed of newspaper editor that would become more and more common as the nineteenth century progressed—one who used his or her press to work for a single reform cause designed to improve life in the United States.

Along with the antislavery press appeared the first newspaper published for the free black community in the North. *Freedom's Journal*, published in New York by John B. Russwurm, the first black college graduate in the United States, and Samuel Cornish, a minister, appealed primarily to African-American readers. However, it also sought to help white Americans better understand their black neighbors.[69] Russwurm and Cornish declared: "We wish to plead our own cause. Too long have others spoken for us. Too long has the publick been deceived by misrepresentations, in things which concern us dearly." Furthermore they planned to publish as much about Africa as possible: "[A]s that vast continent becomes daily more known, we trust that many things will come to light, proving that the natives of it are neither so ignorant nor stupid as they have generally been supposed to be."[70] Ultimately, the editors of *Freedom's Journal* aimed to publish anything that concerned African-Americans. Other newspapers later followed the example set by Russwurm and Cornish.

Antislavery advocates formed only one group that sought to use newspapers to further a cause that they strongly supported. In 1828, the Cherokee Nation established the *Cherokee Phoenix* at New Echota, Georgia. The first Native American paper, the contents appeared partly in English and partly in the Cherokee alphabet developed earlier by Sequoyah.[71] This newspaper had two primary goals: to improve the public image of the Cherokee among white Americans and to help fight the growing drive to remove the Native Americans beyond the Mississippi River: "Those therefore, who are engaged for the good of the Indians of every tribe, and who pray that salvation, peace, and the comforts of civilized life may be extended to every Indian fire side on this continent, will consider us as co-workers together in their benevolent labors."[72] The Cherokee failed to improve their public image, and the original editor of the *Phoenix*, Elias Boudinot, came to believe that removal was inevitable.[73] As was true in this case, newspapers can be used to publicize an issue or a cause, but their use does not guarantee success.

The 1820s also witnessed the beginnings of the labor press as the Industrial Revolution produced a true working class in the United States. The first labor newspaper, the *Journeyman Mechanic's Advocate*, appeared in Philadelphia in 1827. It lasted only a year, but indicated a slowly growing awareness among laborers of the need to work together in some manner in order to achieve better conditions in the factories. The next year, the first successful labor paper, the *Mechanic's Free Press*, began publication. In 1829, two new pro-labor papers appeared in New York, the *Working Man's Advocate* and the *Free Enquirer*. All of these publications worked to improve the public image of the working class and to encourage workers to continue to struggle for improvements in work and life in general. It would be after the Civil War before organized labor began to function well, but parts of the press supported such developments fairly early in the nineteenth century.[74]

The growing diversity in content in the American press also helped encourage the stability of different types of publications. A major benefactor from these developments was the magazine. Magazines had been published in the United States since colonial times, but had met with little long-term or widespread success. One problem for magazines was circulation, for they did not enjoy the same privileges in the mails as did newspapers. Prior to the 1790s, postmasters delivered magazines at their whim. In 1792, rates for magazines were set at the same level as that for letters, resulting in an almost prohibitive cost. In 1794, Congress reduced postage rates for magazines, but postmasters had the right to not deliver them if the post rider's mailbag did not have sufficient room. Delivery costs ran so high that anywhere from 20 percent to 40 percent of the subscription price could be eaten up by postage. In 1815, the postmaster general finally decided that magazines created problems with the delivery of the mail and banned all but religious publications from the postal system. Such a ruling encouraged the growth of denominational publications, but most magazines had to develop alternative delivery systems.[75]

Even with such handicaps, magazines increased in number after 1800. Five had existed in 1794, but by 1800, the number had risen to a dozen. By 1810, there were forty, and by 1825, there were over a hundred. And these were the survivors. Somewhere between 500 and 600 had actually been published at one time or another between 1800 and 1825. One of the primary reasons for the growth of magazines was a developing belief in magazines' ability to encourage moral living. Editors of such publications intended both to teach and to entertain. By 1825, magazines formed a fixed part of the reading materials available to Americans, and the era of the penny press also witnessed the rise of the truly mass circulation magazines in the United States.[76]

One of the first truly successful magazines was the *Port Folio*, published in Philadelphia from 1801 to 1827. The *Port Folio*, originally edited by Joseph Dennie, dominated the field until 1825. Originally Federalist in its political orientation, the *Port Folio* was a "miscellany," containing a variety of materials ranging from general essays to poetry to political commentary. The work of its editors constituted the primary reason for the magazine's success in its first decade of publication. Dennie, a Harvard graduate, began his career as a lawyer, but slowly moved into the field of writing. In 1793, he became the editor of the *Farmer's Museum*, a weekly newspaper published in Walpole, New Hampshire. The newspaper gained a good following, primarily because of a series of essays by Dennie entitled "The Lay Preacher." Before it failed because of financial mismanagement, the *Farmer's Museum* gained subscribers in all of the states but Georgia, Kentucky, and Tennessee.[77] For Dennie, writing came naturally, but he did his best work under pressure. Joseph Buckingham, who served an apprenticeship at the *Museum*, declared that Dennie "generally postponed the task until he was called upon for copy. . . . His copy was often given out in small portions, a paragraph or two at a time; sometimes it was written in the printing office, while the compositor was waiting to put it into type. One of the best of his lay sermons was written at the village tavern, in a chamber where he and his friends were amusing themselves with cards."[78]

Following a change of owners of the *Museum* in 1798, Dennie moved to Philadelphia in 1799 to become the private secretary of Timothy Pickering, the secretary of state. During this time, Dennie also served as editor of the *Gazette of the United States*. Dennie had already established himself as an ardent Federalist in his writings while in New Hampshire, and he continued in this vein while writing for the *Gazette*. He verbally attacked several Republican editors and warned that Jefferson's election as president would result in civil war. Following the change of owners at the *Gazette* and the Federalist loss in the election of 1800, Dennie carried out earlier plans to establish his own magazine.

The *Port Folio* first appeared on January 3, 1801. With a subscription rate of $5 a year, reading the *Port Folio* was an expensive proposition. However, it was worth it. Besides the work of Dennie himself, contributors included John Quincy Adams, Charles Brockden Brown, Royall Tyler, Gouverneur Morris, and others. By mid-1801, the list of subscribers had reached 2,000. Dennie continued his "Lay Preacher" essays, and they provided the centerpiece for the publication. Dennie also continued his attacks on Jefferson and the Republicans, charging that democracy was an unsafe system that always produced the downfall of society and government. One attack on democracy in the April 23, 1803, edition of the *Port Folio* resulted in a charge of seditious libel. Officials finally tried Dennie in November 1805, but the jury quickly found him not guilty.

Although Dennie did not hide his political affiliation and continued his criticism of the Republicans, his publication was much more than a partisan diatribe. Increasingly, the magazine became recognized nationwide primarily as a literary outlet, publishing work by some of the best authors in both the United States and Great Britain. Dennie's responsibilities as editor came to consume so much of his time that he wrote less and less for publication. In 1809, the *Port Folio* dropped its political affiliation and soon dropped politics completely from its pages. Dennie died in 1812, and the magazine was never the same again, even though it continued until 1827.[79]

Following the War of 1812, a variety of more specialized magazines began to make their appearance. "Literary miscellanies," which sought to popularize works by American authors, became common, having appeared in the years immediately following the Revolution. For example, Mathew Carey's *American Museum, or Repository of Ancient and Modern Fugitive Pieces* ran from 1787 to 1792. Wishing primarily to preserve materials previously published in other formats, Carey also published original works by various American authors. The *American Museum* was the most widely read magazine of the day and helped encourage the development of American literature in its own right, separate from the influence of Europe. After the demise of the magazine, Carey used the network developed for the publication as the beginnings of a national book distribution system, which further encouraged American authors in their efforts.[80] Encouragement also came through the efforts of Thomas and James Swords of New York, primarily through the pages of their *New-York Magazine; or, Literary Repository* (1790–1797). The Swords brothers used their magazine to republish materials as well as to present original work to their readers.[81]

After 1800, such literary magazines became more common, but not necessarily longer lived. Charles Brockden Brown, generally described as America's first serious novelist, edited four different literary magazines between 1799 and 1809. None lasted longer than three or four years. In Baltimore, Tobias Watkins, a practicing physician, edited the *Portico: A Repository of Science and Literature* (1816–1818), one of the first serious magazines of literary criticism published in the United States. George Pope Morris met with more success than Brown and published the *New-York Mirror* from 1824 to 1842, filling its pages with essays, stories, and poems by various American authors, such as Nathaniel P. Willis and William Cullen Bryant. Joseph Buckingham and his son Edwin edited the *New-England Magazine* beginning in 1831. Although it lasted for only four years, the *New-England Magazine* changed the direction of literary magazines by shifting the emphasis from long review essays to poetry, sketches, and short stories. By the mid-1830s, literary magazines had become a fixture in the American publishing world.[82]

Along with the literary magazines seeking a national audience came more regional publications. In Cincinnati, Timothy Flint founded the *Western Magazine and Review* (soon renamed the *Western Monthly Review*) in 1827 to encourage recognition for western writers. Although encouraging other authors, much of the work that Flint published in the magazine during its three-year existence came from his own writings and stories about life west of the Appalachian Mountains. William Gibbes Hunt set up shop in Lexington, Kentucky, publishing a newspaper as well as two magazines designed to provide outlets for local authors. The South also developed its own publications as sectional tensions increased.[83] In 1828, Hugh Swinton Legaré founded the *Southern Review*, a literary magazine designed to appeal to southern readers and "to offer to our fellow citizens one Journal which they may read without finding themselves the objects of perpetual sarcasm, or of affected commiseration." The first of several important southern antebellum magazines, the *Southern Review* appeared for four years.[84]

More specialized magazines aimed at particular audiences also began to appear. For example, the first truly successful scientific and legal journals began publication during the early 1800s. By 1833, the *American Journal of Science* was firmly established in New Haven, and Boston boasted the *American Jurist and Law Magazine*. Other types of magazines that appeared for the first time during the first decades of the nineteenth century were theatre reviews, comic periodicals, and college publications. Most of these publications did not last much longer than a year, but even the attempt of them indicated the variety of potential readers that magazines could attract.[85]

Publications designed for groups who did not generally read newspapers proved particularly popular. Magazines targeted for women appeared throughout the country. Titles in this group included the *Ladies' Literary Bouquet* (Baltimore); *Western Ladies' Casket* (Connersville, Indiana); *Atkinson's Casket, or Gems of Literature, Wit and Sentiment* (Philadelphia); *Godey's Lady's Book* (Philadelphia), the most successful woman's magazine in the nineteenth century; and the first to truly succeed, Sarah Josepha Hale's *Ladies' Magazine* (Boston).[86]

As had been true for women involved in journalism in the past, Sarah Josepha Hale got involved in writing and publishing following the death of her husband. Left with five children under the age of seven, Hale turned to writing to make a living. She became editor of the *Ladies' Magazine* in 1827. Publisher John L. Blake intended the Boston magazine to be "the first magazine edited by a woman for women." For ten years, Hale used the pages of the magazine to crusade for various women's causes, particularly education.[87] Throughout her journalistic career, Hale campaigned for "granting to females the advantages of a systematic and thorough education."[88] She filled the pages of her magazine with stories, letters, and essays primarily designed to appeal to women readers, but also with the purpose of improving the lives of women in a variety of ways. She believed that women should take seriously their role as the moral guides for society and urged women to work to make better the world they lived in. Hale was not a feminist like Elizabeth Cady Stanton or Susan B. Anthony, but in her own way, she, too, called for recognition of women as important individuals who should be involved in the world outside the home. Hale's efforts continued and became even more successful following her appointment as editor of *Godey's Lady's Book* in 1837, a post she held for the next forty years. Other accomplishments included helping to direct the fund-raising campaign for the construction of the Bunker Hill Monument and leading the effort that culminated in 1863 in Abraham Lincoln's creation of Thanksgiving Day as an annual holiday.[89]

Oftentimes, it was difficult to distinguish between specialized newspapers and specialized magazines. The *Saturday Evening Post*, which became a well-known magazine following the Civil War, considered itself a family newspaper when it first appeared in 1821. The editors of the *Post* apparently stopped considering it a local newspaper only in 1871, when they ceased printing wedding notices and obituaries.[90]

Another area in the early 1800s in which newspapers and magazines apparently crossed over and blended was in agricultural journalism. The first agricultural journal in the United States, the *American Farmer*, appeared as a weekly in Baltimore beginning on April 2, 1819. Created by John Stuart Skinner, the *American Farmer* hoped "to collect information from every source, on every branch of husbandry, thus to enable the reader to study the various systems which experience has proved to be the best under given circumstances."[91] Other agricultural publications did not appear for several years, but the *Farmer* indicated their potential success, for it circulated widely throughout the United States and elsewhere, even being subscribed to by the Marquis de Lafayette.[92]

Skinner edited the *American Farmer* for ten years, but other interests led him to sell the magazine in 1830. At that time, he founded the *American Turf Register and Sporting Magazine*, the first sports periodical published in the United States. Skinner's interest in horses reflected a widespread fascination in the southern states, which dated back well into the colonial era. Skinner had originally included a sports column, the "Sporting Olio," in the *American Farmer*, which had stimulated interest in a variety of sporting activities, particularly those involving horses and hounds. Skinner finally decided the topic deserved its own magazine. A monthly publication, the *American Turf Register and Sporting Magazine* appeared until 1844 and provided, both then and now, important information for breeders of thoroughbred horses. Skinner also used his magazine to encourage proper care of all animals, not just horses, and to develop widespread interest in all sorts of sporting events. He published information about results of races and other contests, pedigrees, engravings, and all sorts of material concerning sports. In many ways, Skinner can be credited as the founder of sports journalism.[93]

Many changes occurred in American journalism during the early 1800s. By 1825, diversity characterized the press, and a host of different types of newspapers and magazines appeared throughout the country. Diversity did not always mean success, but more and more publications proved economically viable and established themselves a stable reading audience. The partisan press common in the 1790s had faded, but was not gone completely. It had experienced a revival during the 1820s and 1830s with the rise to power of Andrew Jackson. However, it was becoming increasingly clear by this time that a publication would survive not through patronage, but rather through the support of loyal readers and advertisers. The changes that characterized much of the penny press after 1833 were basically in place by 1825 and ready for some enterprising person to put them all together.

NOTES

1. Noble E. Cunningham, *The Jeffersonian Republicans in Power: Party Operations, 1801–1809* (Chapel Hill: University of North Carolina Press for the Institute of Early American History and Culture, Williamsburg, Va., 1963), 236; S. N. D. North, *History and Present Conditions of the Newspaper and Periodical Press of the United States* (Washington, D.C.: U.S. Government Printing Office, 1884), 47.

2. Bernard A. Weisberger, *The American Newspaperman* (Chicago: University of Chicago Press, 1961), 66–68; Robert A. Rutland, *Newsmongers: Journalism in the Life of the Nation, 1690–1972* (New York: Dial Press, 1973), 125.

3. Lawrence C. Wroth, *The Colonial Printer* (Charlottesville: University Press of Virginia, 1964), 79–80.

4. Weisberger, *American Newspaperman*, 73; Alfred McClung Lee, *The Daily Newspaper in America* (New York: Macmillan, 1937), 115–16.

5. "Stereotyping," in *American Dictionary of Printing and Bookmaking* (New York: Howard Lockwood, 1894), 527.

6. David Paul Nord, "The Evangelical Origins of Mass Media in America, 1815–1835," *Journalism Monographs* 88 (May 1984): 7–12. Religious organizations were some of the first to take advantage of these printing improvements in reaching a mass audience with religious tracts. However, newspapers and magazines soon followed, and the industry changed drastically.

7. William J. Gilmore, *Reading Becomes a Necessity of Life: Material and Cultural Life in Rural New England, 1780–1835* (Knoxville: University of Tennessee Press, 1989), 21–22; Richard D. Brown, *Knowledge Is Power: The Diffusion of Information in Early America, 1700–1865* (New York: Oxford University Press, 1989), 218; Rutland, *Newsmongers*, 124. In his study of Yankee farmers and their access to information, Richard Brown concluded that the growth of the economy influenced the desire to know, but was not necessarily the essential element. Knowledge of the outside world was not always needed to function on a day-to-day basis, but many rural farmers sought to know more anyway, for reasons that went beyond just economics. "Information and Insularity: The Experiences of Yankee Farmers, 1711–1830," in Brown, *Knowledge Is Power*, 132–59.

8. In "The History of Literacy in America: An Introduction" (Paper presented at the White House Conference on Library Information Services, Reston, Va., 1–4 April 1979, ERIC, ED 176241, microfiche), Carl F. Kaestle reviewed several studies on literacy rates in the late 1700s. Using the capability of men to sign their names to wills, Kenneth Lockridge concluded that 90 percent of the men in New England and 68 percent of the men in Virginia and Pennsylvania were literate. Lee Soltow and Edward Stevens used army enlistment signatures, resulting in rates of 75 percent in New England and 50 to 60 percent in the South. Lawrence Cremin studied four cities (New York, Philadelphia, Elizabeth City, Va., and Dedham, Mass.) and found rates of 82 to 97 percent for men and 67 to 78 percent for women. Ibid., 6–8. For further information, see Kenneth A. Lockridge, *Literacy in Colonial New England* (New York: Norton, 1974); Lee Soltow and Edward Stevens, *The Rise of Literacy and the Common School in the United States: A Socio-Economic Analysis to 1870* (Chicago: University of Chicago Press, 1981); Lawrence A. Cremin, *American Education: The Colonial Experience* (New York: Harper & Row, 1970).

9. Brown, *Knowledge Is Power*, 11–12.

10. Gilmore, *Reading Becomes a Necessity of Life*, 17–27; John C. Nerone, *The Culture of the Press in the Early Republic: Cincinnati, 1793–1848* (New York: Garland, 1989), 43.

11. Gilmore, *Reading Becomes a Necessity of Life*, 193–94.

12. *Salem* (Mass.) *Literary & Commercial Observer*, 22 July 1826.

13. *Village Record, or Chester and Delaware Federalist* (West Chester, Pa.), 5 January 1820, 3 January 1821; *Saturday Evening Post* (Philadelphia), 27 December 1823, 3 April 1824, 4 December 1824; Letter from E. Jackson of Savannah, Ga., to Joseph Dennie, 28 February 1801, Letters to Joseph Dennie, 1806, ed. Joseph Dennie, *Records of the Port Folio*, 1801–1807, Meredith Papers, *Port Folio* Group, Historical Society of Pennsylvania, Philadelphia; Gilmore, *Reading Becomes a Necessity of Life*, 194.

14. Gilmore, *Reading Becomes a Necessity of Life*, 19, 129, 354–55; Brown, *Knowledge Is Power*, 287–88, 292–93.

15. Daniel Webster, "The Bunker Hill Monument," *The Works of Daniel Webster*, 6 vols. (Boston: Charles C. Little and James Brown, 1851), 1:71.

16. Brown, *Knowledge Is Power*, 287–88; Nathan O. Hatch, "Elias Smith and the Rise of Religious Journalism in the Early Republic," in *Printing and Society in Early America*, ed. William L. Joyce, David D. Hall, Richard D. Brown, and John B. Hench (Worcester, Mass.: American Antiquarian Society, 1983), 260. Hatch points out that both Alfred F. Young and Howard B. Rock have shown the important role of the press in the growing political involvement of artisans and mechanics in the early 1800s. See Alfred F. Young, *The Democratic Republicans of New York* (Chapel Hill: University of North Carolina Press, 1967), and Howard B. Rock, *Artisans of the New Republic: The Tradesmen of New York in the Age of Jefferson* (New York: New York University Press, 1979).

17. Karl Anton Postl was a Moravian-born traveler and novelist who became a citizen of the United States. Writing under the name of Charles Sealsfield, he produced numerous books about his world travels.

18. Charles Sealsfield [Karl Anton Postl], *The United States of North America As They Are* (London: W. Simpkin and R. Marshall, 1828), 113–14, quoted in Rutland, *Newsmongers*, 113.

19. Frances Trollope, a British author, traveled in the United States from 1827 to 1831. Following this trip, she wrote *The Domestic Manners of the Americans* (London: Whittaker, Treacher, and Co., 1832), in which she satirized the American people and criticized American culture because of the inferior social position of American women.

20. Quoted in Nerone, *Culture of the Press*, 10.

21. Alexis de Tocqueville, *Democracy In America* (New York: Alfred A. Knopf, 1946), 1:186–88; 2:111.

22. Anything that seemed to promote elitism proved an easy target for political attacks during the Jacksonian era. Jackson himself would use similar charges to bring down the Bank of the United States during the campaign of 1832.

23. Gerald J. Baldasty, "The New York State Political Press and Antimasonry," *New York History* 64 (July 1983): 267–68, 274.

24. *Evening Journal* (Albany, N.Y.), 22 March 1830.

25. *Norristown* (Pa.) *Herald*, 12 April, 24 May, 21 June 1826.

26. *American Daily Advertiser* (Philadelphia), 1 January 1801; *Norristown Herald*, 9 August 1805, 7 November 1821, 12 January 1825, 10 January 1827; *Village Record, or Chester and Delaware Federalist*, 26 July 1820; *Saturday Evening Post*, 19 November 1825.

27. *Aurora* (Philadelphia), 3 October 1815.

28. *Norristown Herald*, 27 November 1822.

29. Ibid., 15 June 1825. Although the editor uses "might," apparently referring to physical strength, the context indicates a desire for his customers to contribute their "mite" in order to improve his financial status.

30. For example, see the *Baltimore* (Md.) *Weekly Price Current*, 17 February 1810, 1 February 1812; *Relf's Philadelphia Gazette and Daily Advertiser*, 20 January 1812.

31. Newspapers led the fight in western states for improvements in the postal system. Nerone, *Culture of the Press*, 33–35.

32. *Aurora*, 25 June 1805.

33. Ibid., 16 November 1816.

34. Carter to Joseph Dennie, 9 September 1806, Letters to Joseph Dennie, 1806, ed. Joseph Dennie, *Records of the Port Folio*, 1801–1807, Meredith Papers, *Port Folio* Group, Historical Society of Pennsylvania, Philadelphia.

35. For a discussion of this process in Cincinnati, primarily after this period, see Nerone, *Culture of the Press*, 53–55.

36. *Aurora*, 12 September 1810; *True American and Commercial Advertiser* (Philadelphia), 12 September 1810; *Relf's Philadelphia Gazette and Daily Advertiser*, 14 September 1810.

37. Lee, *Daily Newspaper*, 133–37; Proposed Price List, 17 September 1810, Lydia Bailey Waste Book, 1794–1829, Robert and Francis Bailey Records, 1794–1856, Historical Society of Pennsylvania, Philadelphia.

38. *Balance and State Journal* (Albany, N.Y.), 1 January 1811.

39. John Nerone finds this change occurring in Cincinnati a decade later in the 1820s. Nerone, *Culture of the Press*, 69–70.

40. *Norristown Herald*, 13 June 1827.

41. Frederick B. Marbut, "Early Washington Correspondents: Some Neglected Pioneers," *Journalism Quarterly* 25 (1948): 369–74, 400.

42. Donald R. Avery, "The Emerging American Newspaper: Discovering the Home Front," *American Journalism* 1 (1984): 51–66. Professor Avery's careful study of the content of American newspapers prior to the War of 1812 has resulted in several publications discussing the time frame for the change of interest from foreign news to domestic news. His conclusions that the shift came in the years prior to the war have overturned previous assumptions that the War of 1812 had produced the change in focus because it had cut off regular contact with sources of European news. See articles by Avery in *Journalism Quarterly* 63 (1986) and *Studies in Journalism and Mass Communication* 1 (1982).

43. *American Watchman and Delaware Republican* (Wilmington), 22 February 1814.

44. *New-York Mirror, and Ladies' Literary Gazette* (New York), 24 January 1824.

45. *Inquisitor and Cincinnati* (Ohio) *Advertiser*, 23 June 1818.

46. *Rural Visiter* (Burlington, N.J.), 30 July 1810.

47. Henry S. Stroupe, "The Beginnings of Religious Journalism in North Carolina, 1823–1865," *North Carolina Historical Review* 30 (January 1953): 1; Wesley Norton, *Religious Newspapers in the Old Northwest to 1861: A History, Bibliography, and Record of Opinion* (Athens: Ohio University Press, 1977), 1–2; Henry S. Stroupe, *The Religious Press in the South Atlantic States, 1802–1865* (Durham, N.C.: Duke University Press, 1956), 5. The religious press has not received the scholarly attention that it deserves. Henry S. Stroupe and Wesley Norton are two of a small group of historians who began to remedy this problem by cataloging religious publications in particular sections of the country and making some general study of what they found.

48. Prospectus for *Christian Journal* (Richmond), published in *Family Visitor* (Richmond), 8 October 1825.

49. The earliest religious publications in the United States were magazines. First was *Christian History*, founded by Thomas Prince in Boston on March 5, 1743. Several others appeared before 1800, but religious periodicals were rarities until several years into the nineteenth century. Stroupe, *Religious Press*, 3.

50. Stroupe, *Religious Press*, 10–11; Norton, *Religious Newspapers*, 3.

51. *Methodist Magazine* (New York), January 1823.

52. David Benedict, *Fifty Years Among the Baptists* (New York: n. p., 1860), 25.

53. Hatch, "Elias Smith," 271.

54. Norton, *Religious Newspapers*, 6, 15–17, 24–28; Stroupe, *Religious Press*, 3–4; Rutland, *Newsmongers*, 117; Nerone, *Culture of the Press*, 197–98.

55. Norton, *Religious Newspapers*, 33–34.

56. Plan for *Christian Herald*, printed in *Religious Remembrancer* (Philadelphia), 17 February 1816.

57. *Religious Remembrancer*, 13 January, 25 November, 30 December 1815, 17 February, 25 May 1816, 4 January 1817; *Christian Gazette and Youth's Herald* (Philadelphia), 15 May, 31 July 1824; Stroupe, *Religious Press*, 5–7.

58. *Religious Chronicle* (New York), 13 May 1826.

59. *Religious Remembrancer*, 17 February 1816.

60. *Christian Gazette and Youth's Herald*, 20 March 1824.

61. Ibid., 25 December 1824.

62. *American Daily Advertiser*, 24 November 1819.

63. *Aurora*, 23 December 1820.

64. *Columbian Reporter* (Taunton, Mass.), 15 October 1823.

65. Ibid., 2 July 1823.

66. *Religious Remembrancer*, 26 October 1816.

67. John A. Ledingham, "Lundy, Benjamin," in *Biographical Dictionary of American Journalism*, ed. Joseph P. McKerns (Westport, Conn.: Greenwood Press, 1989), 437–38; J. Welfred Holmes, "Some Antislavery Editors at Work: Lundy, Bailey, and Douglass," *CLA Journal* 7 (1963): 48–55.

68. *Genius of Universal Emancipation* (Baltimore, Md.), 24 May 1828.

69. Bernell Tripp, *Origins of the Black Press: New York: 1827–1847* (Northport, Ala.: Vision Press, 1992), 14–15.

70. *Freedom's Journal* (New York), 6 March 1827.

71. Ralph Henry Gabriel, *Elias Boudinot, Cherokee, & His America* (Norman: University of Oklahoma Press, 1941), 106–33; Sam G. Riley, "*The Cherokee Phoenix*: The Short Unhappy Life of the First American Indian Newspaper," *Journalism Quarterly* 53 (Winter 1986): 666–71; Barbara F. Luebke, "Elias Boudinot, Indian Editor: Editorial Columns from the *Cherokee Phoenix*," *Journalism History* 6 (Summer 1979): 48–53.

72. *Cherokee Phoenix* (New Echota, Ga.), 21 February 1828.

73. Ibid., 11 August 1832.

74. Weisberger, *American Newspaperman*, 86.

75. Frank Luther Mott, *A History of American Magazines, 1741–1850* (Cambridge: Belknap Press of Harvard University Press, 1957), 119–20.

76. Ibid., 120–21; Nerone, *Culture of the Press*, 203.

77. Harold Milton Ellis, *Joseph Dennie and His Circle: A Study in American Literature from 1792 to 1812* (Austin: University of Texas, 1915), 84–109.

78. Joseph T. Buckingham, *Specimens of Newspaper Literature* (Boston: Charles C. Little and James Brown, 1850), 2:196–97.

79. Ellis, *Joseph Dennie*, 110–51, 174–215; Mott, *History of American Magazines*, 123, 223–27, 233, 238–39.

80. Earl L. Bradsher, *Mathew Carey: Editor, Author and Publisher* (New York: Columbia University Press, 1912), 8–16.

81. June N. Adamson, "Thomas Swords and James Swords," in *Dictionary of Literary Biography*, vol. 73, *American Magazine Journalists, 1741–1850*, ed. Sam G. Riley (Detroit: Gale Research, 1988), 306–309.

82. Mark J. Schaefermeyer, "Charles Brockden Brown," in ibid., 21–22; James Boylan, "Joseph Tinker Buckingham and Edwin Buckingham," in ibid., 41; Jean Folkerts, "George Pope Morris," in ibid., 221; June N. Adamson, "Tobias Watkins," in ibid., 331–34.

83. Elizabeth M. Fraas, "Timothy Flint," in ibid., 95–98; William E. Huntzicker, "William Gibbes Hunt," in ibid., 184.

84. Quoted in Edward L. Tucker, "Hugh Swington Legaré," in ibid., 218–19.

85. Mott, *History of American Magazines*, 149–52, 154–56, 165–73.

86. *New-York Mirror, and Ladies' Literary Gazette*, 24 January 1824.

87. Ruth E. Finley, *The Lady of Godey's: Sarah Josepha Hale* (Philadelphia: J. B. Lippincott, 1934), 17–40; Isabelle Webb Entrikin, *Sarah Josepha Hale and Godey's Lady's Book* (Lancaster, Pa.: Lancaster Press/Entrikin, 1946), 17–58; Sherbrook Rogers, *Sarah Josepha Hale: A New England Pioneer, 1788–1879* (Grantham, N.H.: Tompson and Rutter, 1985), 28–58.

88. *Ladies' Magazine* (Boston, Mass.), January 1828.

89. Finley, *The Lady of Godey's*, 17–40; Entrikin, *Sarah Josepha Hale and Godey's Lady's Book*, 17–58; Rogers, *Sarah Josepha Hale*, 28–58. Most historians have emphasized that women did not take much interest in politics in the first half of the nineteenth century. Rather, they concentrated their reading efforts on fiction such as novels and short stories. Ronald J. Zboray and Mary Zboray disagree. In a study of antebellum Boston based on personal letters and diaries, the Zborays found middle-class women to be well-informed concerning political events reported in the newspapers. In their correspondence, women discussed a variety of political issues, going far beyond "women's issues" such as benevolence and reform. These discussions reflect a considerable knowledge of both domestic and international political issues, concerns which previous historians have failed to recognize as being of interest to women readers. See Ronald J. Zboray and Mary Zboray, "Political News and Female Readership in Antebellum Boston and Its Region," *Journalism History* 22 (Spring 1996): 2–14.

90. *Saturday Evening Post*, 28 August 1824; Winifred Gregory, ed., *American Newspapers, 1821–1936* (New York: H. W. Wilson Co., 1937), 617.

91. *American Farmer* (Baltimore, Md.), 2 April 1819.

92. Lafayette to John Stuart Skinner, 20 January 1826, John Stuart Skinner Papers, Virginia Historical Society, Richmond.

93. Jack W. Berryman, "John Stuart Skinner," in *Dictionary of Literary Biography*, Vol. 73, ed. Riley, 293–97; *New York Sun* (New York), 3 April 1932.

10

Reflections on the Press of the Young Republic

Between 1783 and 1833, the American press grew and developed from the small operations of the colonial period to the large-scale productions of the penny press era. During this fifty-year period, the American press experienced a series of events that produced developments totally unforeseen by those who had first started newspapers in the British colonies in the early 1700s.

The most obvious changes were physical in nature. During these fifty years, the American population had grown, so some increase in the press was to be expected. However, the growth outstripped the population increase. The growth in literacy provided one obvious reason for such development, but that is not enough. During the early decades of the nineteenth century, reading a newspaper or magazine became an essential part of everyday life for many people. More than ever before, and possibly as much as at any time in United States history, the press sold itself to the American reading public as a necessity of personal existence. The result was a mushrooming in the number of publications.

The growth in numbers is impressive, for in 1783 there were just thirty-five newspapers published in the United States. By 1833, the number had grown to over 1,200. In 1783, the American press primarily hugged the Atlantic coastal areas and consisted primarily of weekly news sheets, "miscellanies" that tried to keep subscribers informed of world events, but also to publish a little bit of everything, such as poetry, essays, and book excerpts. By 1833, the press stretched to the Great Plains, and publication schedules ranged from daily newspapers to monthly magazines. Also by then, content had become more specialized. Most newspapers continued to seek to inform readers of news events, but the emphasis had shifted from foreign to domestic news. Magazines had begun to carry out the role of providing materials primarily designed to entertain and enlighten such as poetry and essays. Magazines had also started specializing in order to attract a par-

ticular audience, such as women or farmers, whereas most newspapers continued
to seek a more broad-based readership. The result was a variety of publications
that seemed almost overwhelming when considered in its entirety.

The growth in the number of publications opened up endless possibilities. Prior
to the Revolution, newspapers provided information about events, primarily in far-
off places. During the Revolution, printers reported the news in particular ways
designed to convince readers to support or oppose the move for independence. But
the press believed it had to appeal to all readers, so printers tried to include a little
bit of everything. Thus, the press of the eighteenth century (excepting the Loyalist
newspapers during the Revolution) spoke with a fairly united voice.

After the Revolution, however, more and more printers became aware that a
publication could survive just as well, and maybe even better, if it appealed to a
more select group of people. As publishers chose to target a particular audience—
women, farmers, African-Americans, etc.—they gave up on presenting a variety of
materials that would appeal to all readers. As a result, publications narrowed their
focus and often ignored important issues that had little to do with their specific
concerns. For example, in the *Genius of Universal Emancipation*, editor Benjamin
Lundy gave little discussion of social and political issues that he believed were un-
related to slavery. Elias Boudinot's *Cherokee Phoenix* discussed politics only as it
related to the fate of the Cherokee Nation. Such specificity of content, while encouraging the growth of the press through diversity, also fostered division and conflict as more and more people argued in print over solutions to various problems.
The perceived unity of the eighteenth-century press was shattered by 1833 because physical growth had produced diversity and variety.

The business of journalism also changed during this era. During the colonial
and Revolutionary eras, most printing shops had been family operations, with possibly one or two extra employees. As the press grew during the years of the early
Republic, diversification occurred. The first specialized job to appear was that of
editor, primarily because of the need for someone to guide the newspaper's public
stands on politics during the partisan conflicts of the 1790s. As the editor became
the recognized controller of content in a newspaper, the person who printed the
paper became an employee who simply produced the final product without really
being involved in its substance. Other specializations took place as the desire grew
for more accurate and personal coverage of news events. By the time of Andrew
Jackson's presidency, reporters and correspondents were becoming fairly common, particularly in Washington, D.C., which was increasingly becoming the center of attention for the nation's press.

The rise of editors reflected another change in the American press. Throughout
this period, many people perceived the press as part of the political process because each newspaper represented a particular point of view. Publications were
supposed to take sides in political conflicts and work to convince people to support their positions or their candidates. In many ways, the press of this period was
more honest and open than the press of today. People expect the press today to be
objective and to editorialize about important issues all at the same time, and they

get upset when the press seems incapable of carrying out this task. The journalists of the late eighteenth and early nineteenth centuries considered such a goal to be impossible, for ultimately the two roles could not be separated. As stated earlier, William Cobbett said it well: Not to take sides in a political controversy was to be "a poor passive fool, and not an editor."[1]

From the perspective of the editors of the period, the press succeeded admirably in its assigned task. Beginning in the 1790s and continuing past the 1830s, many newspapers preached a political cause. Even in the period after 1815 when the Federalist Party disappeared on the national scene, numerous editors continued to support that political group and its ideas at the state and local levels. And the influence of editors increased with the passage of time. During the 1790s, newspaper producers worked for the political parties, providing outlets for the official party lines in their publications. By the 1820s, editors had become personal advisers of national leaders, as in the case of Francis P. Blair and Andrew Jackson.

Such influence, however, did not last. The changes in the political parties from the 1790s to the 1830s contained the seeds of destruction for the partisan press. The Federalists and the Republicans, although different in their emphasis, both stressed republicanism and the idea that the best in society should lead. Even Thomas Jefferson, with his strong desire to involve the common people in government, did not see them in leadership positions. Rather, they should vote and voice their opinion, but the better-educated citizens should hold office.

The Whigs, who appeared in the 1830s, maintained some of the ideas of the Federalists and Republicans, but the Democrats that arose around Andrew Jackson emphasized the idea that all men should have equal access to power and influence. Jackson himself stated that anybody could hold a federal job and that these positions should be spread around to many different people. He supported such "rotation in office" as an example of American democracy, but his opponents accused him of using government jobs to increase his political support. Whatever the reality of the situation, these developments encouraged a growing belief that no person's ideas or advice was better than anyone else's and that wealth and position did not guarantee someone a better place in the political system.

The growing emphasis on democracy undermined the political party press in many ways. As publications became larger and more successful, many people identified editors and publishers as part of the elite. Someone who sat in an office and wrote all day could not possibly understand the life of a farmer in Tennessee or a village blacksmith in Connecticut or even a wage laborer in New York. Even newspaper producers who did not succeed financially were often seen as elitist because they seemed to preach to people in the columns of their papers. Partisan editors continued to be influential and effective for many years to come, as they had been since the 1790s, but their impact slowly diminished as people increasingly saw them either as trying to dictate ideas or policies in inappropriate ways or as not truly understanding the situation because they had little in common with their readers. With the growing diversity of publications, readers could just choose another newspaper or magazine when they became disenchanted with the one they had been reading. That possibility had not existed in the eighteenth century, primarily because most communities did not have a multiplicity of publications and also because the means for delivering newspapers and magazines over a long distance in a short period of time did not exist.

Even with these problems, however, the press of the early years of the United States had an enormous influence, primarily because people turned to printed publications as the only source of information concerning the larger world in which they lived. Local news continued to circulate by word of mouth in many towns, but residents of cities found newspapers essential for knowing what was going on in their community and elsewhere in the country and across the globe. People who lived in rural areas found newspapers and magazines to be their primary contact with the outside world. As a result, newspapers became the place for political discussion. They became the public forum, a domination that lasted well into the twentieth century. As communities grew beyond the point where everyone knew everyone else, newspapers became the place for the debates that had once occurred in town meetings.

Throughout this period, newspapers and magazines discussed all the major political and social issues of the day. During the 1780s, the press provided a place for consideration of the various problems that arose after the victory over Great Britain. The new nation went through some growing pains in those years. With the end of the fighting and the coming of peace in the early 1780s, people began to consider future directions for the United States. Many Americans became quickly convinced that the Articles of Confederation government, created under duress during time of war, could not provide adequate guidance and control for the new country. The final result was a move to replace the Articles government with a new system, eventually embodied in the Constitution. The press played an important part in this development because it was in the pages of weekly newspapers that most Americans read of the troubles of the national government and the need to make some changes. To totally redo the nation's system of governance in less than ten years was nothing short of remarkable, and the newspapers helped push the people in this directon by publicizing the many problems, real and imagined, that necessitated such a change. Although newspapers discussed a variety of concerns, economic issues predominated because the editors feared that the United States faced bankruptcy if the nation failed to solve its financial problems. The Constitution may not be an economic document as stated by historian Charles Beard, but the United States' newspaper printers clearly believed that economic troubles provided a strong reason for scrapping the Articles of Confederation and starting anew with a stronger central government.

The press also provided the forum for the first debates over the meaning of the First Amendment's protection for a free press. During the 1790s, the United States experienced a series of political controversies as leaders sought to organize the new government in a stable manner. The climax of these contests came in 1798 with the passage of the Alien and Sedition Acts. These laws presented a challenge to the nation that threatened the basis for political discussion and forced a serious debate over individual rights. The Alien and Sedition Acts grew out of the conflict with France following the French Revolution and were intended by the Federalists to silence their Republican opponents. Since each group did not trust the other, believing that its members were plotting to undermine the nation, such legislation is not surprising. All of the major Republican newspaper editors faced legal prosecution, either directly or indirectly, because of the Sedition Act. The Federalists had hoped to silence all of them, but they failed. Ultimately, the persecution helped Thomas Jefferson win the presidential election of 1800.

The challenge of the Sedition Act was important because it forced editors and politicians to discuss seriously just what it meant to have a free press. All agreed that there should be no prior restraint of publication, but here agreement ceased. Division over whether one could openly criticize or disagree with the government abounded, with the Federalists denying that one could do so, while the Republicans declared that a representative government could not exist if ideas could not be discussed and debated. Ultimately, the Federalists and Republicans did not settle this argument because the Federalists were voted out of office in the midst of the debate. However, the discussions over the Sedition Act provided the basis for a definition of a free press that allowed wide latitude in discussing and criticizing the actions of government. By the middle of the nineteenth century, such an attitude was commonplace.

The return of war with Great Britain brought up new concerns. The War of 1812 was not a great military success for the United States, but the nation did not ultimately lose. For the press, however, this war differed from the Revolution. There was considerable press criticism of the conflict, particularly in New England. During the Revolution, Loyalist papers had been put out of business or limited to areas under British control. During the War of 1812, opposition newspapers appeared throughout the country. Several newspaper offices were destroyed by mob activity, but President Madison refused to take any official action to silence the press opposition. His lack of action helped to reinforce the idea first put forth during the debate over the Sedition Act, the idea that a newspaper could legitimately disagree with the activities of the national government and not be charged with treason or sedition.

Ultimately, the press of this period gave the young nation a sense of national identity. Prior to 1783, what became the single nation of the United States had been thirteen separate colonies and a "wilderness" of western territory unsettled by people of European background. By 1833, the states were well on the way to identifying the "Union" as a single unit with a common history and a common sense of self. This perception of nationhood found its greatest expression in the newspapers and magazines published during this period. Whether a daily paper in a big city or a monthly magazine meant primarily for farmers, all the publications of this era emphasized the greatness of the United States and the glorious future that lay ahead. Furthermore, the press created a set of heroes for the young nation by praising the various officers and political leaders of the Revolution. Most important among these heroes was George Washington. The newspapers made his name a household word and created around him an aura that bordered on divinity.

Continuing an oral tradition that had begun at Jamestown and Plymouth, the press called on all citizens to remember the successes of the past and to face the future with faith and optimism. The United States had shaken off the shackles of the European past and could now establish its own unique Republic, which would lead the rest of the world to a greater future. The partisan editors, no matter what their party affiliation, all sought this goal in their effort to convince readers that their party knew the right way to achieve this end. The reform editors such as Benjamin Lundy sought to reach this goal by pushing the nation to solve the problem(s) that stood in the way of success. Editors such as Sarah Hale and John Stuart Skinner, while appealing to a focused group of readers, also sought to improve the future of the United States by advancing the efforts of their readers in the context in which they lived. Partisanship was the mainstay of the press in this period, but everyone had the same ultimate ambition of a great nation, and all the editors, whether political in their emphasis or not, helped to create the national sense of self-identity and self-awareness that was needed for the United States to become a stable nation in the world community.

NOTE

1. *Porcupine's Gazette* (Philadelphia), 5 March 1797.

Bibliographical Essay

Almost from the moment the United States came into being, journalism history has been seen as a part of its overall growth and development up until the present day (whenever the present day happened to be). As a result, much of the history of the press has been overlooked or discounted because it seemed not to play an important role in getting journalism and its practitioners to the present. This trend has been particularly true for the party press, for most historians have either downplayed the era because it was so out of step with what true journalism is supposed to be like or failed to look at the big picture, concentrating instead on individuals and specific papers.

It is strange that the party press has not been studied in more depth and detail, for primary sources abound and are readily available. Most of the publications from the era still exist, and many either have been republished or are available on microform. Also, there are numerous personal records of editors and other newspapermen scattered throughout the country. Many have been used, but generally only when studying a specific person or publication. Historians have failed to make good use of the wealth of material available on the party press.

Basically, historical writing about journalism has gone through four stages. The historiography of the party press has tended to follow a pattern similar to that of the study of American history in general. The earliest scholars, generally titled Nationalist historians, emphasized the growth of American democracy and the role newspapers played in that process. The next group to appear, the Developmental historians, stressed the growth of the press to its modern-day state of maturity. Next came the Progressive historians, who emphasized the idea of conflict in history and the role of newspapers in such conflicts. Finally, the Cultural historians appeared. Their study of the newspapers and magazines underscored how the press functioned in its environment. For most of these different groups of histori-

ans, the party press seemed all bad—the "Dark Ages of American journalism"—
or all good—the essential era for the growth of the press. Only recently have journalism historians managed to judge the party press by the standards of that era
rather than those of a later time.

The historians of the press who lived during the nineteenth century readily fall
into the all-good or all-bad pattern by their emphasis on the role of the press in the
early growth of the United States. They followed the lead of George Bancroft and
other Nationalist historians in praising the move toward democracy that the new
nation experienced. People like Isaiah Thomas and Joseph T. Buckingham rejoiced over the growing liberty in the United States and praised the newspapers for
helping in that development. Isaiah Thomas's *The History of Printing in America*
(1810) is the first history of journalism in the United States. While not really
studying journalism past the Revolutionary era, Thomas's work reflects the
widespread belief in the importance of the press in the new and budding democratic nation. Joseph T. Buckingham's *Specimens of Newspaper Literature* (1850)
discusses the party press era more, but basically in a series of anecdotes and personal remembrances. Buckingham's decision to organize the work primarily
around individual newspapers makes it difficult to get a broad overview, but he
provides much information about individual people and papers.

Other Nationalist historians studied the important papers or individuals of the
party press era. In 1860, Charles Lanham discussed the *National Intelligencer* in
Atlantic Monthly. Even with the partisanship that existed, the editors of the *National Intelligencer* succeeded and developed good reputations among their peers.
In a similar vein, Horace Scudder's *Noah Webster* (1883) praises the journalist
whose efforts in the field of letters encouraged the growing cultural independence
of the United States. Four years later, G. G. W. Benjamin, in discussing "Notable
Editors Between 1776 and 1800" in the *Magazine of American History*, stressed
the influence of newspaper editors in the push for liberty and democracy

While the National historians emphasized the role of the press in the rise of
American democracy, the next group narrowed the focus to the growth of journalism itself. The perspective of the Developmental historians, the first to develop beyond the contemporaneous generation, became the major influential outlook in the
study of American journalism in the party press era. Their ideas dominated from
the late nineteenth century until well past the mid–twentieth century. As indicated
by their descriptive title, these historians emphasized the growth and development
of journalism as a profession. For them, more than any other group, all trends led
up to the present. Most of the major survey histories fall into this category. Fred-
eric Hudson's *Journalism in the United States, from 1690 to 1872* (1873) describes
the early nineteenth century as a troublesome period for American journalism because newspapers were in the hands of the politicians and thus were unable to develop professionally. Later studies reflect the same outlook. In 1941, Frank Luther
Mott's survey work, *American Journalism: A History of Newspapers in the United
States Through 250 Years, 1690–1940*, gave the party press period its ultimate pe-
jorative title when he described it as the "Dark Ages of American journalism."

Developmental historians produced many biographies of individuals important in the growth of the press. In 1887, Benjamin Ellis Martin wrote *Transition Period of the American Press: Leading Editors Early in This Century*. In studying the political editors from 1790 to 1820, Martin concluded that the partisan press displayed the worst attributes possible in its discussion of politics. Charles Levermore's "The Rise of Metropolitan Journalism" in the *American Historical Review* (1901) continues the theme of transition. He concluded that the party press played an important role for the political parties at the time, but that its long-term influence was limited because of those attachments. For most of these historians, the late eighteenth to the mid–nineteenth centuries were times best looked at quickly and then almost forgotten because they produced very little of benefit in the history of American journalism.

Developmental historians also emphasized the "firsts" by taking a great interest in the mechanics of journalism and who did what first. One study of nineteenth-century journalists, Frederick B. Marbut's "Early Washington Correspondents: Some Neglected Pioneers" in *Journalism Quarterly* (1948), emphasizes the development of the correspondent in the nation's capital in an attempt to identify the first one. Also in *Journalism Quarterly*, Alan R. Miller's "America's First Political Satirist: Seba Smith of Maine" (1970) discusses the pioneer of political satire in the United States and how he influenced other writers during the mid–nineteenth century.

Another interpretation of the party press appeared in the early 1900s alongside the Developmental outlook. It has been called the Progressive view because of its sympathies with the Progressive reform efforts of the early twentieth century. These historians perceived the move toward republicanism and democracy under Presidents Jefferson and Jackson and their supporters as a move toward improvement. Jefferson and Jackson both sought to protect and enlarge the rights of the people, and the press sought to aid these efforts. For the Progressives, the Republican and Democratic editors who fought for individual liberty were the heroes of the era, as they led the fight between the conservatives who sought to maintain control and the working-class people who hoped to increase their role in the political system. Conflict was to be expected, and so the argumentative newspapers of the party press era were necessary in order for democracy to triumph. One of the first histories to reflect this outlook is George Henry Payne's *History of Journalism in the United States* (1920). Payne still belittled the party press era as relatively unimportant in the overall history of journalism in the United States, but the newspapers did play an important role in the overthrow of aristocratic (read Federalist) control of the government. One of the leading Progressive historians, Richard Hofstadter, entered the fray through a study of "William Leggett, Spokesman of Jacksonian Democracy" in *Political Science Quarterly* (1950). Hofstadter praised Leggett for his attempt to democratize the American economy by giving all of the people access to sources of opportunity and profit.

The Progressive historians also produced numerous studies of individual newspapers and journalists. All of them emphasized the role of the press in the growing influence of the people. Richard Hooker's *The Story of an Independent Newspa-*

per: One Hundred Years of the Springfield Republican, 1824–1924 (1924) describes the paper as fighting aristocracy through its opposition to Federalism. In discussing the career of William Duane in a 1929 sketch for the *Dictionary of American Biography*, Claude Bowers praised the Republican journalists for their efforts in support of democracy. In 1933, Bernard Fäy wrote *The Two Franklins: Fathers of American Democracy*. He applauded Benjamin Franklin and Benjamin Franklin Bache for pushing the United States toward independence and democracy. Henry P. Rosemont also studied Benjamin Franklin from a Progressive perspective. In his article in *Labor History* (1981), Rosemont discussed Franklin's sympathies with militant workers during a 1786 strike of typefounders against their employers.

With all of these historians emphasizing the backwardness of the newspapers of the party press era, few have studied the journalism of this period in any depth. The image of the party press era as one of unethical journalism has resulted in its being ignored by many historians. Since the 1920s, however, this outlook has changed somewhat, and that has produced some detailed study of the period as a whole. Beginning with the work of sociologist Robert E. Park in 1925, some journalism scholars, generally referred to as Cultural historians, have sought to consider the press as part of the larger society. The result has been attempts to place newspapers and magazines in the context of the era they existed in, a process that has benefited the study of the partisan press of the 1790s–1830s. While still accepting the idea of the party press era as one of underdevelopment, historians such as Edwin Emery, Michael Emery, and Sidney Kobre have sought to understand the media and their interaction with the society in which they operated. Other historians—primarily Donald H. Stewart, in *The Opposition Press of the Federalist Period* (1969), and Jerry W. Knudson, in a series of journal articles published from 1969 to 1976—sought to better understand the partisan era through careful study of the press during the political career of Thomas Jefferson and his contemporaries.

The Cultural outlook has also resulted in the first real attempt to rethink the overall evaluation of the party press. With a growing emphasis among all historians on considering people and events in the context in which they lived and operated, rather than from a modern perspective, journalism historians have attempted the same type of study of the press. The result has been a reevaluation of the concept of the party press as the "Dark Ages of American journalism."

The first scholar to take a second look at the party press was William E. Ames in his studies of the Washington, D.C., press in the 1820s. Ames concluded that, rather than being regressive, the party press provided more outlets of information for the people. In *Newsmongers: Journalism in the Life of the Nation, 1690–1972* (1973), Robert A. Rutland described the party press era as the "Golden Age of American journalism," a period in which the newspapers played a more central role in national life than at any other time in American history. Gerald Baldasty, in his studies of the Jacksonian press, and Wm. David Sloan, in considering the newspapers of the 1790s, have both concluded that partisan editors played an essential and central role in the party system by presenting the party line to their readers.

Other recent historians have tried to go beyond the designation of "party press period" to look at the media as a whole. John C. Nerone, in *The Culture of the Press in the Early Republic: Cincinnati, 1793–1848* (1989), approached the issue of the party press and its environment from this perspective by studying all of the print media for a particular community over a lengthy period of time. As a result, Nerone has painted a more complete picture of the function of the press in one area by combining a study of all the media, both the political/commercial publications and the specialized journals. He discovered that the press of the partisan era went much beyond what many previous scholars have pointed out.

All of these recent historians conclude, in one way or another, that scholars have missed the point in studying the party press by using modern standards of evaluation. By design, newspapers from the 1790s to the 1830s were primarily meant to trumpet the cause of a particular group, generally a political party. Objectivity was not an issue, for it was irrelevant. With this goal as a guide, the party press succeeded very well, for the newspapers worked hard to forward the cause of their candidates or their groups. This reevaluation has helped force historians to judge the party press by their own standards rather than by those of today. When that is done, one finds that the press from the late eighteenth to the mid–nineteenth century consisted of a rich and complex variety of publications with many goals and aspirations. Politics provided the centerpiece, but it was not the only issue under consideration.

Ultimately, when one considers the scholarship about the party press era, one finds that much is missing. The emphasis on the political papers leaves out many publications that did not fit this guideline. The emphasis on biographies and specific papers fails to draw a big picture. The past two or three decades have seen attempts to remedy this situation, but many people, unfamiliar with recent scholarship, still see the party press era as one of depravity and unethical behavior on the part of journalists. To leave these hard-working editors and printers so judged is to do them a disservice by failing to take them at their word and to judge them by their own standards of success and ethics.

Sources

UNPUBLISHED PAPERS AND DOCUMENTS

Aurora, Office Account Books, Historical Society of Pennsylvania, Philadelphia.
Robert and Francis Bailey Records, Historical Society of Pennsylvania, Philadelphia.
Joel Barlow Papers, American Antiquarian Society, Worcester, Mass.
Biddle Papers, Library of Congress, Washington, D.C.
Book Trades Collection, American Antiquarian Society, Worcester, Mass.
William Henry Brodnax Papers, Virginia Historical Society, Richmond.
Richard Keith Call Letter, Virginia Historical Society, Richmond.
Francis Asbury Dickins Papers, Virginia Historical Society, Richmond.
Fontaine Family Papers, Virginia Historical Society, Richmond.
James Mercer Garnett Papers, Virginia Historical Society, Richmond.
Robert Selden Garnett Papers, Virginia Historical Society, Richmond.
Gooch Family Papers, Virginia Historical Society, Richmond.
Greene Family Papers, Virginia Historical Society, Richmond.
Hugh Blair Grigsby Papers, Virginia Historical Society, Richmond.
William Hammett Papers, Virginia Historical Society, Richmond.
Harrison Family Papers, Virginia Historical Society, Richmond.
Haxall Family Papers, Virginia Historical Society, Richmond.
Henry Lee Papers, Virginia Historical Society, Richmond.
Mercer Family Papers, Virginia Historical Society, Richmond.
Meredith Papers, *Port Folio* Group, Historical Society of Pennsylvania, Philadelphia.
John Stuart Skinner Papers, Virginia Historical Society, Richmond.
Spragins Family Papers, Virginia Historical Society, Richmond.
Isaiah Thomas Papers, American Antiquarian Society, Worcester, Mass.
Woodhouse Collection, Historical Society of Pennsylvania, Philadelphia.

PUBLISHED PAPERS AND DOCUMENTS

Annals of Congress. House of Representatives, 5th Congress, 2nd Session. Washington, D.C.: Gales and Seaton, 1834.

Binns, John. *Recollections of the Life of John Binns*. Philadelphia: Parry and M'Millan, 1854.

Buckingham, Joseph T. *Specimens of Newspaper Literature*. 2 vols. Boston: Charles C. Little and James Brown, 1850.

The Debates and Proceedings in the Congress of the United States. 2nd Congress, 1791–1793. Washington, D.C.: Gales and Seaton, 1849.

Dennie, Joseph. *The Lay Preacher*. Philadelphia: Harrison Hall, 1817.

General Court of Massachusetts. *The Perpetual Laws of the Commonwealth of Massachusetts, 1780–1788*. Worcester, Mass.: Isaiah Thomas, 1788.

Hamilton, Alexander. *The Papers of Alexander Hamilton*. Edited by Harold C. Syrett et al. 27 vols. New York: Columbia University Press, 1974.

Hamilton, Alexander, John Jay, and James Madison. *The Federalist Papers*. Edited by Clinton Rossiter. New York: New American Library, 1961.

Jackson, Andrew. *Correspondence of Andrew Jackson*. Edited by John Spencer Bassett. 6 vols. Washington, D.C.: Carnegie Institution of Washington, 1926–1933.

Jefferson, Thomas. *The Papers of Thomas Jefferson*. Edited by Julian P. Boyd et al. 25 vols. to date. Princeton, N.J.: Princeton University Press, 1950– .

Jefferson, Thomas. *The Writings of Thomas Jefferson*. Edited by Paul Leicester Ford. 12 vols. New York: G. P. Putnam's Sons, 1904–1905.

Jefferson, Thomas. *The Writings of Thomas Jefferson*. Edited by Andrew A. Lipscomb. 20 vols. Washington, D.C.: Thomas Jefferson Memorial Association, 1903–1904.

Jensen, Merrill, ed. *Ratification of the Constitution by the States: Delaware, New Jersey, Georgia, and Connecticut*. Vol. 3 of *The Documentary History of the Ratification of the Constitution*. Madison: State Historical Society of Wisconsin, 1978.

Kaminski, John P., and Gaspare J. Saladino, eds. *Commentaries on the Constitution, Public and Private*. Vol. 1. Vol. 13 of *The Documentary History of the Ratification of the Constitution*. Madison: State Historical Society of Wisconsin, 1981.

Madison, James. *The Complete Madison: His Basic Writings*. Edited by Saul K. Padover. New York: Harper, 1953.

Madison, James. *Notes of Debates in the Federal Convention of 1787*. Edited by Adrienne Koch. Athens: Ohio University Press, 1966.

Madison, James. *The Papers of James Madison*. Edited by Thomas A. Mason, Robert A. Rutland, and Jeanne K. Sisson. 17 vols. Charlottesville: University Press of Virginia, 1985.

Nevins, Allan, ed. *American Press Opinion: Washington to Coolidge*. Boston: D. C. Heath, 1928.

Pickett, Calder M. *Voices of the Past: Key Documents in the History of American Journalism*. New York: Macmillan, 1977.

Schwartz, Bernard. *The Bill of Rights: A Documentary History*. 2 vols. New York: Chelsea House, 1971.

Van Winkle, C. S. *The Printers' Guide*. New York: C. S. Van Winkle, 1818.

Waldo, S. Putnam. *The Tour of James Monroe, President of the United States, Through the Northern and Eastern States, in 1817*. Hartford, Conn.: F. D. Bolles, 1818.

Webster, Daniel. *The Works of Daniel Webster*. 6 vols. Boston: Charles C. Little and James Brown, 1851.

NEWSPAPERS AND MAGAZINES

The contemporary publications produced between 1783 and 1833 are scattered in several repositories throughout the United States. Major collections are at the American Antiquarian Society, Worcester, Mass.; the Library Company, Philadelphia, Pa.; and the Library of Congress, Washington, D.C. Many of the newspapers have been reproduced in microform. The major collection available in microform is the American Antiquarian Society's *Early American Newspapers*, which contains most American newspapers published prior to 1820.

SECONDARY SOURCES

Alexander, John K. *The Selling of the Constitutional Convention: A History of News Coverage*. Madison, Wis.: Madison House, 1990.

Ammon, Harry. "The Fifth President and the Press: Monroe." *Media History Digest* 3 (1983): 22–28.

———. *James Monroe: The Quest for National Identity*. New York: McGraw-Hill, 1971.

Anderson, David A. "The Origins of the Press Clause." *UCLA Law Review* 30 (February 1983): 455–537.

Ashley, Perry, ed. *Dictionary of Literary Biography*. Vol. 43, *American Newspaper Journalists, 1690–1872*. Detroit: Gale Research, 1986.

Avery, Donald R. "The Emerging American Newspaper: Discovering the Home Front." *American Journalism* 1 (1984): 51–66.

Baldasty, Gerald J. "The New York State Political Press and Antimasonry." *New York History* 64 (July 1983): 261–79.

———. "The Press and Politics in the Age of Jackson." *Journalism Monographs* 89 (August 1984).

———. "The Washington, D.C., Political Press in the Age of Jackson." *Journalism History* 10 (Autumn/Winter 1983): 3–4, 50–53, 68–71.

Bemis, Samuel Flagg. *A Diplomatic History of the United States*. New York: Henry Holt, 1936.

———. *Jay's Treaty: A Study in Commerce and Diplomacy*. Rev. ed. New Haven, Conn.: Yale University Press, 1962.

Blanchard, Margaret A. "Freedom of the Press, 1690–1804." In *The Media in America*, 2nd ed., edited by Wm. David Sloan, James G. Stovall, and James D. Startt, 93–122. Scottsdale, Ariz.: Publishing Horizons, 1993.

Bleyer, Willard Grosvenor. *Main Currents in the History of American Journalism*. Boston: Houghton Mifflin, 1927.

Bowers, Claude G. *The Party Battles of the Jackson Period*. Boston: Houghton Mifflin, 1922.

Brant, Irving. *The Bill of Rights: Its Origin and Meaning*. Indianapolis: Bobbs-Merrill, 1965.

———. *James Madison*. 6 vols. Indianapolis: Bobbs-Merrill, 1941–1961.

Brigham, Clarence S. *History and Bibliography of American Newspapers, 1690–1820*. 2 vols. Worcester, Mass.: American Antiquarian Society, 1947.

————. *Journals and Journeymen: A Contribution to the History of Early American Newspapers.* Philadelphia: University of Pennsylvania Press, 1950.

Brown, Richard D. *Knowledge Is Power: The Diffusion of Information in Early America, 1700–1865.* New York: Oxford University Press, 1989.

Brown, Robert E. *Middle-Class Democracy and the Revolution in Massachusetts, 1691–1780.* Ithaca, N.Y.: Cornell University Press for the American Historical Association, 1955.

Buel, Richard, Jr. *Dear Liberty: Connecticut's Mobilization for the Revolutionary War.* Middletown, Conn.: Wesleyan University Press, 1980.

Chidsey, Donald Barr. *The Birth of the Constitution.* New York: Crown, 1964.

Christie, Ian R. *War and Revolutions: Britain, 1760–1815.* Cambridge: Harvard University Press, 1982.

Clason, Augustus W. "The Convention of Massachusetts." *Magazine of American History* 14 (December 1885): 529–45.

Collier, Christopher. *Roger Sherman's Connecticut: Yankee Politics and the American Revolution.* Middletown, Conn.: Wesleyan University Press, 1971.

Commager, Henry Steele. "The Search for a Usable Past." *American Heritage*, February 1965, 4–9, 90–96.

Cox, Archibald. *The Court and the Constitution.* Boston: Houghton Mifflin, 1987.

Cremin, Lawrence A. *American Education: The Colonial Experience.* New York: Harper & Row, 1970.

————. *In Pursuit of Reason: The Life of Thomas Jefferson.* Baton Rouge: Louisiana State University Press, 1987.

Cunningham, Noble E., Jr. *The Jeffersonian Republicans in Power: Party Operations, 1801–1809.* Chapel Hill: University of North Carolina Press for the Institute of Early American History and Culture, Williamsburg, Va., 1963.

Dangerfield, George. *The Era of Good Feelings.* London: Methuen, 1953.

Daniell, Jere. *Experiment in Republicanism: New Hampshire Politics and the American Revolution, 1741–1794.* Cambridge: Harvard University Press, 1970.

DeConde, Alexander. *The Quasi-War: The Politics and Diplomacy of the Undeclared War with France, 1797–1801.* New York: Charles Scribner's Sons, 1966.

Dicken-Garcia, Hazel. *Journalistic Standards in Nineteenth-Century America.* Madison: University of Wisconsin Press, 1989.

Dickerson, Donna Lee. *The Course of Tolerance: Freedom of the Press in Nineteenth-Century America.* Westport, Conn.: Greenwood Press, 1990.

Dumbauld, Edward. *The Bill of Rights and What It Means Today.* Norman: University of Oklahoma Press, 1957.

Duniway, Clyde Augustus. *The Development of Freedom of the Press in Massachusetts.* Cambridge: Harvard University Press, 1906.

Eaton, John. *The Life of Andrew Jackson.* Cincinnati: Hatch & Nichols, 1827.

————. *Memoirs of Andrew Jackson.* Boston: C. Ewer, 1828.

Edmunds, R. David. *The Shawnee Prophet.* Lincoln: University of Nebraska Press, 1983.

————. *Tecumseh and the Quest for Indian Leadership.* Boston: Little, Brown, 1984.

Emery, Michael, and Edwin Emery. *The Press and America: An Interpretive History of the Mass Media.* 6th ed. Englewood Cliffs, N.J.: Prentice-Hall, 1988 (1954).

Ershkowitz, Herbert. "Andrew Jackson: Seventh President and the Press." *Media History Digest* 5 (1985): 10–16, 40.

Farrand, Max. *The Framing of the Constitution of the United States*. New Haven, Conn.:
    Yale University Press, 1913.
Fehrenbacher, Don Edward. *The South and Three Sectional Crises*. Baton Rouge:
    Louisiana State University Press, 1980.
Ferguson, E. James. "State Assumption of the Federal Debt During the Confederation."
    Mississippi Valley Historical Review 39 (December 1951): 403–24.
Ford, Franklin L. *Europe, 1780–1830*. London: Longman, 1970.
Friedman, Leon, and Fred L. Israel, eds. *The Justices of the United States Supreme Court,
    1789–1969*. Vol. 1. New York: Chelsea House, 1969.
Gatell, Frank Otto, ed. *Essays on Jacksonian America*. New York: Holt, Rinehart & Win-
    ston, 1970.
Gilmore, William J. *Reading Becomes a Necessity of Life: Material and Cultural Life in
    Rural New England, 1780–1835*. Knoxville: University of Tennessee Press, 1989.
Gregory, Winifred, ed. *American Newspapers, 1821–1936*. New York: H. W. Wilson,
    1937.
Hall, Van Beck. *Politics Without Parties: Massachusetts, 1780–1791*. Pittsburgh: University
    of Pittsburgh Press, 1972.
Hamilton, Milton W. *The Country Printer*. Port Washington, Long Island, N.Y.: Ira J. Fried-
    man, 1964 (1936).
Handlin, Oscar. "The Bill of Rights in Its Context." *American Scholar* 62 (Spring 1993):
    177–86.
Harding, Samuel B. *The Contest over the Ratification of the Federal Constitution in the
    State of Massachusetts*. New York: Longmans, Green, 1896.
Hart, Jim Allee. *The Developing Views on the News: Editorial Syndrome, 1500–1800*. Car-
    bondale: Southern Illinois University Press, 1970.
Hench, John Bixler. "The Newspaper in a Republic: Boston's *Centinel* and *Chronicle*,
    1784–1801." Ph.D. diss., Clark University, 1979.
Hickey, Donald R. *The War of 1812: A Forgotten Conflict*. Urbana: University of Illinois
    Press, 1989.
Holcombe, Arthur N. "Massachusetts and the Federal Constitution of 1787." In *Common-
    wealth History of Massachusetts*. Vol. 3, edited by Albert Bushnell Hart, Chap. 13.
    New York: States History Co., 1929.
Horsman, Reginald. *The Causes of the War of 1812*. Philadelphia: University of Pennsyl-
    vania Press, 1962.
Howe, Daniel Walker. *The Political Culture of the American Whigs*. Chicago: University of
    Chicago Press, 1979.
Joyce, William L., David D. Hall, Richard D. Brown, and John B. Hench, eds. *Printing and
    Society in Early America*. Worcester, Mass.: American Antiquarian Society, 1983.
Katz, Judith Maxen. "Connecticut Newspapers and the Constitution, 1786–1788." *Con-
    necticut Historical Society Bulletin* 30 (1965): 33–44.
Knudson, Jerry W. "Political Journalism in the Age of Jefferson." *Journalism History* 1
    (1974): 20–23.
Kobre, Sidney. *Development of American Journalism*. Dubuque, Iowa: William C. Brown,
    1969.
Kohn, Hans. *American Nationalism*. New York: Macmillan, 1957.
Lee, Alfred McClung. *The Daily Newspaper in America*. New York: Macmillan, 1937.
Levy, Leonard. *Emergence of a Free Press*. New York: Oxford University Press, 1985.

————. *Essays on the Making of the Constitution.* 2nd ed. New York: Oxford University Press, 1987.

————. *Jefferson and Civil Liberties: The Darker Side.* Cambridge, Mass.: Belknap Press of Harvard University Press, 1963.

Lockridge, Kenneth A. *Literacy in Colonial New England.* New York: Norton, 1974.

Luxon, Norval Neil. *Niles's Weekly Register: News Magazine of the Nineteenth Century.* Baton Rouge: Louisiana State University Press, 1947.

McCaleb, Walter Flavins. *The Aaron Burr Conspiracy.* New York: Wilson-Erickson, 1936.

McDonald, Forrest. *Alexander Hamilton: A Biography.* New York: Norton, 1979.

McKerns, Joseph P., ed. *Biographical Dictionary of American Journalism.* Westport, Conn.: Greenwood Press, 1989.

McNulty, John Bard. *Older Than the Nation: The Story of the Hartford Courant.* Stonington, Conn.: Pequot Press, 1964.

Main, Jackson Turner. *The Antifederalists: Critics of the Constitution, 1781–1788.* Chapel Hill: University of North Carolina Press for the Institute of Early American History and Culture, Williamsburg, Va., 1961.

Malone, Dumas. *Jefferson and His Times.* 6 vols. Boston: Little, Brown, 1948–1981.

Marbut, Frederick B. "Early Washington Correspondents: Some Neglected Pioneers." *Journalism Quarterly* 25 (1948): 369–374, 400.

May, Ernest R. *The Making of the Monroe Doctrine.* Cambridge: Belknap Press of Harvard University Press, 1975.

Meyers, Marvin. *The Jacksonian Persuasion: Politics and Belief.* Stanford, Calif.: Stanford University Press, 1960.

Middlekauff, Robert. *The Glorious Cause: The American Revolution, 1763–1789.* New York: Oxford University Press, 1982.

Miller, John C. *Alexander Hamilton: Portrait in Paradox.* New York: Harper, 1959.

————. *The Federalist Era, 1780–1801.* New York: Harper & Brothers, 1960.

Mitchell, Broadus. *Alexander Hamilton.* 2 vols. New York: Macmillan, 1957–1962.

Moore, Glover. *The Missouri Controversy, 1819–1821.* Lexington: University of Kentucky Press, 1953.

Morris, Richard B. *Witnesses at the Creation: Hamilton, Madison, Jay, and the Constitution.* New York: Henry Holt, 1945.

Mott, Frank Luther. *American Journalism: A History of Newspapers in the United States Through 250 Years, 1690–1940.* New York: Macmillan, 1941.

————. *A History of American Magazines, 1741–1850.* Cambridge: Belknap Press of Harvard University Press, 1957.

————. *Jefferson and the Press.* Baton Rouge: Louisiana State University Press, 1943.

Myers, Denys P. *Massachusetts and the First Ten Amendments to the Constitution.* Washington, D.C.: U.S. Government Printing Office, 1936.

Nerone, John C. *The Culture of the Press in the Early Republic: Cincinnati, 1793–1848.* New York: Garland, 1989.

Nevins, Allan. *The Evening Post: A Century of Journalism.* New York: Boni and Liveright, 1922.

Nord, David Paul. "The Evangelical Origins of Mass Media in America, 1815–1835." *Journalism Monographs* 88 (May 1984).

North, S. N. D. *History and Present Conditions of the Newspaper and Periodical Press of the United States.* Washington, D.C.: U.S. Government Printing Office, 1884.

Norton, Wesley. *Religious Newspapers in the Old Northwest to 1861: A History, Bibliography, and Record of Opinion.* Athens: Ohio University Press, 1977.

Onuf, Peter S., ed. *Jeffersonian Legacies.* Charlottesville: University Press of Virginia, 1993.

Osthaus, Carl R. *Partisans of the Southern Press.* Lexington: University Press of Kentucky, 1994.

Owen, John B. *The Eighteenth Century, 1714–1815.* London: Thomas Nelson and Sons, 1974.

Padover, Saul K. *Jefferson.* New York: Harcourt, Brace, 1942.

Parton, James A. *Life of Andrew Jackson.* 3 vols. Boston: Houghton Mifflin, 1885 (1861).

Payne, George Henry. *History of Journalism in the United States.* New York: D. Appleton, 1920.

Perkins, Bradford, ed. *The Causes of the War of 1812.* New York: Holt, Rinehart & Winston, 1961.

Perkins, Dexter. *A History of the Monroe Doctrine.* Boston: Little, Brown, 1955.

———. *The Monroe Doctrine, 1823–1826.* Cambridge: Harvard University Press, 1932.

Peterson, Merrill D. *The Great Triumvirate: Webster, Clay, and Calhoun.* New York: Oxford University Press, 1987.

———. *Thomas Jefferson and the New Nation.* New York: Oxford University Press, 1970.

Polishook, Irwin H. *Rhode Island and the Union, 1774–1795.* Evanston, Ill.: Northwestern University Press, 1969.

Pollard, James E. *The Presidents and the Press.* New York: Macmillan, 1947.

Prescott, Frederick C., ed. *Alexander Hamilton and Thomas Jefferson.* New York: American Book Co., 1934.

Rakove, Jack N. *The Beginnings of National Politics: An Interpretive History of the Continental Congress.* Baltimore, Md.: Johns Hopkins University Press, 1979.

Remini, Robert V. *Andrew Jackson and the Course of American Democracy, 1832–1845.* New York: Harper & Row, 1984.

———. *Andrew Jackson and the Course of American Empire, 1767–1821.* New York: Harper & Row, 1977.

———. *Andrew Jackson and the Course of American Freedom, 1822–1832.* New York: Harper & Row, 1981.

———. *Henry Clay: Statesman for the Union.* New York: W. W. Norton, 1991.

———. *The Life of Andrew Jackson.* New York: Harper & Row, 1988.

Riley, Sam G., ed. *Dictionary of Literary Biography.* Vol. 73, *American Magazine Journalists, 1741–1850.* Detroit: Gale Research, 1988.

Risjord, Norman K. *Forging the American Republic, 1760–1815.* Reading, Mass.: Addison-Wesley, 1973.

Ritcheson, Charles R. *Aftermath of Revolution: British Policy Toward the United States, 1783–1795.* Dallas: Southern Methodist University Press, 1969.

Rock, Howard B. *Artisans of the New Republic: The Tradesmen of New York in the Age of Jefferson.* New York: New York University Press, 1979.

Ronda, James P. "Jefferson and the Imperial West." *Journal of the West* 31 (July 1992): 13–19.

Rosewater, Victor. "The Constitutional Convention in the Colonial Press," *Journalism Quarterly* 14 (December 1937): 364–66.

Ross, Steven T. *European Diplomatic History, 1789–1815: France Against Europe.* Garden City, N.Y.: Anchor Books, 1969.

Rossiter, Clinton. *1787: The Grand Convention.* New York: W. W. Norton, 1987 (1966).

Rutland, Robert A. *The Birth of the Bill of Rights, 1776–1791*. Chapel Hill: University of North Carolina Press for the Institute of Early American History and Culture, Williamsburg, Va., 1955.

———. *James Madison: The Founding Father*. New York: Macmillan, 1987.

———. *Newsmongers: Journalism in the Life of the Nation, 1690–1972*. New York: Dial Press, 1973.

———. *The Ordeal of the Constitution: The Antifederalists and the Ratification Struggle of 1787–1788*. Norman: University of Oklahoma Press, 1965.

Schachner, Nathan. *Alexander Hamilton*. New York: D. Appleton-Century Co., 1946.

Schlesinger, Arthur M, Jr. *The Age of Jackson*. Boston: Little, Brown, 1945.

Shipton, Clifford K. *Isaiah Thomas: Printer, Patriot, and Philanthropist, 1749–1831*. Rochester, N.Y.: Printing House of Leo Hart, 1948.

Simister, Florence Parker. *The Fire's Center: Rhode Island in the Revolutionary Era, 1763–1790*. Providence: Rhode Island Bicentennial Foundation, 1979.

Sloan, Wm. David. "The Early Party Press: The Newspaper Role in American Politics, 1788–1812." *Journalism History* 9 (Spring 1982): 18–24.

———. "Examining the 'Dark Ages' Concept: The Federalist-Republican Press as a Model." *Journal of Communication Inquiry* 7 (1982): 105–19.

———. "The Federalist-Republican Press: Newspaper Functions in America's First Party System, 1789–1816." *Studies in Journalism and Mass Communcation* 1 (Spring 1982): 13–22.

———. "Historians and the Party Press: 130 Years of Scholarship." *Studies in Journalism and Mass Communication* 2 (Spring 1983): 27–32.

———. " 'Purse and Pen': Party-Press Relationships, 1789–1816." *American Journalism* 6 (1989): 101–25.

———. "Scurrility and the Party Press, 1789–1816." *American Journalism* 5 (1988): 97–112.

Sloan, Wm. David, and Julie Hedgepeth Williams. *The Early American Press, 1690–1783*. Westport, Conn.: Greenwood Press, 1994.

Smith, J. Eugene. *One Hundred Years of Hartford's Courant: From Colonial Times Through the Civil War*. New Haven, Conn.: Yale University Press, 1949.

Smith, James Morton. *Freedom's Fetters: The Alien and Sedition Laws and American Civil Liberties*. Ithaca, N.Y.: Cornell University Press, 1956.

Smith, Jeffrey A. "Public Opinion and the Press Clause." *Journalism History* 14 (Spring 1987): 8–17.

Soltow, Lee, and Edward Stevens. *The Rise of Literacy and the Common School in the United States: A Socio-Economic Analysis to 1870*. Chicago: University of Chicago Press, 1981.

Stein, M. L. *When Presidents Meet the Press*. New York: Julian Messner, 1969.

Stewart, Donald H. *The Opposition Press of the Federalist Period*. Albany: State University of New York Press, 1969.

Stroupe, Henry S. "The Beginnings of Religious Journalism in North Carolina, 1823–1865." *North Carolina Historical Review* 30 (January 1953): 1–22.

———. *The Religious Press in the South Atlantic States, 1802–1865*. Durham, N.C.: Duke University Press, 1956.

Szatmary, David P. *Shays's Rebellion: The Making of an Agrarian Insurrection*. Amherst: University of Massachusetts Press, 1980.

Taylor, George Rogers, ed. *Jackson v. Biddle's Bank*. Lexington, Mass.: D. C. Heath, 1972.

Tebbel, John. *The Media in America*. New York: Thomas Y. Crowell, 1974.

Tebbel, John, and Sarah Miles Watts. *The Press and the Presidency: From George Washington to Ronald Reagan*. New York: Oxford University Press, 1985.

Thomas, Isaiah. *The History of Printing in America*. Worcester, Mass.: Isaiah Thomas, Jr., 1810; reprint (edited by Marcus A. McCorison) Barre, Mass.: Imprint Society, 1970.

Thorpe, Francis Newton. *The Constitutional History of the United States*. Chicago: Callaghan, 1901.

Tocqueville, Alexis de. *Democracy in America*. New York: Alfred A. Knopf, 1946.

Van Doren, Carl. *The Great Rehearsal: The Story of the Making and Ratifying of the Constitution of the United States*. New York: Viking Penguin, 1948.

Ward, John William. *Andrew Jackson: Symbol for an Age*. New York: Oxford University Press, 1955.

Warren, Charles. *The Making of the Constitution*. New York: Little, Brown, 1937 (1928).

Weisberger, Bernard A. *The American Newspaperman*. Chicago: University of Chicago Press, 1961.

Whitaker, Arthur Preston. *The United States and the Independence of Latin America, 1800–1830*. Baltimore, Md.: Johns Hopkins University Press, 1941.

Williamson, Chilton. *Vermont in Quandary, 1763–1825*. Montpelier: Vermont Historical Society, 1949.

Wright, Esmond. *Fabric of Freedom, 1763–1800*. New York: Hill & Wang, 1961.

Wroth, Lawrence C. *The Colonial Printer*. Charlottesville: University Press of Virginia, 1964.

Young, Alfred F. *The Democratic Republicans of New York*. Chapel Hill: University of North Carolina Press, 1967.

Index

About the Author

CAROL SUE HUMPHREY is Associate Professor of History at Oklahoma Baptist University. She is the author of *"This Popular Engine": New England Newspapers During the American Revolution, 1775–1789* (1992).